CECIL RHODES

BUST OF CECIL JOHN RHODES

BY J. M. SWAN

IN THE MEMORIAL ON TABLE MOUNTAIN DESIGNED BY HERBERT BAKER.

CECIL RHODES

BY

BASIL WILLIAMS

GREENWOOD PRESS, PUBLISHERS
NEW YORK

Originally published in 1921 by Henry Holt & Co.

First Greenwood Reprinting, 1968

Library of Congress Catalogue Card Number: LC 69-14152

PRINTED IN THE UNITED STATES OF AMERICA

TO

THE RIGHT HON. J. X. MERRIMAN

Forsan et haec olim meminisse juvabit.

PREFACE

THIS book, first planned in 1914, was interrupted by the war. The delay has enabled me to see many papers previously inaccessible. In the Bibliography at the end of the book I acknowledge my obligations to those who have been good enough to talk to me about Rhodes, and to the books that have been helpful. To Lord Charnwood I am grateful for some valuable suggestions on the proofs. My wife has helped me at every stage. I should also like to mention my special debt of gratitude to Lord Milner, a Trustee, to Mr. Geoffrey Dawson, Acting Secretary, and to the Staff of the Rhodes Trust; to Mr. Wilson Fox, M.P., and Mr. D. Malcolm, Directors of the British South Africa Company; and to Colonel Amery, M.P., for their readiness to let me see papers in their charge and the interest they have taken in my attempt to portray Rhodes.

Even if I have failed in this attempt, I trust that something of the love I have for the South African land and people may be found to breathe through these pages.

B. W.

CHELSEA,
Michaelmas Day, 1920.

CONTENTS

ILLUSTRATIONS

CHAPTER I

INTRODUCTORY

DURING the sittings of the South African Convention at Cape Town, some seven years after Rhodes's death, an Englishwoman, recently landed, the daughter of an English statesman, was describing to some of us her first impressions of the Cape Peninsula. The charm of Cape Town and its surroundings, Rondebosch, Wynberg, Sea Point, Muizenberg, lovely even in their names; the Mountain dominating them all; the clear, clean South African air and its wonderful light—these she felt and saw as all must who have ever touched there; but there was something more, a haunting sense of some dominating personality present but unseen everywhere. Table Mountain with the town and villages nestling in its kloofs seemed to have some great spirit brooding over it, and in men's talk there was always a reserve as of some idea too familiar yet too impressive to be much talked about. Then it had dawned upon her that the haunting personality was that of Rhodes; and the mystery was explained. For everything appeared to call up associations with Rhodes. The statue of the old Dutch governor, Van Riebeeck, on the quay, to greet the stranger on his arrival in South Africa, was his gift; the road round the Mountain was planned by him with the loving thought that "human beings would walk that road long after he had gone"; the old Dutch block-house on the Mountain was preserved from destruction by him; Groote Schuur at Rondebosch, with its ample grounds and its masses of hydrangeas, was his home, left for the public service of a united South Africa; in the tiny cottage by the sea at Muizenberg he breathed his last painful breath; the monument on the Mountain side marks the seat where he used to sit musing and staring at the view of both oceans, or gazing towards his own country in the north,

> Like stout Cortez . . .
> Silent upon a peak in Darien.

The very work of Union, for which the chosen men of every state in South Africa were then assembled at Cape Town, was his constant preoccupation, and was now recalling him at every turn. "Oh, if we only had Rhodes here!" exclaimed a Dutchman from the Transvaal, when some almost fatal obstacle had presented itself in the Convention—a Dutchman, who in Rhodes's lifetime had been fighting him and his countrymen. "Let us not bother about these details, we are out for the big thing," said another delegate, this one a dear friend of Rhodes, unconsciously echoing almost the very words of his chief.

Nor were these experiences singular or confined to the period of the National Convention, when men's minds were all intent on one of Rhodes's great ideas. The German Colonial Secretary, Dernburg, who visited South Africa a little later, had the same vivid sense of his personality; for what, he said, impressed him most in the country was the omnipresent glamour of Rhodes. Later still, on the eve of the war, the feeling of his presence is as fresh and living. "The spirit of the man permeates the place," writes a visitor to Groote Schuur in 1914, an ancient opponent of Rhodes, not merely because of the books, the old Dutch objects and furniture he collected there, the rare trees he planted and the animals he acclimatized in the grounds, and his favourite view from the stoep, still remembered, but for the passions he aroused and the ideas he stimulated.

This vivid remembrance of Rhodes was not confined to the Cape Peninsula, his home, if he can be said ever to have had one, for the last ten years of his life. For many years after his death it was the same throughout South Africa. In Natal, where he was least known, the few men who knew or worked with Rhodes are pointed out to the stranger at the Club as among those specially to be noted and talked to; and sooner or later the visitor is bound to hear the story of Rhodes winning over their Prime Minister, Escombe, till then somewhat suspicious, by the invitation to Groote Schuur, to discuss South African Union, with its postscript: "besides, the hydrangeas are in full beauty: it would be a pity to miss them." In the Transvaal and the Free State, where he was once regarded by many besides old President Kruger as "Apollyon, a financier, and the foul fiend himself . . . if Rhodes had not been born . . . South Africa would have been little less than a paradise," his death has mellowed men's judgements, and it is remembered that with all his faults and in spite of the Raid he was a great South African, while in Johannesburg it is not forgotten that he was one of the founders of its prosperity. In the native territories of the Cape his creation, the Glen Grey system, has profoundly modified the condition and outlook of the black community. Among the Dutch of the Cape he is not only remembered for the betrayal of the Raid but as a farmer such as themselves, who loved the land as they do and felt with them in all their troubles. The Kimberley of to-day, for good or evil, is merely what he made it by the De Beers amalgamation; and Bechuanaland, "the Suez Canal to the interior," might never have been British, but for Rhodes. For Rhodesia he is the one man; Jameson indeed is remembered with affection; Grey and Milton and all the directors of the Chartered Company had their good qualities; but since he died it has never been quite the same there for white men or natives. The lame dogs among the whites he helped materially or cheered with brave words; the stalwart felt that his curt approval was worth working for; and all knew that, whatever might be the difficulties, he would surely be there to see the country through. By the natives he was trusted blindly for his just dealings and the respect he showed them; to him alone among white men they gave the royal salute of their tribe. Here above all his memory is cherished, in the country he won and loved; and here he rests on the hill called the View of the World, amid the grandeur and loveliness of the Matoppos.

Even South Africa's wide expanses were too narrow a

field for Rhodes. He is the only colonial statesman who has to such extent struck the imagination and affected the thoughts of Englishmen at home and throughout the world. The very suddenness with which he loomed upon the outer world helped to concentrate attention upon him. A few years before he became Prime Minister of the Cape he had hardly been heard of in England. During a debate of 1884 Lord Randolph Churchill spoke scornfully of "some cypher" appointed to supersede the missionary Mackenzie in Bechuanaland, a "cypher" whose appointment the Minister was hard put to it to defend as of "a gentleman of some distinction, who had always shown himself to be a great sympathizer with the native races." Less than six years later the "cypher's" name was on every tongue as the autocrat of one of the greatest industrial undertakings in the world, as Prime Minister of his colony and as the founder of what promised to be a vast new dominion for the Empire. At home, indeed, the quality of his eminence was never so incontestable as at one time it was in South Africa. To many he was a bugbear—the type of the dishonest and unscrupulous politician, who uses politics to rig the market and the wealth thus acquired to corrupt politics, a man who filched away an empire and slaughtered innocent savages or plotted against a friendly state to put money into his own and his fellow-conspirators' pockets. "Rank selfishness and an inextinguishable love of power and renown, of adulation and of praise are the prevalent characteristics which distinguish this eminent statesman and conqueror from the small fry," such is another, perhaps extreme, instance of the form of obloquy to which he was exposed. On the other hand, to many more he had soon become a national hero, on a par with a Clive or a Warren Hastings, and by the few who consorted familiarly with him he was treated as little short of infallible and impeccable. Since his death Oxford and its Rhodes scholars have helped to keep his memory green and to further his ideals even beyond the shores of England. At Oxford his statue looks proudly down upon The High, taking rank above the sovereigns of his day, as a Founder no less than William of Wykeham, Chichele, Waynflete or Wolsey.

In our law courts Rhodes's words of some thirty years ago still have weight in a decision on the fate of a vast territory in the heart of Africa; and for long ardent young missionaries of Empire have been devoting themselves to the problems of Imperial government on principles which he initiated.

To-day, except in his own Rhodesia, the glamour of his great name is somewhat dulled. Many of the faithful friends, men like Jameson and Grey, jealous guardians of the reputation and tradition of Rhodes, which they themselves had helped to form, have passed away. The war, which raised so many new problems and brought forward so many new men, has for the time being obscured Rhodes and the Rhodes ideas. South Africa itself, where he played his chief part, no longer holds that prominent place in the world's eye which it held for ten years and more before his death and during the decade which succeeded it. Perhaps by very reason of this partial eclipse it is opportune to attempt another judgement on Rhodes. Hitherto most of the lives or sketches of him have been written under the attractive magnetism of his living personality. To-day it may be possible to take a more dispassionate view. Most of the written material ever likely to be available for his life is now accessible, and so much has happened in the last eighteen years that his career can be judged not only by the passions which it raised but by the test of the effects which it has produced. On the other hand, it has still not been too late to gather living impressions of the man from those who saw him plain, who knew him and listened to his actual words, who can describe his gestures, the tone of his voice, and some of his unguarded moments. Such evidence is especially valuable in the case of a man like Rhodes, who wrote very few intimate letters and received few. For the account of such a man depends for its value not so much on what he did as on why and how he did it; and that can only be obtained by close acquaintance with the man himself.

This book is not intended to be an unrelieved panegyric of Rhodes or a tract for the imperialism he preached and worked for. But it frankly sets forth with the belief that he was, with all his grievous faults, a great man, and that at the root of his imperialism were qualities that have done good service to mankind. His character was cast in a large mould, with enormous defects corresponding with his eminent virtues. But, from the recital of these shortcomings no less than that of his achievements, help, we think, may be gained by those moved by the same spirit of devotion to what they believe best for England and the world. As to his creed of imperialism, a worthy spirit will be engendered if we look, not to the blatant and exaggerated manifestations of national arrogance it contained, but to its deep sense of public duty, the tenacity of purpose it implied, and above all to the underlying sympathy and desire for co-operation even with opponents, without which it was meaningless.

CHAPTER II

EARLY YEARS

CECIL JOHN RHODES, the fifth son of the Rev. F. W. Rhodes, Vicar of Bishop Stortford, was born on July 5, 1853. Since the seventeenth century his paternal ancestors had been farmers, first in the Midlands and in Cheshire, then on the outskirts of London near the Gray's Inn Road. His great-grandfather Samuel besides his farm had large brick and tile works at Dalston, on a property now built over and still owned by the Rhodes trustees. His grandfather William was a cowkeeper in a large way at Islington and also had property at Leyton Grange in Essex. Rhodes, therefore, had good reason in after life for his boast to the Dutch farmers that he was one with them, as he also came of farming stock. The father, F. W. Rhodes, who was born in 1806, and educated at Harrow and Trinity, held the vicarage of Bishop Stortford for twenty-seven years, until two years before his death in 1878. Himself one of a large family, he also had many children, a daughter by a first wife and nine sons and two daughters by his second wife, Louisa Peacock, one of a Lincolnshire family, whom he married in 1844. Two of the nine sons died in infancy, leaving, besides the daughter of the first marriage, Edith and Louisa, Herbert, Frank, Cecil John, Ernest, Elmhirst, Arthur and Bernard, to be sent out into the world by the vicar and his wife Louisa.

The vicar, tall and spare in appearance, was a man of system and of strong prejudices. To his parishioners he gave good sound doctrine in his sermons, which always lasted ten minutes, no more and no less; he saw to the education of their children, being a generous benefactor to the old grammar school of the place and establishing a training school for mistresses in elementary schools; he was also noted for his charity and his courteous bearing to all, and is said to have had a horror of lawyers. He kept his large family in due respect of him and brought them up on strictly religious principles. They were all expected to take their turn teaching in the Sunday school, and received pious books as a reward for their pains. His hope was that all his sons should follow his own example by taking Orders and become, as he was wont to say, "the angels of the Seven Churches," a hope doomed to complete disappointment. The mother, who died when Cecil was twenty, is said to have been a woman of great charm and ease of manner, whose sympathy and tenderness gave some relief from the vicar's Spartan principles. Thanks to her sympathy, perhaps quite as much as to the father's pungent originality, many of the children developed on unconventional lines. It was not the custom for this crowd of brothers and sisters, so one of them records, to confide much in one another, and each grew up on his own lines; but at least they learned not only to hold their own with one another but also, in spite of passing quarrels, to stick together and face the world as no mean clan. Throughout life Cecil, though he may have passed disparaging remarks on the pursuits of some of his brothers and sisters, never left any of them in the lurch, but saw that they had the opportunities he was able to give them. The favourite brother of the clan was the second son, Frank, who inherited all his mother's charm but, though a gallant soldier, little of the father's force.

Herbert, the eldest son, went to Winchester and Frank to Eton, but when it came to Cecil, at the age of nine, he was put as a day-boy to the local grammar school. Here he gave no signs of great distinction. A school-fellow writing to him when he had become famous recalls that he gained the silver medal for elocution, an art in which he afterwards showed but little proficiency, and he is stated to have taken interest in history, geography and classics; but he must have been a good cricketer, for he attained the glory of the school XI. at the age of thirteen. He was always rather a shy, reserved boy, with a delicate appearance, though never wanting in spirit and power of concentration. The motto he chose at the age of thirteen for one of those quaint confessional albums, so dear to the Middle Victorians, was "to do or to die"; even then he had decided that a single life was better than to be married; and in one of Frank's early letters home he is already spoken of as "long-headed Cecil," as if this were a well-recognized trait in his character.

Though reserved at home, he appears to have blossomed out more in what was a second home to several of the Rhodes children in Lincolnshire. Mrs. Rhodes's sister, Sophia Peacock, lived at Sleaford Manor in the Belvoir country, where she often had one or more of the vicar's children to stay, her special favourite being Frank, whom she practically adopted. Cecil was often there for the holidays, and found himself in a circle of relations and acquaintances. His aunt Sophy was always a good friend to him, and she was one of the few to whom in those early days he confided his plans and aspirations. Some Willson cousins lived two miles away at Ranceby; the Finch Hattons at Haverholm close by, and the family of Mr. Yerburgh, rector of Sleaford, were close friends; and Frank had Eton companions to stay there. In those days Cecil could put up a good fight with his fists, as one of his friends, a much bigger boy, whom Cecil had thought too "cheeky," had ruefully to admit. One of those who remembered him best at Sleaford was the rector's son, Robert, a lifelong friend. The two used to go riding about the country together, Cecil fond of the exercise but even then remarkable for his bad seat in the saddle, a fault of which practice in the Belvoir country itself never cured him. Though quite a young lad at the time, Cecil, Yerburgh used to say, showed a most precocious power of observation; instead of gazing at the pretty girl looking over a gate, he was all eyes for the country he passed through, and always remembered which farm was well cultivated and which slackly managed. These early Lincolnshire friendships completed the good grounding for life which he got from the give and take of the large family at the Vicarage and the rough and tumble of the Grammar School. Unconventional and original he always was, and his unconventionality was no doubt accentuated by the turbulent life on the Diamond Fields; but he also always kept an air of good breeding and a dignity of bearing, sure passports to the most exclusive as to the roughest society; and he very early learned the gift of appraising men at their true value to himself To this atmosphere of squire and parson in which he was reared at Bishop Stortford and Sleaford he owed, too, his reverence for the feudal traditions of the old squirearchy, with its high if limited sense of public duty, and his lifelong respect for the profession of a landowner.

In 1869, at the age of sixteen, Cecil left the Grammar School and continued his studies under his father's eye. Herbert and Frank had already disappointed the vicar's hope that they should take orders, Frank being bent on Sandhurst and Herbert having already taken to a roving life abroad. Ultimately four of the brothers joined the army. "My father," afterwards said Rhodes, "was anxious that they should enter the Church as a preliminary step to becoming angels: they prefer being angels through the Army and I don't blame them"; the other three all went to the Colonies. But at sixteen Cecil had not entirely rejected the idea of the Church as a profession, although his first choice lay elsewhere. "I cannot deny," he wrote to his Aunt Sophy, "for it would only be hypocrisy to say otherwise, that I still above everything would like to be a barrister; but I agree with you it is a very precarious profession. Next to that I think a clergyman's life is the nicest; and therefore I shall most earnestly try to go to College, because I have fully determined to be one of these two, and a College education is necessary for both. I think that as a barrister a man may be just as good a Christian as in any other profession"; nor should the jolly ending of the letter be omitted, if only to show that even in those early years he was not too much of a prig: "How proud you must have been of Frankie's success [in the Eton and Harrow match]! I can assure you we were in the highest state of excitement . . . a great cricketer . . .

said he preferred Frank's play to any on the field, because he had never seen anything equal to his defence."

However, neither College nor the Bar were yet to be approached by this determined young man. His health was weakly, and there were even fears that he might be consumptive, a disease of which several of the family showed symptoms. His father, therefore, determined to send him abroad to try the effect of a sea voyage and a better climate. Herbert had already set up as a planter in Natal, so to join Herbert in Natal Cecil was despatched on a sailing vessel. The voyage to Durban took him seventy days, and on September 1, 1870, he first set foot on African soil, a tall, lanky, anæmic, fair-haired boy, shy and reserved in bearing. Nelson boarding a man-of-war for the first time, when "nobody had been apprised of the boy's coming," could hardly have felt more solitary and forlorn than this seventeen-year-old boy on landing upon the scene of his life's work. For Herbert, the only soul he knew in South Africa, was away upon some expedition; he had, however, left a message with his friend Dr. Sutherland, the Surveyor-General of the Colony, to befriend his brother. So to Dr. Sutherland's house at Pietermaritzburg Cecil found his way. There he was kindly entertained until his brother's return. He is said to have spent most of his time there reading, and still apparently used to talk of taking Orders to his host, who used to prophesy that he would end his days as a village parson in England.

Towards the end of the year Herbert returned from his expedition, and the two brothers started off for the Umkomanzi Valley, south of Pietermaritzburg, where the elder had already taken a farm. It was in a settlement where a first attempt was being made to start cotton-planting in Natal; their friends in town all warned them that the attempt would prove a dismal failure. However, they found that the pioneer of the settlement, one Conyngham, and Powys, the owner of a neighbouring farm specially noted for its beauty, had had some success. Their own farm had first to be cleared of the dense bush which grew luxuriantly in the hot steamy valley; this they did with the help of their Kaffir labourers in time for a first year's crop. The crop proved a failure, as their friends had predicted; the cotton, planted too closely in rows, had become tangled and matted, and fell a prey to the caterpillar and bore-worm. A few bales were picked, but not enough to pay expenses. Nothing daunted, they cleared off more bush for the second year's crop and planted the forty-five acres they now had for cotton on a new system, with much greater intervals between the plants, and at every 80 feet a small patch of mealies, which attracted the grub from the cotton; the numerous monkeys in the district were also attracted by the mealies, but the brothers had no objection to their visits as long as they confined their depredations to the corn cobs. On this second year's crop they made a good profit, and obtained a prize for their cotton at a local agricultural show. By the end of 1872 the Rhodes brothers expected to have 100 acres cleared for planting, and were already regarded as among the most successful planters of the settlement;[1] their method of ploughing instead of hoeing between the rows being looked on as a specially commendable innovation.

The life on the settlement was hard and simple, but had its attractions. Herbert and Cecil had built themselves two little huts, one for sleeping, the other as a store and living room; here they lived, waited on by a Kaffir servant. They had pleasant neighbours within riding distance, one, with whom Cecil formed a close friendship, being H. C. Hawkins, the son of a Natal magistrate, and a relation of the Provost of Oriel. With him Cecil kept up his classics, and formed plans for saving up enough money to go to Oxford, an ambition which only one of them fulfilled. Cecil, it is also recorded, no doubt as the scholar and the youngest member of the settlement, was chosen to respond to the toast of The Ladies at the banquet of the agricultural show at which his cotton samples were exhibited. Herbert, a restless and adventurous fellow, was more noted for his feats of daring, especially for an exploit in swimming into the Umkomanzi, when in raging flood, and cutting the traces of a team of oxen which were being helplessly swept

[1] See *Notes on Natal*, by John Robinson. 1872.

down with their wagon, and so enabling them to swim ashore.

Though Cecil in the intervals of bush clearing and cotton planting studied his classics and dreamed of Oxford, he also gave early evidence of his practical eye for a business bargain, keeping a shrewd look out for investments and openings in the colony. At this stage he had no capital to spare, but during the year after he had left Natal, when he had scraped some together, he put his previous observation to good use. To his friend, Dr. Sutherland, who acted as his agent, he wrote several anxious letters on the placing of the few pounds he had available. Farms had been suggested to him, but he would have nothing to say to farms, unless he had seen them for himself and was assured of their accessibility and good water-supply; and finally, after much consideration, he pitches on the new railway under construction between Durban and The Point at the landing-stage, which this wise young man of nineteen quite rightly judged to be a profitable investment.

The little settlement on the Umkomanzi was short-lived. By the end of 1871 one neighbour of the Rhodes's, finding that the sluit, on which he depended for water, had dried up, was forced to leave; Powys, the owner of the lovely farm, had all his cotton dried up and was burned out of his house. Others went to try their luck at the newly discovered diamond diggings, whither Herbert also went to prospect in May 1871. Cecil looked after the cotton by himself till October, when he followed Herbert to Griqualand West; but the Natal plantation was not finally abandoned till the end of 1872, after Herbert had returned to put in one more crop. "It really seems an ill-fated valley," was Cecil's parting verdict, and he thought his brother wise not to drop any more money on it. "You would be surprised," he wrote to Dr. Sutherland, "if I told you what a sink it has been. I believe if one only kept on, it has a capacity to absorb any amount of capital." But though an expensive experiment, this plantation was a good training-ground for Rhodes. He learned here to understand something of the difficulties of South African farming and how to overcome them; he gained his first experience of natives, improved in health, developed business capacity, and was enabled, before he was of age, to be self-reliant and fend for himself as few young Englishmen of his class are qualified to do. Above all, he acquired those habits of work, and that loathing of a loafer which he kept to the end. It is indeed amusing to find him writing home at this tender age to urge that his elder brother Frank should " come out here before he gets his commission, as it will be very good for him, so much better than the do-nothing life he is leading now."

" Ah yes," he would say in later days to the critics who told him a thing was impossible, " they told me I couldn't grow cotton."

CHAPTER III

THE OPENING OF THE DIAMOND FIELDS

IN the year 1867 Schalk van Niekerk, a Dutch farmer, was calling at his friend Jacobs's house near the Orange River. The Jacobs children were playing at marbles, and Van Niekerk's eye was attracted by the extraordinary brilliancy of one of the stones they were using. "Take it away with you, by all means," said Jacobs, "if you fancy it," and accordingly Van Niekerk, who regarded it merely as a curiosity, pocketed it. Shortly afterwards he met the trader John O'Reilly and pulled it out to show him. O'Reilly thought it might be valuable and took it off to get the opinion of some diamond merchants; they told him it was worth nothing; but when it was passed on to the Colesberg magistrate, Lorenzo Boyes, he was so convinced of its value that he sent it to the Cape mineralogist, Dr. Atherstone, who pronounced it to be a diamond worth £500. At this price it was bought by the Governor, Sir Philip Wodehouse. The next important find was two years later, when a native witch-doctor brought the same van Niekerk a large and brilliant stone he had found near the Orange River, and was using as a charm in the course of his calling; the Dutchman, now awake to the value of such stones, at once offered the witch-doctor all he stood possessed of, namely 500 sheep, 10 oxen, and one horse, for his charm. Van Niekerk did well by his bargain, for he sold the diamond, an exceptionally fine one that turned 83 carats, for over £11,000 to a Hopetown trader, who sold it again to Lord Dudley for £25,000. This diamond became famous as "The Star of South Africa."

At first it was imagined by many people that these

discoveries were mere freaks; in fact, a Mr. Gregory, the expert agent of a London jeweller, reported that there were no signs of diamond-bearing soil in South Africa.[1] But many colonists on the look out for adventure and an easy fortune were less incredulous, and began to search on the banks of the Orange River and along the Vaal, near its junction with the Hart River. In the latter half of 1869 diamonds were found in the bed of the Vaal, near the mission station of Hebron, and parties of diggers flocked to that neighbourhood. Among the first were J. B. Robinson and Stafford Parker, long well-known names in the Diamond Fields, and a party from Natal under Captain Rolleston. Within a short space of time the bend of the Vaal for eighty miles from Hebron to the junction with the Hart River was dotted all along with little mining camps designated Gong Gong, Forlorn Hope, Blue Jacket, Larkin's Flat, etc., outlandish names to our ears but familiar enough among the red sands and the white ants of Kalgoorlie, the snows of the Yukon, the scrub and sand-storms of the veld, or wherever the strange wild brotherhood of prospector and digger may chance to be gathered together. Large settlements sprang up at Pniel, on the south bank of the river, and at Klipdrift, now Barkly West, on the opposite bank, which by 1870 already had brick buildings and shops, and boasted of a newspaper of its own. The soil from the river-bed was sifted in rough hand-cradles by the diggers, and so successful were they that within a few months some 10,000 prospectors had been attracted to a district hitherto inhabited only by a few missionaries and wandering natives.

Soon, however, the river diggings were entirely thrown into the shade by a new discovery on the open veld. In September 1870, diamonds were found on the farm Dutoitspan, only twenty miles from Klipdrift. Speculators, scenting a profit, soon appeared on the scene and offered what seemed fabulous prices to the simple farmers of the district. Dutoitspan was sold for £2600, Bultfontein near by for £2000, and Voruitzicht for £6000, the purchasers of

[1] Hence the Diamond Fields euphemism for any outrageous misstatement as "a Gregory."

the last being the Port Elizabeth firm of D. A. & N. J. de Beers. All these farms could have been contained within a ring fence of fifteen miles. The new owners, however, were unable to stem the rush of prospectors on to their property, and the most they could do was to exact a monthly licence fee of 7s. 6d. or 10s. for each claim of thirty feet square. Dutoitspan was rushed at the end of 1870, Bultfontein a few months later; part of the De Beers farm in May; in the following July Rawstorne, a prospector from Colesberg in Cape Colony, discovered the first diamond on the kopje, under the roots of an old thorn tree which crowned its grassy knoll. The original claims on Voruitzicht were then christened Old De Beers; the kopje ground, some ten acres in extent, Colesberg Kopje or De Beers New Rush and later Kimberley, after the Colonial Secretary of the day. The river diggings were soon deserted for these dry diggings, where the diamonds were more plentiful and easier to find; for along the Vaal pits had to be sunk in the heavy gravel, thick with boulders, whereas here the diamonds could be picked out of the light surface soil like plums out of a cake. As the fame of the new Diamond Fields near the Vaal spread, prospectors kept arriving thither not only from every part of South Africa, but from Europe, Australia and America, and within their radius of five miles a huge canvas city sprang up where there had hitherto been nothing but bare veld, an even more marvellous transformation than that of the eighty mile bend in the Vaal River.

The discovery of the Diamond Fields opened a new chapter in South African history, in which the eighteen-year-old cotton planter of the Umkomanzi valley was destined to play a principal part. Hitherto South Africa, with its two colonies of the Cape and Natal and its two Boer republics named after the Orange River and the Vaal, had been a poor and rather unhappy land, troubled with internal dissensions among the whites and with constant danger from the natives. In 1871 Cape Colony was bounded on the east by the Great Kei River and on the north by the Orange River. On its eastern borders it was subject to constant alarms of raids from the large native territory of Kaffraria, extending from the Great Kei to the Natal borders, over which the Imperial government exercised a shadowy protectorate. In that year it had added to its difficulties by taking over from the Imperial authorities the administration of Basutoland, a native state nowhere touching its own borders. It still had that unhappy form of government, an executive directly appointed by the governor, and an elected parliament responsible for legislation and finance but with no authority over the executive: the controversies to which this system gave rise were accentuated by the cleavage between the original Dutch colonists, who predominated in the western province, and the English settlers of 1820 in the eastern province, the Dutch in the aggregate being in the majority. Except for the merchants, forwarding agents and shopkeepers in the ports and towns, the population was almost entirely agricultural and pastoral, pursuits to which the Dutch took more kindly than the English. It could, it is true, boast of the only completed railway in South Africa, a line sixty miles long from Cape Town to Wellington, but financially it was at a low ebb, with a Budget showing a revenue of only £543,583 to meet an expenditure of £604,926. Natal was happier in having a more homogeneous population, for most of the original Boer emigrants, who had borne the brunt of the fighting against the Zulu invaders, had retired in disgust to the Transvaal when Natal was finally proclaimed a British colony in 1843. The chief difficulty there was the enormous preponderance of the native over the white population and the proximity of the ferocious Zulu race; but the English and Scottish settlers were an independent, self-reliant people, who were not averse to the isolation from other parts of South Africa which their geographical position imposed upon them. Besides these two colonies there were the two Boer republics. The Free State had first been settled in 1828; in 1848 it was annexed by Sir Harry Smith and the Boer leader Pretorius defeated at Boomplaats; six years later, much against its will, its independence was restored because the Imperial government had changed its mind and decided to have no responsibilities north of the Orange River.

Since then its people had been ruled wisely and successfully by their President, John Brand, though with occasional wars against their neighbours, the Basutos, who could not be controlled either by the Imperial authorities or the Cape. The Transvaal to the north of the Free State had not had a happy history since its first invasion by the Cape Boers of 1835, who were anxious to escape from British interference. Its independence was not recognized by Great Britain till 1852, and for eight years longer it contained four separate republics. Its unification in 1860 did not much mend matters, for it had constant fights with the native tribes in the north and west and was always on the verge of bankruptcy.

One important result of the large influx of strangers, chiefly of the English race, to the Diamond Fields was to redress somewhat the balance between the Dutch and English races in South Africa. It also for the first time introduced an industrial element into the country ; for not only diamond digging itself soon developed into a regular industry, but it stimulated others required to supply the needs of the diggers. Again, agriculture throughout South Africa was in time encouraged to increased production by the wants of the large and extravagant new population. All this additional prosperity affected for the better the public as well as the private finances of South Africans, not only in Cape Colony, the state most concerned, but elsewhere also. The state of the natives was even more profoundly influenced. Hitherto they had for the most part lived isolated in their tribes, comparatively little changed by the advent of the Europeans : some indeed did agricultural work for neighbouring farmers and a few were employed as house servants or grooms. But soon the diggers required an almost inexhaustible supply of natives to help them with the drudgery of their labour, and the supply in the neighbourhood of the fields was extremely limited. They offered high wages for natives, and in an incredibly short time the rumour of these good wages and the good food offered, and of the chance of buying European firearms and ammunition, spread to every native kraal throughout South Africa. Natives came trudging hundreds of miles from Kaffraria beyond the eastern province, from Zululand, from the northern fastnesses of the Transvaal, from the far distant regions of the Zambesi and even beyond to take up the new work. And they never came to stay. They remained long enough to earn their good wages, and to buy their guns and ammunition, and then trudged back to their far-away homes, bringing news to their own tribes of other tribesmen they had met and of the ways of the white men. Thus the solidarity and isolation of the tribes was gradually modified, and the natives themselves acquired new wants and became more ready to secure their satisfaction by closer association with Europeans. In a word, the influence of the Diamond Fields proved a first and most important step to the penetration by Europeans of vast native districts, where they had hitherto been almost unknown or dreaded as a terrible danger.

Unfortunately another result of the discovery of the Diamond Fields was to add one more to the many causes of grievance of the Dutch, and to reveal one more change in the kaleidoscopic policy of the Imperial government in South Africa. Great Britain, which since the cession of 1806 had paid heavily in warfare and expense for its South African possessions, had chopped and changed its frontier policy with successive secretaries of state and governors of the Cape, sometimes aggressive, sometimes taking a long step backwards. By 1871 nearly everybody at home was tired of South Africa: the onerous charge of Basutoland had been shuffled off on to the Cape and it had been laid down as a definite instruction that the Orange River was to be the northern limit of our responsibilities. It so happened, however, that both the river diggings and the dry diggings were discovered in Griqualand West, virtually a no-man's land north of the Orange River, west of the Free State and south-west of the Transvaal, over which a small tribe of Griquas, ruled by the chief Waterboer, roved at will. It was obvious that this large influx of adventurers, many of them lawless and turbulent, could not be left without a government or be subjected to the whims of a semi-savage chieftain. The question arose who should govern them. The Transvaal Boers had never been disposed to abide by any arbitrary limits to their roaming disposition, and had for some time cast a covetous eye on the pasture grounds of the Griquas along the Vaal and Hart Rivers and the neighbouring settlements of the Batlapins and Barolongs farther north on the edge of Bechuanaland.

Accordingly when the river diggings were opened President Pretorius claimed the right of keeping order there with his Transvaal police and magistrates, and even had the happy thought of giving an exclusive concession for diamonds to three of his countrymen. The Diggers Committee, elected by the diggers to maintain order, riposted by proclaiming themselves an independent republic, and though the President withdrew the obnoxious concession and tried the effect of a personal visit to the diggings, he made no impression on the headstrong community on his borders. The dry diggings in their turn were claimed as coming within the jurisdiction of the Free State; and it must be admitted that the claim seemed reasonable. It was hardly disputed that Waterboer's country had been treated as part of the Orange River Sovereignty until that territory was returned to the Free State Boers in 1854; and, though Waterboer had disputed their authority, the Boers had never abandoned their claim. Accordingly Brand sent his magistrates and police to Pniel and the dry diggings. He failed, it is true, in his attempt to stop a rush at Bultfontein, for the miners refused to regard the Free State commando sent to maintain order otherwise than as a huge joke and invited its members to dismount and have a drink with them. But on the whole he managed to establish some sort of order in a very unruly community: a school, a courthouse and a prison were built, and the Free State magistrate became popular and respected.

But the Colonial Secretary in the Cape Executive had from the outset made up his mind that the Diamond Fields must be brought within the British dominions. Robert Southey was a remarkable man When quite young he had come out with the hardy settlers of 1820 and by this time had become the most efficient and powerful Minister in the Government of Cape Colony. Some of his ideas were not unlike those with which Rhodes after him was inspired. Apart from any question of financial advantage to the Cape, he was convinced that a bankrupt state like the Transvaal or a small pastoral community such as the Free State were quite incapable of governing the turbulent crowd on the Diamond Fields ; he also had taken a longer view in being the first, perhaps, of his generation to realize the importance of securing the territory north of the Orange River and west of the two republics as a corridor for Great Britain into the interior of Africa. If Griqualand West were given over to the Free State and the rest of Waterboer's territory with the Batlapin and Barolong lands in Bechuanaland to the Transvaal, he saw that this "Suez Canal into the interior," as Rhodes described it later, might be closed for ever to English enterprise.

To carry out his designs Southey got into communication with Waterboer, or rather with his agent, David Arnot. Both Waterboer, the head of the Griqua tribe, and the chieftains of the Barolongs and Batlapins, realizing that they could not hope to carry on unaided intricate boundary disputes with the Boers, had appointed agents to conduct their case. Arnot and the successive agents for the Batlapins and Barolongs, Theodor Doms and the Rev. Joseph Ludorf, were troubled with few scruples and were suspected with some reason of turning to good account their authority to make grants of land for their principals. Arnot at any rate was also an extremely able man of business and proved more than a match for his Boer opponents. At Southey's instigation he persuaded the chieftain to ask that his territory should be incorporated in the British dominions, thus making the British Government responsible for his claims. Lord Kimberley's assent to the incorporation was obtained, subject to proof of Waterboer's case and on condition the Cape agreed to annex the territory. A magistrate from the Cape was sent to take over the administration of justice at the river diggings ; and the new High Commissioner, Sir Henry Barkly, at an interview with President Pretorius at Klipdrift, then re-named Barkly West persuaded him to submit all the frontier disputes with Waterboer and the Bechuana chieftains to arbitration. The Transvaal Government, unlike Arnot and Ludorf for the natives, presented its case very badly, and when Governor Keate of Natal, with whom the decision rested, made his award in October 1871, it entirely set aside the Transvaal claims. Thus the river diggings were adjudged to Waterboer, or in other words the British Government, and the Batlapin and Barolong pasture lands declared outside the Transvaal boundaries. Pretorius and his advisers had themselves largely to blame for this decision and were forced to resign office, but none the less the Keate award long rankled with the Transvaal Boers as a fresh grievance against the British, and more than ten years later Rhodes found them still attempting to evade it.

Keate's decision against the Transvaal was well founded on the evidence available, but there is no such justification for Barkly's and Southey's high-handed proceedings in regard to the Free State claims to the rest of Waterboer's territory. Four days after the Keate award the High Commissioner proclaimed the whole of Griqualand West to be part of the British dominions, and sent up British magistrates and officials to take over the administration of the dry diggings: this in spite of the fact that Lord Kimberley's condition of annexation to the Cape could not be fulfilled; for the feeling against Southey and the Government among the Dutch colonists was so bitter that they did not venture even to introduce a bill for that purpose. There is no doubt that, had diamonds never been discovered, Waterboer would have been left to his fate with the Free State, and the policy of the British Government not to advance beyond the Orange River, laid down in 1854 and since reiterated, would have been observed. The only excuse for the British Government and Southey is that English authority was more likely to ensure respect among the 40,000-50,000 turbulent emigrants, chiefly of English race, in the new Crown colony than that of the petty republic.

Brand was indeed given the offer of arbitration on his claims to Waterboer's territory, but not on terms that he could accept. Recognizing, however, that resistance was hopeless he withdrew his magistrates and calmed the hot-heads among his burghers who were eager for a fight. But he never ceased protesting and appealing to the British sense of justice, while Southey was employed in drawing up the best answer he could to his detailed statements of claim. Finally, in 1876, Lord Carnarvon, the Conservative Secretary of State, who for reasons of his own wished to allay ill-feeling in South Africa, tacitly admitted the wrong done by paying over £90,000 to the Free State as a solatium for the loss of Griqualand West. Southey had won in his duels with the Transvaal and the Free State; for he had secured the Diamond Fields and taken the first step in the road to the north. But it was at a heavy cost. Not only were the two republics given a grievance, which the Transvaal at any rate never forgot, but the Dutch in Cape Colony were once more estranged from us and their English fellow-colonists and drawn closer to their brothers in the republics. Carnarvon within the next few years came up against this stubborn opposition in attempting to carry through his scheme for a confederation of South Africa; and after him Rhodes found the same obstacle, rendered more formidable by fresh blunders of Downing Street, in his endeavours to proceed along Southey's line into the interior.

CHAPTER IV

THE YOUNG DIGGER

In October 1871 Rhodes left his Natal farm, never to return. His luggage comprised a few digger's tools, some volumes of the classics and a Greek lexicon ; heaping these into a Scotch cart drawn by oxen he started on his 400-mile journey to the Diamond Fields. In those days this journey was at best a long and tiresome business ; J. W. Matthews, travelling about the same time as Rhodes, took seven days and nights in Walsh's post cart ; another prospector, who enjoyed the comparative ease and leisure of a conveyance drawn by six mules and two horses, took eleven days ; Rhodes in his ox-cart must have taken over a month. In that month he had plenty of time for solitary meditation, an occupation which never came amiss to him, while his oxen crawled through a country of singular beauty and grandeur. From Pietermaritzburg the road climbs steadily past the Mooi River to Blaauwkrantz and Colenso ; it crosses Natal's chief river, the Tugela, and thence steeply rises to Van Reenen's Pass over the Drakensberg range. From this point Rhodes could see the great Basuto mountains on his left and in front the broad plains of the Free State stretching into the distance. Across these he journeyed slowly through the Boer villages of Harrismith, Bethlehem, and Winburg to Bloemfontein, the capital, meeting few creatures by the way except the great herds of buck that still abounded in the country.

Here he had his first experience of the high veld, the real South Africa. The part of Natal where he had hitherto lived, with its deep valleys, its rushing rivers, its steamy heat and its luxuriant, semi-tropical vegetation, is characteristic of a mere fringe of South Africa. It has a beauty and a charm of its own, but it is not a soul-expanding country. Perhaps for that reason the men of Natal with all their industry and perseverance, their courage and their local patriotism, have remained somewhat parochial and have never as a community had the same wide outlook on South African affairs as men from the other colonies. For the great unconfined spaces of the world one must go to Cape Colony, the Free State, the Transvaal or Bechuanaland and the country beyond. Here are the vast plains, unending to the view :

> Mile upon mile
> Of ridge and kopje, bush and candid waste
> Sun-dried and empty, tacit as the sea ;

their level uniformity broken only by some clear-cut, flat-topped kopje rising plumb out of the veld, or by some tiny clump of green trees, the sign of water and of a Boer farmer's homestead. There is no monotony in this wide level expanse. The light of the sun by day is always changing, like the light upon the sea ; the whole country is bathed in a glory of light. At night the stars look down with eyes more shining than in our confined spaces ; or a sudden bush-fire sweeping over the distance with lightning speed and strength lights up the darkness with its glowing radiance. And there is no such air as that of the veld, an exhilarating air, an uplifting air that gives a man hope and courage. In these vast plains of the veld that he saw for the first time on his journey to the diggings and on which he spent most of his remaining years, Rhodes must have gained that clear direct gaze characteristic of those who have dwelt long in those sun-washed spaces, a gaze that seemed to be straining out to a far distant horizon and never finding the goal of his visions.

A day's farther ride from Bloemfontein brought Rhodes to Dutoitspan, which he thus describes in a letter written to his mother shortly after his arrival. " Fancy an immense plain with right in its centre a great mass of white tents and iron stores, and on one side of it, all mixed up with the camp, mounds of lime like ant-hills ; the country round is all flat with just thorn trees here and there: and you have some idea of Dutoitspan, the first spot where dry diggings for Diamonds was begun." Here were the principal hotels of the place, all in the Market Square: Benning and Martin's, which floated the Union Jack, Parker's opposite with the Stars and Stripes, and next door a hotel with the Prussian Eagle. Martin, the friendly host of the Union Jack hotel, generally managed to find a bed for the English new-comer, even if it were only a shake-down on the table, where a noisy party was playing loo till dawn. Staying here, no doubt, on the night of his arrival, Cecil went on next day to Colesberg Kopje or New Rush, where Herbert had already secured three claims "in the richest diamond mine the world ever produced. . . . Imagine," he continues to his mother, "a small round hill at its very highest part only 30 feet above the level of the surrounding country, about 180 yards broad and 220 long; all round it a mass of white tents, and then beyond them a flat level country for miles and miles, with here and there a gentle rise. . . . I should like you," he says, "to have a peep at the kopje from my tent door at the present moment. It is like an immense number of ant-heaps covered with black ants, as thick as can be, the latter represented by human beings; when you understand there are about 600 claims on the kopje and each claim is generally split into 4, and on each bit there are about 6 blacks and whites working, it gives a total of about ten thousand working every day on a piece of ground 180 yards by 220." He then describes how the kopje is divided off into claims. "Take your garden, for instance," he tells his mother, "and peg the whole off into squares or claims 31 ft. by 31 ft., and then the question is how to take all the earth out and sort and sieve it. All through the kopje roads have been left to carry the stuff off in carts like the following [here comes a rough diagram]; that is of every claim of 31 ft., 7 ft. 6 inches are not allowed to be worked, but is left for a road . . . the roads are the only ground that remain of the original level. . . . The carting on the kopje is done chiefly by mules, as they are so very hardy, and have so few diseases. There are constantly mules, carts and all going head over heels into the mines below as there are no rails or anything on either side of the roads, nothing but one great broad chasm below. Here and there where the roads have fallen in, bridges have been put, and they are now the safest part of the kopje. . . . On each side of every road there is now a continuous chasm from top to bottom of the kopje varying in depth from 30 to 60 ft."

He then explains the rough system of digging and sifting then used on the Fields, and some of the difficulties to be overcome. "To begin with the ground is first picked, then the lumps mashed up and you put the stuff through a very coarse wire sieving, this lets the fine stuff pass through and keeps all the stones, which are thrown on one side; it is then hoisted out of the claim, and either carried or carted to the sorting table, where it is first put through fine wire sieving, which sieves all the lime dust away; what remains is put on the sorting table, and then one sorts away with a small scrapper, spreading the stuff out on the table with one scoop and then off with the next. The diamonds are found in all ways; the big ones generally in the hole by the caffre, or else in the sieving; and the small ones on the table. . . . They are only found on these kopjes, and along the river, where they very likely have been carried by water. There are reefs all round these diamond mines, inside which the diamonds are found. The reef is the usual soil of the country round, red sand just at the top and then a black and white stony shale below. Inside the reef is the diamondiferous soil. It works just like Stilton cheese, and is as like the composition of Stilton cheese as anything I can compare it to. . . . They have been able to find no bottom yet, and keep on finding steadily at 70 ft. You will understand how enormously rich it is, when I say that a good claim would certainly average a diamond to every load of stuff that was sorted—a load being about 50 buckets. . . . The question now of course is, how are the roads to be worked? Every claim-holder has an interest in them, as a portion of every man's claim is the road, and one has no idea of leaving ground, every load of which stands a fair chance of holding a diamond. . . . Some day I expect to see the kopje one big basin where once there was a large hill." In this prediction Rhodes showed himself a true prophet; for in the place of Colesberg Kopje now stands a huge crater, from the edge of which men working at the bottom look no bigger than ants.

He concludes the letter with a business-like statement of his own and his brother's prospects. "Have you ever read those tales," he asks his mother, "where they find some wonderfully big diamonds? Well! on this kopje I should think nearly every day they find a diamond over 50 carats. The only misfortune is, that they almost all have a slightly yellow tinge, and are getting quite unsaleable. Diamond buyers now give only £4 per carat for yellow stones of any size or shape, that is a 70 carat would not fetch more than £280. I found a 17⅝ carat on Saturday, it was very slightly off, and I hope to get £100 for it; does it not seem an absurd price? Yesterday I found a 3½ perfect stone, but glassy, which I sold for £30 as they are rather dangerous stones to keep, having a nasty habit of suddenly splitting all over. . . . You must not however think that every diamond one finds is a beauty, the great proportion are nothing but splints—but still even of these you very seldom find one that is not worth 5s. Rough diamonds are of all shapes, sizes and colour under the sun, some are flat, some round, some like two pyramids with their bases joined, some have black spots in the centre, others are yellow, and in fact they take every form you can think of. . . . I find on an average 30 carats a week and am working one of the few whole claims in the kopje: a claim in fact that will take me 4 years to work out at the present rate. Diamonds have only to continue a fair price and I think Herbert's fortune is made. When I tell you at the present moment he owns in all 3 whole claims on this kopje: the one I am working, 1 whole claim, Beecher's 1 quarter, Chadwick a half, another whole claim at the top of the kopje and another ¼ I bought. Mine and Beecher's however yield far the most. I average about £100 per week.—Yrs., C. RHODES."

Rhodes was once more left to his own resources when he wrote this letter home, for soon after he arrived at the Fields Herbert had gone back to Natal to see to the last cotton crop, leaving his brother to look after the claims by himself. Within the last year and a half he had had pretty severe training in self-reliance. At seventeen he arrives in Natal friendless and alone, at eighteen he takes sole charge of a farm of 250 acres and a gang of native labourers, and now at eighteen and a half he has claims valued at £5000 to look after, more raw natives to keep in order and to hold his own in a rough undisciplined crowd, consisting, as Froude saw it two years later, of "diggers from America and Australia, German speculators, Fenian head-centres, traders, saloon keepers, professional gamblers, barristers, ex-officers of the Army and Navy, younger sons of good family who have not taken to a profession or have been obliged to leave; a marvellous motley assemblage, among whom money flows like water from the amazing productiveness of the mine; and in the midst of them a hundred or so keen-eyed Jewish merchants, who have gathered like eagles over their prey, and a few thousand natives who have come to work for wages, to steal diamonds and to lay their earnings out in rifles and powder." In such a crowd a man had to depend on his own resources if he was to keep his head above water. And he shows signs of the severe training. This letter, abrupt and to the point without a word in it of family gossip or home allusions, is a precocious production for such a youth, and, when Frank, following Cecil's advice, comes out a few months later, "Nobody," he says, "believes I am older than Cecil"; in fact, one who knew the brothers well out there speaks categorically of Cecil as the elder. Within a few months of his arrival Mr. Merriman, another of his Kimberley friends, speaking to Frank, "praises Cecil up to the skies. He says he is such an excellent man of business"; Frank continues in his letter home, "that he has managed all the business in Herbert's absence wonderfully well and that they were all so very fond of him. . . . He says most young fellows when they get up there and do well get so very bumptious, but that Cecil was just the contrary. Cecil seems to have done wonderfully well as regards the diamonds. . . . I have not repeated half the nice things he said about Cecil."

Frank went from Cape Town to join Herbert at the

Natal cotton plantation, and then both came over to join Cecil at Kimberley. "We found Cecil," writes Frank, "down in the claim, measuring his ground with his lawyer and in a tremendous rage with another man in the next claim to him, who has encroached on his ground. . . . I know the Father will be horrified at the idea of Cecil going to law." Here the three brothers, with a hideous tailless cur picked up by Cecil, lived in a tent, 16 by 18 feet, stretched over a rough skeleton framework and shared a mess with four or five other young fellows. Housekeeping must have taxed Cecil's powers of organization to the full, for most necessaries and all luxuries were hard to come by. Beef and mutton at 6d. a lb. and meal at 7s. to 10s. a bushel, the produce of the few Boer farmers of the district, were cheap enough: but water cost 3d. a bucket, firewood, brought from long distances, £3 to £4 a load, and vegetables were almost as valuable as small diamonds. Everything else had to be brought up 400 miles from Port Elizabeth or 700 from Cape Town by ox-transport, so that the prices for building material, mining gear, clothes, blankets, groceries, liquor and any kind of luxury were correspondingly enormous. But the men who had come for a life of adventure and freedom to the diggings cared little about discomfort, Cecil least of all. From the motley crowd gathered from the ends of the earth the brothers picked out for their mess and their special friends some of the best of the young men. Among these were C. D. Rudd of Harrow and Trinity, Cambridge, George Paton, Becher, and Dr. Thorne, who all made their mark in business; Seppings Wright, the *Graphic* artist, was one of them; Scully, then a lad of sixteen and later notable for his gift of interpreting the fascination of South African life and scenery, another; Norman Garstin, who soon abandoned the Fields for the studios of Paris and finally settled down as an artist at Newlyn, always retained a lively memory of his early friendship here with Rhodes. Above all, there was John X. Merriman, son of the Dean of Grahamstown, keen and hot-headed like his father, who was a very firebrand in ecclesiastical circles. We have seen what he thought of Cecil Rhodes, who in his turn wrote home of Merriman as "a pleasant young fellow." These two used to go out riding together, Rhodes on his rusty black pony, Bandersnatch, discussing the affairs of the Fields and of South Africa, the classics and universal history. Mr. Merriman still recalls his companion's remarkable interest in politics and the compact they both made to take a part in public affairs, the only intellectual pursuit, so they agreed, open to a colonist. Rhodes on his side must have gained greatly in general knowledge and in breadth of outlook from his association with the best read man and the best talker in South Africa.

For the time being, however, Rhodes, busied with his claims, took no very active part in the politics of Griqualand West, as the new Crown Colony was called. Sir Robert Southey had, appropriately enough, been sent up as the first Lieutenant-Governor, with J. B. Currey as Government Secretary. Politics there were apt to be volcanic in those early days, for the turbulent diggers had many real or fancied grievances, which they were inclined to redress by rioting and rough attempts at mob justice;[1] and at one time the military had to be called in to quell them. Southey's ideas of northern expansion, however, must have found a ready sympathiser in the young digger, who also formed a lasting friendship with Currey and his family. It is even recorded that Rhodes and Merriman between them concocted for Southey's benefit a draft of the anti-gambling law, which was enacted in 1873; but that is his only excursus into politics before 1880.

His strenuous life as a digger did not prevent his having his jokes at times. Scully describes a party of Rhodes and four others returning late one night from a mild spree at Dutoitspan and sending him as the smallest of the party on to the roof of the little tin church to ring the bell, much to the alarm of the diggers, who all came rushing out of their tents to see what was up. There is also a pleasant

[1] Diamond thieves and illicit diamond buyers (I.D.B.) were the chief causes of grievance. But the mob sometimes showed some sense of fairness. The house of a butcher suspected of diamond thefts was burned to the ground, but when the mob discovered that he was innocent the hat was sent round and ample means collected to restore the butcher's property.

picture by Scully of himself and Rhodes sitting down on the ground with a meal-bag as card-table between them to decide in three rounds of euchre whether Rhodes should pay £25 or £30 for Scully's wagon, brought back in parlous condition after the eight months' trek to the Transvaal. The luck was against Rhodes, who paid up cheerfully. He even danced on occasion, though he generally was content to choose the ugliest partners in the room, asserting that he enjoyed it chiefly for the exercise: his more susceptible brother Frank found it "quite a mistake to suppose that there are no nice girls out here." But Cecil had no more eye for a pretty face at Kimberley than he had in Lincolnshire: "I do not believe," says one contemporary, "if a flock of the most adorable women passed through the street, he would go across the road to see them." But what struck all his contemporaries at this time was his faculty of silent concentration on his own thoughts. There is a vision of him "silent and self-contained, dressed in white flannels and leaning moodily with hands in his pockets against a street wall. He hardly ever had a companion and seemingly took no interest but in his own thoughts." On the sorting ground he is described as a tall, fair boy with a ruddy complexion and aquiline features, "wearing flannels of the school playing field, somewhat shrunken with strenuous rather than effectual washings that still left the colour of red dust . . . his tall figure crumpled up on an inverted bucket, as he sat scraping his gravel surrounded by his dusky Zulus," . . . "moody and deaf to the chatter around him, his blue eyes fixed intently on his work or on some fabric of his brain"; and one of his mess-mates used to chaff him on his absent-mindedness after dinner, when he would lean forward on both elbows, his mouth slightly open, rubbing his chin with his forefinger—yet not so entirely abstracted but that he would suddenly wake up and join in the talk. For with all his absent-mindedness he had a shrewd idea of what was going on about him. The letter to his mother already quoted shows a precocious power of observation and that uncanny capacity for business which stands out so clearly as the main element of his success in after life. Nobody who presumed on his casual manner remained in error long, or failed to discover in this dreamer a practical acumen most dangerous to anybody who tried to get the advantage of him. As Lord Rosebery said of him, he was that most formidable of all men of action, the practical visionary.

CHAPTER V

OXFORD AND KIMBERLEY

A SERIOUS illness, when he was alone in Kimberley, had warned Rhodes that he must not presume on his delicate constitution. He had found kind friends in the Curreys to nurse him back to health; but he was still weak when the brothers arrived. To complete his recovery he went off with Herbert some time in 1872 for a long trek into the Transvaal, Frank being left to look after the claims. Herbert, an unquiet, roving spirit, had heard of gold discoveries in the Transvaal and wanted to investigate the new diggings. Borrowing young Scully's wagon, the two brothers travelled along the missionaries' road into Bechuanaland as far as Mafeking, then turning eastwards into the South African Republic past Pretoria to Marabastad in the Low Country and eastwards to the Murchison Range, both districts where gold had been found. Thence by slow stages they turned back, striking the high veld again at Middleburg, and reached Kimberley after several months' absence. During that long trek the great love he bore to the country, the people and even the animals of South Africa became rooted in his being. It is a love that breathes in every speech of his and often gives him quaint and apposite illustrations of his meaning. Talking, for example, many years later, of his own isolation, he found an analogy to his case in the life he had observed on the veld. "It has been my lot in life," he said, "to travel through many regions of this country, and it has been my fortune to see a solitary springbok separated from the herd. I have often pitied his feelings and wondered how he works out the day; but I have a sort of idea that the time comes when he returns to his old associates, and perhaps the temporary dissociation will have strengthened the original ties." He bought a farm of 3000 acres, when he was up in the Transvaal, but it proved, so he told his friend Dr. Sutherland, a mere sink for money and of no earthly good; however, his experience gave him the right to boast to the South Africa Committee of 1897 that he had known the Transvaal for twenty-five years, and he never forgot the hospitality and other sterling qualities that he found among his Boer fellow-beings.

What he saw of the country he passed through and of its problems and his long meditations during this almost solitary trek made a lasting impression on him and turned his thoughts definitely to schemes of greater moment than diamond digging. For the immediate present the trek seems to have confirmed him in his cherished design of going to Oxford, "to help himself in his career," a career which he always intended to be something more than that of amassing money. Not that he objected to money: on that he was quite frank. He desired it partly to pay for Oxford and for other ambitions, but also because he liked and was amused by the game of winning it. But before leaving Kimberley he had to settle his affairs. Herbert, tired of diamond mining, sold his claims in De Beers New Rush and disappeared into the wilds and out of Cecil's life.[1] Rhodes then went into partnership with C. D. Rudd, who was to stay out to look after their properties: at this time, probably, he deserted the New Rush and began to buy up claims in Old De Beers, which he used to speak of as "a nice little mine," and which soon became the mainstay of his fortunes.

[1] In 1875 Herbert is heard of as a gold miner at Pilgrim's Rest in the Transvaal and he became a representative for that place in the Volksraad. He is heard of in prison at Lourenço Marques for an unsuccessful attempt at smuggling through Portuguese territory an old cannon destined for Sekukuni, a rebel chief in the Transvaal, and lastly in Nyassaland, where he was burnt to death in his hut in 1879. Cecil took great pains to have a gravestone erected to his memory and carefully preserved; and among his papers are several photographs of it sent to him a year before his own death.

I

Cecil and Frank returned to England together in 1873, Frank to take up his commission in the cavalry and Cecil to matriculate at Oxford in the Michaelmas term. He tried to get into University College, where his old friend Robert Yerburgh was; but that foundation, having already sent down Shelley for distributing revolutionary pamphlets, now with better excuse refused to take this other more Philistine dreamer, because he failed to qualify in Latin prose. So Rhodes went to Oriel as a passman. He never had rooms in college but lived in lodgings with Yerburgh and other friends, mostly Christchurch or University undergraduates, in King Edward Street or The High. In fact he seems to have gone very little into Oriel; and it is known what he thought of the quality of its dinners.

Certainly few undergraduates had so chequered and broken a sojourn at Oxford as Cecil Rhodes, and no man with less determination would, in face of all his difficulties, have carried out his purpose of obtaining his degree. Almost at the outset not only his Oxford career but even his life seemed in jeopardy. He had not yet thrown off his youthful delicacy and found the dampness of Oxford very trying to his lungs: in his second term he caught a chill rowing, which so affected his constitution that his doctor gave him only six months to live, even if he went back at once to the clear invigorating air of South Africa.[1] Two years, however, of the climate of Kimberley, more treks and the care of his friends the Curreys set him up again and he was back at Oxford for the Easter term of 1876. For the next two years he kept every term and found time for a visit to Kimberley during a long vacation, but he did not keep his last term or take his degree till 1881, when he was twenty-eight, had earned a large fortune for himself and was a rising member of the Cape Parliament.

Although he had become a rich man when he took his degree, as a freshman and even later he was sometimes embarrassed for money. Writing to Rudd in his first term

[1] Rhodes himself at a later date saw the entry "only six months to live" in the doctor's case-book.

he says: "I wake up fancying myself meeting various little bits of paper ranging over four or five months with my blessed signature at the bottom," and he admits having been obliged to borrow money on credit from Rudd's brother: "It is very unpleasant being under an obligation to any one . . . but I had not a sixpence and do not like to bother my father. People in England are so blastedly suspicious: they also charge 4 % for drafts." Two years later a payment of £50 leaves him so straitened that he determines to economize by reading at home in the Long Vacation. But such money difficulties were purely temporary; the claims of his Kimberley business were a more permanent and distracting call on his attention at Oxford. For, besides the flying visit to Kimberley on business during one long vacation, even in term time this singular undergraduate rarely loses sight of his growing interests in South Africa. In his letters to his partner Rudd he discusses the pros and cons of buying new claims, and is very strong against abandoning old ones because of bad times, for a rally is bound to come; he describes his interviews with the secretaries of rival companies or his visits to the diamond merchants of Hatton Garden, and sends his views on the state of foreign politics and their influence on the diamond market. He discusses ice machines and pumping engines, required for contracts undertaken by the partners, and asks Rudd to note his precise instructions to the makers about special winding drums and clutch gears to suit the conditions at Kimberley. He is also lavish in his instructions to his partner to "accumulate the ready" even more industriously than pumping engines. One letter, for instance, has an interesting apologia for his decision to eat dinners at the Temple while he is completing his terms at Oxford: "on a calm review of the preceding year," he writes, "I find that £3000 had been lost, because, owing to my having no profession, I lacked pluck on three occasions, through fearing that one might lose; and I had nothing to fall back on in the shape of a profession. . . . I am slightly too cautious now": besides the profession for himself, as a second string to their bow, he proposes a "nest-egg" in the form of a "marvellously solvent property" at Hampstead, which he has bought for £6200 and in which he offers to go halves with Rudd; "it is prettily situated and from all accounts is likely to increase in value . . . owing to a railway about three minutes which discharges in the centre of the city." With this nest-egg in reserve they would feel much safer as all Diamond Field securities are necessarily very risky.[1] "By all means," he concludes, "try and spare me for two years: you will find I shall be twice as good a speculator with a profession at my back. I will be reading hard all the summer."

In spite of this distracting background of business and speculation Rhodes took his life at the university more seriously than most passmen. It is true he read in his own way and rarely attended lectures: "Now, Mr. Butler," he said to his Dean, "you let me alone and I shall pull through somehow"; and he was quite right, for though his reading was spasmodic he took real interest in books he thought useful and made them part of his own life. He had his own ideas, too, of college discipline. "My dons and I have had some tremendous skirmishes," he wrote to Rudd, "I was nearly caught going to Epsom, but still do not think I shall be sent down. The change [from Kimberley] was at first rather odd." He also belonged to clubs more celebrated for good fellowship than for study, such as the Bullingdon, Vincent's and the Freemasons. At the banquet following his initiation as a Mason he created some scandal by his levity in revealing the secrets of the craft in spite of the president's reproofs and attempts by his friends to pull him down by the coat tails. For a time, too, he was master of the drag. His friends were most of them quiet men who kept to themselves, and many of whom afterwards took a more or less prominent part in politics or business. Robert Yerburgh was one of the leaders of the set, others were Dunbar Barton, afterwards a judge in Ireland; Maguire, who became a Fellow of All Souls and is now a director of the Chartered Company, and Sir Charles

[1] Rudd does not seem to have availed himself of Rhodes's offer, and Rhodes was obliged to realize and be content with £800 profit on his Hampstead speculation.

Metcalfe. Among less intimate acquaintances were Bodley, the historian of modern France, the present Lords Desborough and Downham, Arnold Forster, Tennyson d'Eyncourt, and G. W. E. Russell. Rhodes is noted in this set as one who was always talking, and some rather objected to the low views of human nature he at times expressed, derived no doubt from Kimberley acquaintances. He had rather a naïve habit, too, of bringing up some well-known phrase he had just read in Plato or Aristotle and insisting that all present should discuss it from his own and every other point of view. This habit of starting a debate, even with the most unsympathetic audience, on a subject or phrase, which happened to seize his attention for the moment, persisted throughout his life: it often wearied those who could not see his drift, but he found it most useful in clearing his own mind and making certain that he had grasped an idea in all its bearings before he acted upon it. He was indeed somewhat apart even from men in his own set. He was older than most of them, had not been to one of the regular public schools as they generally had, possessed far more acquaintance with life than any of them; and had queer unconventional ways. He would suddenly bring out a pocketful of diamonds to induce a man to join him in Kimberley, and he had a disconcerting way of impressing his creed of hard work on people. "Shouldn't do that," he said to a friend who expressed a desire to make his living by writing, "it is not a man's work—mere loafing. Every man should have active work in life."

But though he was so different from most of his undergraduate contemporaries, the Oxford spirit, so hard to define and yet so easy to recognize, sank into his nature. Aristotle's Ethics, the groundwork and the special glory of the Oxford system, with its virile appeal to young men to exercise their best faculties to the full, in order to attain a life of happiness and virtue, became to him a lasting source of inspiration: Gibbon, too, most characteristic, if most ungrateful, of Oxford's sons, gave him a basis for his political creed, that Rome's burden of governing the world had now fallen on England's shoulders. There, too, during

Rhodes's years at Oxford, was John Ruskin, preaching a new gospel of beauty and of public service to an age wearied of ugliness and commercial self-interest; the whole university thronged to his lectures; at his bidding dons and undergraduates went out daily to Hinksey and took off their coats to labour at Ruskin's road and learn the meaning of hard, unselfish toil; in language rarely surpassed for eloquence and burning conviction he was setting before them their duty as citizens of no mean city. "There is a destiny now possible to us," so spake the prophet in words yet ringing in the ears of young Oxford, when Rhodes came up, "the highest ever set before a nation to be accepted or refused. We are still undegenerate in race; a race mingled of the best northern blood. We are not yet dissolute in temper, but still have the firmness to govern and the grace to obey. . . . Will you youths of England make your country again a royal throne of kings; a sceptred isle, for all the world a source of light, a centre of peace; mistress of learning and of the Arts, faithful guardian of time-tried principles, under temptation from fond experiments and licentious desires; and amidst the cruel and clamorous jealousies of the nations, worshipped in her strange valour, of goodwill towards men? . . . This is what England must either do, or perish: she must found colonies as fast and as far as she is able, formed of her most energetic and worthiest men; seizing every piece of fruitful waste ground she can set her foot on, and there teaching these her colonists that their chief virtue is to be fidelity to their country, and that their first aim is to be to advance the power of England by land and sea: and that, though they live on a distant plot of ground, they are no more to consider themselves therefore disfranchised from their native land than the sailors of her fleets do, because they float on distant seas. . . . If we can get men, for little pay, to cast themselves against cannon-mouths for love of England, we may find men also who will plough and sow for her, who will behave kindly and righteously for her, and who will bring up their children to love her, and who will gladden themselves in the brightness of her glory, more than in all the light of tropical skies. . . . You think that an impossible ideal. Be it so; refuse to accept it, if you will; but see that you form your own in its stead. All that I ask of you is to have a fixed purpose of some kind for your country and for yourselves, no matter how restricted, so that it be fixed and unselfish."

It is for words such as these that Rhodes ever afterwards held the Inaugural Lecture as one of his greatest possessions. Among his papers there is a rough jotting in his handwriting: "You have many instincts, religion, love, money-making, ambition, art and creation, which from a human point of view I think the best, but if you differ from me, think it over and work with all your soul for that instinct you deem the best. C. J. Rhodes"—a jotting clearly suggested by these words of Ruskin. They were words that gave form and direction to the vague and troubled thoughts which, in the wide expanses of South Africa, had already been simmering in his brain.

But to Rhodes, as to most university men, teachers however inspired and lectures however sublime were not the most valuable part of Oxford life. The freedom and unconventionality of the undergraduate, untrammelled as he is by pompous precedents, yet insensibly moulded by a tradition of fastidious scholarship and exact research of truth, the interminable discussions wherein generation after generation of Oxford men renew the investigation of common beliefs in politics, religion and morals, and constantly bring currents of fresh air into the nation's creeds—all this delighted and impressed him. At Oxford he lost something of the hardness and cynicism which some of his friends there had deplored; and he never lost his sense of what he owed to those years. On his return to South Africa he showed a touching belief in the power of Oxford to give others what he owed her himself. "Bishop," he once said to his friend Dr. Alexander, "have you ever thought how it is that Oxford men figure so largely in all departments of public life? The Oxford system in its most finished form *looks* very unpractical, yet, wherever you turn your eye—except in science—an Oxford man is at the top of the tree." So, whenever he wanted a young man to carry on his work, he was always on the look out for one from his old university; he always gave a specially warm welcome to young Oxford men on a visit to South Africa; and it is related that in the last year of his life, when he was sad, suffering and desolate, his whole face lighted up when a chance visitor began quoting to him the first lines of Matthew Arnold's tribute to the "Beautiful city, so venerable, so lovely. . . ." "Go on," he said, "quote the whole passage," and as he listened he seemed to forget his pain. Finally, he could think of no better gift to the Empire he loved than to bring its young men to Oxford to draw from her the inspiration which had helped him so powerfully in his own career.

II

The ship carrying Rhodes home to England in 1873 crossed in mid-Atlantic an outgoing ship that had among its steerage passengers one Barnett Isaacs, the grandson of a rabbi and son of a little shopkeeper in Whitechapel. He was eighteen years old, and his sole capital consisted of sixty boxes of cigars, the result of many years' savings, but he had been so attracted by glowing reports from his brother Harry of the opportunities for profitable speculation to be found on the Fields that he had determined to try his luck there. Making his way up to Kimberley, he sold his cigars at an enormous profit and then turned his talents to the business known as that of a kopje-walloper. This was to go round the sorting-tables and buy up the diamonds as they were turned out of the gravel for prices which would ensure a large profit on their resale. He changed his name to the more arresting *nom de guerre* of Barney Barnato, hired a shanty as an office for a guinea a day—"worth it," he explained, "if you can make 30s. a day"—and as stock-in-trade bought up an old lame yellow pony from a retiring kopje-walloper; for he had observed this pony stopping of its own accord at the best sorting-tables and dealers' shanties and calculated that he would thereby obtain his business connection. Barney Barnato prospered in all his dealings, and in 1876, the year Rhodes returned to Oxford, found his capital increased to

£3000, which he expended on the purchase of the four best sections in the Kimberley mine. This shrewd purchase enabled him gradually to buy up more claims and sections in this mine, which Rhodes had now deserted for his " nice little mine," Old De Beers, and seven years after his steerage passage to South Africa with his five dozen boxes of cigars he was rich enough to found the firm of Barnato Brothers, dealers in diamonds and brokers in mining property. Rhodes had also been buying up claims in other mines, and in the course of the eighties the two men were brought face to face in a rivalry for supremacy on the Diamond Fields. Leave we now Barnato and return to Rhodes, still, even as an Oxford undergraduate, the Kimberley digger.

After the first feverish excitement on the discovery of the dry diggings, the diamond industry had passed through a period of serious depression. The causes for this depression were various. The diamond-bearing " yellow ground," though found to a depth of fifty or sixty feet, was worked with such energy that it soon showed signs of giving out. Below it, but still enclosed in the oval-shaped funnel of shale, known as " the reef," was a layer of bluish breccia composite, called the " blue ground," which extended to an unknown depth. The qualities of this blue ground were not much known, but most diggers thought that with the exhaustion of the yellow ground diamonds would cease to be found. Continual disputes with farm owners about licence fees also hampered the industry and were not abated until in 1875 the Crown bought up the farm Voruitzicht, containing both De Beers and the Kimberley mine, through the agency of Mr. Merriman. The roads between each claim were another source of trouble and dispute between the adjoining owners ; and, as they were undermined and fell in, the difficulty of working by a separate system of haulage for each claim created terrible confusion, each mine assuming the appearance of some vast spider's web of chains and ropes, along which buckets were constantly passing from the rim to the interior. Then the encircling reef began to cause serious difficulty, for, as the yellow ground supporting it was scooped out, it fell in, burying large tracts of diamond-bearing soil. Water also oozed through and flooded the mines. Lastly, with the trade depression of 1875 and the succeeding years the market for diamonds became poor and the prices to be obtained were barely remunerative. In consequence of all these difficulties many diggers gave up the business in despair and sold their claims for anything they would fetch.

Rhodes, however, was one of those who never despaired, because he was long-sighted enough to see remedies for all these difficulties. Both he and Barnato were convinced that the prosperity of the Fields would not cease with the exhaustion of the "yellow ground"; without any scientific knowledge to guide them, they believed that the blue ground also contained diamonds, and they were confirmed in their instinct by the Cape mineralogist. With regard to the other difficulties, fall of reef, flooding and the haulage of ground from the mines he had one panacea, economy of working by an amalgamation of interests. Froude, when he visited Kimberley in 1874, had seen the need of this amalgamation of interests to secure the use of the best and cheapest mechanical devices and to regulate the output of diamonds, and Barnato saw it as clearly as Rhodes. It could be effected in two ways: by a combination of claim-holders in a mine to work for objects of common interest, such as pumping out the water or removing blocks of reef; or by an absorption of all claims in a mine or even of the various mines into as few hands as possible.

Rhodes took his share in promoting both methods of united action. When the Mining Boards were established, with his partners Rudd and Alderson he tendered in 1874 for the contract to pump out the Kimberley, De Beers and Dutoitspan mines. By cutting the price very fine they got the contract over the head of some formidable rivals, and then nearly lost it for want of the pumping machinery. However, by dint of shameless importunity and by paying the exorbitant price of £1000 Rhodes obtained his engine from an unwilling seller at Victoria West; he had to pay another £120 to get it transported to Kimberley, and, as he had no more ready money, to persuade the Boer transport rider, who had never seen him before, to accept his cheque. He never forgot this old Boer's readiness to trust him and used to date his increased respect for the Boer race from this circumstance. The pumping contract did not prove all gain: engine and gear were often out of order, and once, when Rhodes was in charge, the boiler burst because he had forgotten to fill it; penalties incurred and incidental expenses also proved costly. But it was useful for the prominence it gave Rhodes on the Fields and was held by the partners for many years. While at Oxford Rhodes used to buy engines for the pumping at £115 to £140, a considerable reduction on the £1000 engine with which it started; and finally assigned the contract as a stock-in-trade to the first company he and Rudd started.

But Rhodes's warning to Rudd to accumulate "the ready" even more than pumping engines was dictated by his policy of purchasing all the claims he could lay hand on and thus doing away with the need of cumbersome mining boards. He and Rudd stuck to their Old De Beers mine and rapidly extended their holding in it, either by buying claims outright or by bringing other claim-holders into partnership with them. They acquired the valuable block known as Baxter's Gully and might once have bought the whole mine for a mere song, some £6000; but after discussing the offer for a whole day they reluctantly decided that they could not afford the capital as well as the licence fees, no doubt one of the occasions missed by Rhodes for "want of pluck." But he could not often blame himself on this score; his more usual tendency was to an invincible optimism. "I suppose our affair at De Beers looks bad now," he writes from his father's vicarage in 1876 [1]; "don't be low-spirited. If ever you were in a good thing that will give you a good income, that will. . . . I suppose you, like the rest, are in a happy state of bills, short cash, and prospective insolvency. All I can say is I envy you. I never was so happy as when in bills up to my neck and pump breaking down." And though he did not buy up the mine for £6000 he was gradually working to that end by more expensive methods. By 1880 R. Graham, Dunsmure, Alderson, Stow and English and other less

[1] Not 1879 as the *Diamond Fields Advertiser*, where the letter was published at Christmas 1906, surmises.

known De Beers claim-holders had joined the Rhodes-Rudd partnership, which on April 1 was floated as a company with the modest capital of £200,000. Some important groups were still outstanding at De Beers, but Rhodes's company already held the chief place. Meanwhile Barnato, who also formed his company in that year, was in much the same position at the Kimberley mine. For some years longer these two long-headed young men were content to work on parallel lines without meeting as rivals. But this was after Rhodes had taken his degree at Oxford, where, it must be remembered, he was still an undergraduate in residence during a considerable portion of the time he was thus carrying on his business as a pumping contractor and consolidating his interests in De Beers.

CHAPTER VI

DREAMS

RHODES had many sides to his character and a rare faculty for keeping all his interests distinct and becoming absorbed in the business of the moment. Within the five years from 1876 to 1881 he was by turns the Oxford passman interested in his Aristotle and in the talk and pastimes of the average undergraduate, the diamond digger immersed in the work of acquiring wealth, the South African politician, and, lastly, the dreamer of dreams. To most of his friends and contemporaries he showed only one side of his activities, and to each of them in turn that seemed the one purpose of his life: hence a strange diversity in his friendships. He had Oxford friends, friends coarsened by the rough and boisterous life of Kimberley, political friends, and a very few to whom he imparted his dreams and his most secret ambitions. Naturally such diverse friends did not always harmonize with one another: the budding statesman or the man of university education could not be expected to appreciate the merits Rhodes found in some of his Jewish financiers and unscrupulous adventurers of the diggings. But Rhodes did not care: once, a Harrow and Cambridge friend relates, he met him coming out of the train with one of his more disreputable acquaintances; while greeting Rhodes he studiously ignored his companion. "You know So-and-so," said Rhodes, but as the coolness was still obvious, "Oh, yes," he continued in the other man's hearing, "I remember, you think him a thorough-paced scoundrel," chuckling as, with a familiar gesture, he rubbed his two hands along his left side. Rhodes himself had the co-ordinating principle which harmonized and united all these interests, though as a natural consequence of his habit of concentration on the work of the moment, the interests of the diamond digger or the Cape politician sometimes seemed to loom too largely in the eyes of the world, and even in his own, and to give a disproportionate bias to the sum total of his activities. But to a few intimates he gave glimpses of his central ideas.

One of the few to whom Rhodes spoke without reserve of his innermost feelings was W. T. Stead, who published during Rhodes's life an article [1] giving his impression of these confidences. Here we get Rhodes's musings on life, on the destiny of the human race and on his own part in that destiny,—jerky musings, much like his jerky speeches and jerky conversations, with the logic implied rather than clearly expressed. Brought up in an orthodox household, he appears during his solitary meditations on the Natal plantation and at Kimberley to have found that his boyish creeds rested on no secure foundation. Soon after its publication in 1872 a book entitled *The Martyrdom of Man* seems to have fallen into his hands and made a lasting impression on his mind. The author, Winwood Reade, was a strange Ishmael, who travelled much in Central Africa studying the native and imported Mohammedan forms of religion he found there; basing his theories on these studies and on conclusions he derived from Buckle and Darwin, after a brilliant, if somewhat prejudiced, survey of the origin and development of all religions, he preaches, with all the passionate zeal of a religious enthusiast, that the only hope for man was in the exercise of his own faculties and energies unaided by appeals to non-existing supernatural powers. Rhodes in his turn, musing on destiny and influenced, no doubt, by this book, came to the conclusion that the Darwinian theory of evolution was the most likely explanation of the world. But this explanation did not lead him far, for he was faced by the further question: Is this evolution merely the result of blind forces or is it the law of some Supreme Being, some God? To this question Rhodes admitted to

[1] Republished by Stead in his little volume on the *Last Will and Testament of Cecil J. Rhodes.*

himself that he neither knew nor was ever likely to know the answer for certain: nevertheless—and here comes the contrast between the practical miner and the more scholarly theorist, Reade—he felt bound to adopt one or other alternative as a working proposition. After weighing all the pros and cons in his own mind, he concluded on a fifty per cent chance that there was a God, and on that fifty per cent chance resolved to base his beliefs and his actions. On this assumption his next step was to determine the end set before Himself by God for the evolution of the world; for, said he to himself, the proper business of man is to forward the end proposed by God. Running through various possible ends, wealth, worldly success and so on, he found that none of these were satisfactory, whereas on the broadest view of life and history, he argued, God was obviously trying to produce a type of humanity most fitted to bring peace, liberty and justice to the world and to make that type predominant. Only one race, so it seemed to him, approached God's ideal type, his own Anglo-Saxon race; God's purpose then was to make the Anglo-Saxon race predominant, and the best way to help on God's work and fulfil His purpose in the world was to contribute to the predominance of the Anglo-Saxon race and so bring nearer the reign of justice, liberty and peace.

It was a clumsy philosophy, like the man: a strange jumble of Darwin, Winwood Reade, and Gibbon, with an admixture of Aristotle and a distinct flavour of Ruskin's Inaugural Lecture, but real and personal to Rhodes by years of more or less disjointed and laborious thought of his own. In these clumsy thoughts we get glimpses of what was passing in his mind as he gazed over the veld in his long treks with the ox-wagon or sat moody and abstracted on his overturned bucket. Pringle, the South African poet, came to a more definite conclusion on the divine ordering of the world, but he sought for guidance from the same sky and the same earth as Rhodes:

> Where the barren earth and the burning sky,
> And the blank horizon, round and round,
> Spreads, void of living sight and sound—
> And here, while the night winds round me sigh,
> And the stars burn bright in the midnight sky,

As I sit apart by the desert stone,
Like Elijah at Horeb's cave alone,
" A still small voice " comes through the wild
(Like a father consoling a fretful child),
Which banishes bitterness, wrath and fear—
Saying, " Man is distant, but God is near ! "

Many, too, have vaguely held the same creed of the divinely appointed mission of the British race ; but few, like Rhodes, have made it a direct spur to action throughout their lives and regarded themselves as the agents of the divine purpose in so doing.

The first known result of these reflections wears a pathetically naïve aspect. During his Long Vacation at Kimberley in 1877 he drew up his will. His wealth was still to make, but he felt assured that he would make it, and was determined that his prospective millions should serve his ultimate purpose, whether he lived or died. With that curious mixture of child and prophet so often found in great men, this boyish document directed that a Secret Society should be endowed with the following objects: "The extension of British rule throughout the world, . . . the colonization by British subjects of all lands where the means of livelihood are attainable by energy, labour and enterprise, and especially the occupation by British settlers of the entire continent of Africa, the Holy Land, the Valley of the Euphrates, the islands of Cyprus and Candia, the whole of South America, the islands of the Pacific not heretofore possessed by Great Britain, the whole of the Malay Archipelago, the sea-board of China and Japan, the ultimate recovery of the United States of America as an integral part of the British Empire, . . . colonial representation in the Imperial Parliament, which may tend to weld together the disjointed members of the Empire, and finally, the foundation of so great a Power as to hereafter render wars impossible and promote the best interests of humanity." Sidney Shippard, the Attorney-General of Griqualand West, and Lord Carnarvon, or the Colonial Secretary for the time being, were appointed by this twenty-four-year-old enthusiast as trustees to carry out his wishes. There is something pathetic in the crudeness of the idea and the grandiose completeness with which the details are filled in. But the scheme appears less absurd if it is considered merely as the first sketch of a plan which Rhodes never lost sight of, and on which, gradually shedding some of the more extravagant details, he worked consistently through life. In 1882, 1888, 1891 and 1893 he made further wills, all with the same intention, less formally expressed perhaps, of forming a society to advance the interests of the British Empire, the only important changes being in the personality of the trustees. He found it difficult to get men who grasped and sympathized with his idea, and was glad to secure Stead as a trustee in 1891; but even he gave dissatisfaction and was expunged by a codicil to the last will of 1899. This will, to be referred to later, contained the final and most explicit directions for a scheme to carry out the purpose already outlined in more ambitious language twenty-two years earlier.

Rhodes was not content to leave what he counted as his main object in life, "the foundation of so great a Power as to hereafter render wars impossible and promote the best interests of humanity," to be attained merely by his heirs. He devoted his own life to it, even when he seemed absorbed by other schemes. To attain his purpose he had come to the conclusion that he needed wealth and that he needed friends. Without wealth he believed that little could be attained in the world. Speaking to Colquhoun about railway schemes in China he said, "You'll never do anything with it, Colquhoun; you've got no money"; and when Gordon told him that he had refused a room-full of treasure offered him by the Chinese Government, Rhodes, in no wise impressed by his magnanimity, replied: "I should have taken it and as many more rooms-full as they offered me: it is no use having big ideas if you have not the cash to carry them out." This conception of wealth as the chief motive power in the world obsessed him, and, in spite of his unselfish aims, was apt to distort his views and debase his standards. Such phrases as "philanthropy + 5 per cent," which he coined to illustrate his view of a guiding principle in British policy, and his belief that men could generally be won over by self-interest are the outcome of this obsession. The pursuit of wealth seemed at times the primary object of a man who cared little for its benefits to himself and had a soul above it. He even came to believe that with the material power wealth gave him he could achieve anything and thus in the end brought on his own undoing.

When it came to the choice of friends to help him in his great object it was far otherwise. He recognized that the men influenced chiefly by money considerations were not the confidants and partners needed for his life-work. Such men had their uses and he employed many of them in his subsidiary schemes for acquiring wealth or in working out the details of his main scheme. Those he trusted with his ideals and to whom he spoke openly were men of the type he sought for his Secret Society. They were not easy to come by, especially in Kimberley. Rhodes told Stead that after the death of the dear friend whom he had at one time named as his trustee, the only man he could then think of to take his place was a financier, to whom he endeavoured to explain his ideas: "but," he added, "I could see by the look on his face that it made no impression, that the ideas did not enter his mind and that I was simply wasting my time." Yet he found a few, and these he trusted whole-heartedly. Pickering, the trustee who died, was one: for him Rhodes had a romantic affection; he probably never loved any one so well: he sat day and night nursing him on his deathbed in 1888, neglecting all business for weeks at one of the most critical times in his fortunes: to him he had written that "the curious conditions of my will can only be carried out by a trustworthy person and I consider you one." With some of his friends of Oxford days he talked freely and tried, with more or less success, to impress them into the service of his great ideas. Among these was Maguire, whom later he brought out to South Africa, and Sir Charles Metcalfe, who came to construct railways. He gradually, too, acquired an extraordinary influence over some of his Kimberley friends and induced the most unlikely people to take up his causes and interests. One rough fellow, who had faithfully served Rhodes in strange corners of South Africa, hearing him once quote an incident of Roman history in a speech, was so abashed by his own ignorance that he forthwith followed his example and became an Oxford undergraduate. Another very different man, Alfred Beit, a Jew from Hamburg and the shrewdest financier of his time in South Africa, having made his fortune at Kimberley, stayed, under the spell of Rhodes's enthusiasm, to put his rare gifts at his command with a generosity and self-effacement rarely equalled.

One, however, of Rhodes's friends stands out as most especially identified with his schemes and fortunes. On his return from Oxford to Kimberley in the autumn of 1878, Rhodes first met a young Scottish doctor, born in the same year as himself, who had come out to share a practice with Dr. Prince, then the best-known doctor of the place. Leander Starr Jameson after taking a brilliant degree had originally come out to South Africa for the same reason as Rhodes and many others, to cure a weak lung. He soon made his mark professionally for his quickness of decision, and for the skilful and successful treatment of his cases. The acquaintance formed between Rhodes and Jameson quickly ripened into a close friendship. Jameson became one of the Twelve Apostles, as the mess presided over by Rhodes was called, and later, after Pickering's death, shared Rhodes's cottage opposite the club. Superficially the two men were a great contrast. Whereas Rhodes was a slow and laborious thinker on lines of his own, Jameson was sharp as a needle and quick at seeing another man's drift. Rhodes to the end retained many of the characteristics of a child: he was constantly surprised by his own thoughts and always anxious in any society to discuss fundamentals long accepted or ignored by his contemporaries; Jameson was brilliant in conversation and too sophisticated a man of the world to talk about fundamentals unless he was very sure of his audience; the one took long views and prepared his plans with infinite labour, the other was impetuous and impulsive; in curious contrast with the lofty idealism of his aims, Rhodes had a strong vein of calculated cynicism in his methods, whereas Jameson's cynical manner was a mere defensive crust assumed in the vain attempt to conceal his natural rashness. Probably these very differences helped to attract the two men to one another. Rhodes may well have felt that his solid, deliberate nature found its right complement in Jameson's sympathy and lightness of touch and that his ambitious plans might be forwarded by the Doctor's readiness in finding ingenious expedients to overcome difficulties. But these bonds would have been slight indeed had it not been for Jameson's whole-hearted devotion to Rhodes and what Rhodes confided to him of his schemes. Merriman had then left Kimberley; Pickering was dead; so Jameson gradually fell into their place as the comrade who cared not, as so many others did, chiefly for the money-making capacity of his friend, but was moved by the same public spirit. During their early morning rides on the veld or in long-drawn-out talks at the club or in their lodgings, he and Rhodes used to discuss plans for a definite policy in South Africa, the first practical outcome of even more ambitious projects. Rhodes came to love Jameson, but it is characteristic of him that, with all his love and genuine admiration for the Doctor's qualities, he was not blinded to his defects of judgement: at any rate, he never made him a trustee for any of his wills until on his deathbed he added his name in a codicil.

In those days Rhodes, when discussing his plans, used to pull out the map of South Africa and, laying a large hand on all the tracts up to the central lakes, say, "All this to be painted red; that is my dream." The idea thus expressed was not so crude as its statement. The political creed he gradually evolved from his musings on destiny and final causes has been conveniently summarized, by one who had several opportunities of talking to him openly,[1] under the following heads:

1. The world is made for the service of men, especially for civilized European men most capable of utilizing the crude resources of nature for the promotion of wealth and prosperity (*i.e.* the Anglo-Saxon race).

2. England is unable to protect herself without overseas dominions.

[1] Sir Sidney Low, *Nineteenth Century and After*, May 1902.

3. The British constitution is an absurd anachronism and should be re-modelled on the lines of the American Union with federal self-governing colonies as the constituent states.

4. The first aim of British statesmanship should be to find new areas of settlement and new markets to avoid penalizing tariffs from foreign rivals.

5. The largest tracts of unoccupied land are in Africa, which should be kept open for British colonization and commerce.

6. As the key of South Africa lies in the Anglo-Dutch states, the federation of these states should be aimed at under the British flag, but without any meddling by the home authorities.

To carry out this comprehensive policy Rhodes was biding his time. For ten years he was content to amass wealth, to make such converts as he could at the Kimberley Club and to gain a sound foundation for political power by the authority he was acquiring as one of the leading men of the diamond industry. He still took little part in local politics, but when occasion offered, such as Sir Bartle Frere's visit to the Fields, had shown a greater power of logic and more eloquence than anybody on the subject of the mining interests. He had shouldered his rifle in 1879 in a punitive expedition against some native marauders, during which he had come under fire near Christiania on the Vaal, and had first attracted the amused interest of the Lieutenant-Governor, Colonel Warren, by his absorption in a divinity cram-book for an Oxford examination during a railway journey. But in 1880, when he had formed his De Beers Mining Company, he felt that the time had come to make his views known to a wider audience. The Home Government had been meddling, with very serious results: so far from any prospect of the South African federation desired by Rhodes, Carnarvon's clumsy efforts to impose it had ended in a fiasco; the Transvaal had been annexed and was on the eve of revolt. As Rhodes remarked bitterly years afterwards, the Transvaal would have been quite happy under British rule had it not been shockingly misgoverned by the Imperial Commissioner, Sir

Owen Lanyon, " who conducted the business on the lines of a second-rate line regiment." The Dutch and English at the Cape, whom Rhodes wished to see united as a preliminary to all his plans for expansion, had been driven farther apart than ever before. The English still regarded the Dutch as a conquered and uncivilized race, the Dutch stood aloof in sullen obstinacy. Rhodes saw that this would not do; he was one of the few Englishmen to respect the Boers and recognize that they were to be reckoned with. The Boer farmer in his eyes was as much a " producer " as the Kimberley miner, and no more to be classed with mere " loafers "; and in his scheme of life he had a use for all " producers." Long before Majuba he used to say to Jameson: " The Dutch are the coming race in South Africa and they must have their share in running the country." All this he felt needed saying, and that he was the man to say it.

His opportunity came at the right moment. In 1880 Griqualand West was at last incorporated with the Cape, partly owing to the strong representations made by Merriman and Rhodes himself, and thereby became entitled to send representatives to the Cape Parliament. Rhodes did not stand for Kimberley, as might have been expected, but chose a rural constituency, the district of Barkly West. Here had been the headquarters of the old river-diggings, but it was now deserted by nearly all save the Dutch farmers who had seen the diggers come and go. This choice of a constituency where there was a large Dutch vote was significant of Rhodes's considered policy and proved a great strength to him. He could speak not only for Kimberley miners with whom his business lay, but also for the Boer farmers who were his constituents; and Barkly West remained faithful to him, through good report and ill, to the end of his life.

CHAPTER VII

THE PLUNGE INTO CAPE POLITICS

RHODES took his seat in the House of Assembly in April 1881 and very soon made himself known to the political world of the Cape. He was still a digger in appearance and in his free and easy manners, and so he remained to the end. Thus he scandalized Hofmeyr and other members of the more formal school by refusing to wear the conventional black coat and top hat: "I am still in Oxford tweeds," he said in one of his speeches, "and I think I can legislate as well in them as in sable clothing." But he had a keen eye for business. To make certain of a paper that would always print his speeches and any information he might give it, he bought a share in the *Cape Argus*, at the same time assuring the editor he should never attempt to interfere with the opinions expressed in its columns, a promise he appears to have kept with this paper, as well as with others in which he was afterwards interested. He made useful friends at Government House. The new Governor and High Commissioner, Sir Hercules Robinson, chosen by Lord Kimberley to inaugurate a less adventurous and more conciliatory policy than his predecessor Sir Bartle Frere, was attracted by the unconventional young digger, sympathized with his views on co-operation with the Dutch and was gradually led on to approve of his more ambitious schemes. The Imperial Secretary, Captain Graham Bower, R.N., proved an even more useful ally: for his knowledge of Cape politics and his fertility of resource gave him great influence over the High Commissioner as well as over the Cape politicians. Another friend at court was the Governor's private secretary, Newton, who had been a friend of Rhodes at Oxford. Sir Richard Southey and J. B. Currey, early friends at Kimberley, made him welcome; and very soon he was accepted by the rough and ready society of Cape Town in the genial colonial fashion which suited him well. He struck up a great friendship with Penfold, the port-captain, and under his tuition became an enthusiastic yachtsman in Table Bay. As usual with things that interested him, this sport gave him a happy analogy for one of his speeches. " It is as if," he said, " I were a little sailing boat in Table Bay and knew exactly what I am starting for. There are honourable members opposite who have racing boats, but I dare to challenge them and to say that they do not know what ports they are sailing for; and though they may be manned with a smarter crew, what with their backing and filling I am not sure they will not scuttle and go to the bottom." Once, too, when he was Prime Minister, he put his nautical experience to more practical use. During one of those tremendous storms which sometimes sweep over the Bay he heard that two lighters had got adrift and were in deadly peril; he not only saw to it that the port tug should put out to their rescue but insisted in going out with her himself, and for a whole night was buffeted and tossed about by the angry seas in very serious danger.

Above all, he revelled in the talk and arguments of the politicians and civil servants who foregathered at the Civil Service Club or at Poole's for lunch, or at odd times invaded the rooms he shared with Captain Penfold in Adderley Street. In those days there were some good talkers and thinkers among them: Molteno, the first Prime Minister of the Cape; Upington, the wild Irishman, witty and perennially in debt; Sauer, shrewd and caustic; Saul Solomon, the friend of the natives, who, in spite of his physical insignificance, had by his eloquence and passionate conviction won for himself a place apart in the House of Assembly; Schreiner, the brilliant young advocate, incorruptible and conscientious, ready to split a hair or prolong an argument to any hour of the night, who, with his brilliant sister Olive, was enormously attracted by Rhodes's personality. There, too, he found his old friend

Merriman, sparkling with wit, and ever ready with the pungent phrase that clung to his victims for life; full of strange lore, culled from every source, ancient or modern; caustic without malice to his opponents but generous to a fault with friends, such as Rhodes, in whom he believed; and always bubbling over with enthusiasm for some great cause or principle.

But the man with whom, more than any in the Cape Parliament, Rhodes had for long the closest political affinity was not usually to be found in these jovial parties. Jan Hofmeyr, Onze Jan as he became known throughout South Africa, was some eight years older than Rhodes, having been born in 1845 at Welgemeend, a farm on the slopes of Table Mountain. The ancestor who founded the Cape branch of the family landed at Table Bay a century earlier and lies buried in the grounds of Groote Schuur, the Dutch Company's great barn at Rondebosch. By ancestry and birth rooted to the soil of the Cape Peninsula, Hofmeyr had all his education there too, and at sixteen took to journalism in Cape Town; at twenty-six he was editor of the *Zuid Afrikaan*, the leading Dutch newspaper. He had become member for Stellenbosch two years before Rhodes took his seat, and was already one of the most powerful forces in Cape politics, for by his paper he had made himself the mentor of the Dutch party not only at the Cape but throughout South Africa. He had two great political objects in life: to awaken his Dutch fellow-countrymen to a sense of their own importance and, secondly, to form a federation of all South African states. With the first object he founded a union of Boer farmers, afterwards merged into the better known Afrikander Bond; he urged Dutchmen to stand for parliament and encouraged the revival of the Dutch language. "I am a little bit of an Englishman," he once said, "as far as language is concerned. The Englishman loves his language and I mine. . . . The language question is a question of life and death. Despise the language and you despise your nationality; honour your language and you honour your nationality." South African union he advocated as early as 1865 and even supported Carnarvon's and Froude's crazy scheme of federation, speaking at a banquet in Froude's honour in 1874: in 1880, it is true, he voted against it, but only as a protest against the annexation of the Transvaal. Though a reformer in these respects he had all the conservative instincts of his own Dutch landowners. He supported protection and privilege for the farmer, wrote and spoke against responsible government in 1872, upheld strict orthodoxy in the Church and resisted Saul Solomon's progressive views on native policy. When Rhodes came to Capetown, he found Hofmeyr the unchallenged leader of the Dutch contingent in parliament, enlarged and brought to discipline by his exertions; and, though his supremacy in the country districts was challenged by Du Toit's actively disloyal Afrikander Bond, he was on the eve of capturing that body and forcing it to abandon some of its extreme tenets. For his cautious and secret methods of political intrigue Merriman gave him the nickname of "The Mole." This had some justification. He was always inclined to overcome opposition by conciliatory methods and, like Rhodes himself, preferred to deal with a man by finding some common basis of agreement than to fight him. By nature he was cautious and averse to undertaking personal responsibility. Thus he only once held office in a ministry, and that for a very brief spell, preferring to be the Warwick of ministries that displeased him and the secret counsellor of those that supported his views. He several times gave considerable umbrage to his Transvaal cousins by his timidity: recently, for example, he had disapproved of the republicans' revolt because he feared they would be beaten by England, and even after Majuba urged them at once to desist from further hostilities. But, though economical of his dogmatic assertions, on questions of principle he never had any hesitation in coming out into the open and expressing his views, however unpopular they might be. He had protested vehemently against the annexation of the Transvaal, and supported that country in its efforts to regain freedom, while as a political organizer he did more than any man to make the Dutch a force in South Africa.

Both in appreciation of the Dutch element in South Africa and in a desire for federation Rhodes had points in common with Hofmeyr. But in April 1881 the divergence between them seemed more marked than the agreement. Majuba had just been fought and negotiations for the retrocession of the Transvaal opened. Nearly every Englishman in South Africa had a sense of bitter humiliation, and Rhodes would hardly have been human had he not shared in this feeling. An acquaintance speaks of the "unspeakable anger of the militant young Englishman" at Gladstone's surrender and his determination "not to be trampled on by these Dutchmen." Hofmeyr he regarded as a dangerous man full of machinations against England. Hofmeyr for his part had been told that Rhodes was "a regular beefsteak, John Bull Englishman," and what was perhaps worse, "a young Oxford Englishman, full, some said, of the exclusive traditions of Oxford." But these feelings did not last: in the same conversation in which he expressed his indignation Rhodes admitted that he did not dislike the Dutch and that the best plan would be to work with Hofmeyr: and when the two men were brought together by a friend their distrust of one another vanished. Fourteen years later, at a banquet to Hofmeyr, each gave his account of this first meeting. While still finding many points of disagreement, Rhodes said of Hofmeyr that he was the fairest opponent he had ever met. and Hofmeyr declared that this talk had laid the foundation of a lasting friendship; "the secret," he added, "of this friendship was this: I found in Mr. Rhodes the true Englishman but at the same time the man who could make allowances for true nationalism existing in other people. Also, I remember, about the time we were introduced, the Transvaal War broke out, and Mr. Rhodes—perhaps as it behoved him as an Englishman [1]—was all against the Boers and Transvaal independence. I was on the other side. But when the war was over we had a talk with one another, and I said to Mr. Rhodes, 'It is an awful pity that the war broke out.' I was surprised when Mr. Rhodes

[1] This is a characteristic instance of the Dutchman's high standard of honour even for an enemy. Louis Botha had the same standard. The story is told that shortly after the Boer War he met an Englishman in London who said to him effusively: "I always hoped you would win," whereupon Botha turned his back on him.

said: 'No, it is not. I have quite changed my opinion. It is a good thing. It has made Englishmen respect Dutchmen and made them respect one another.' Well, when an Englishman could speak like that to a Dutchman, they are not far from making common cause with one another." They thus found that they had aims in common, the one, as it has been well said, with his British point of view, which he looked at from the colonial angle, the other with his colonial point of view, which he tried to broaden from the standpoint of Britain and the Empire as a whole. Misunderstandings as to important details and methods were not entirely removed at first, but with growing acquaintance the two men found it possible to work as allies.

Rhodes's first three sessions were chiefly taken up with discussions on the Basuto War, which had been brought on by the decision of the Prime Minister, Sir Gordon Sprigg, to disarm the Basutos under some forgotten statute. Rhodes and the Kimberley people disliked the war, because they had many Basutos working for them in the mines, and as one man said, "After all, we sold them the guns; they bought them out of their hard-earned wages, and it *is* hard lines to make them give them up again." Early in the first session Sprigg fell, partly for his mismanagement of this business, partly owing to the general dissatisfaction with his government: the Diamond Fields members, for example, headed by Rhodes, bluntly told him they must withdraw their support because of his failure to extend the railway to Kimberley; he had also alienated Hofmeyr and the Bond, who had originally helped him to office and who now transferred their support to his successor, Scanlen. The Basutoland question itself has no great interest to-day except as an illustration of the Home government's unfortunate indecision in South African affairs. In 1854, when the Orange River sovereignty had been given back to the Free State Boers, Basutoland, the native state on its eastern border, had been left in the air: fifteen years later, after a succession of wars between the Boers and the Basutos, it had been proclaimed under British protection, then two years afterwards given over to the Cape. Finally, in 1883, when the inability of the Cape to deal with the problem had been proved by three years of desultory and inconclusive fighting, the Imperial Government agreed to take back the country under its protection, in which condition it has fortunately remained ever since.

From the outset Rhodes had advocated this solution, not from any love of "meddling by the Home Government," but simply on the ground that the Cape was not in a position to deal effectively with a country so far removed from its natural interests; and on the score of expense. "Are we a great and independent South Africa?" he asked: "No, we are only the population of a third-rate English city spread over a great country," and in these circumstances he declared that it was the duty of the Imperial Government to bear the burden. But Scanlen did not dare to call in the Imperial Government, such was its unpopularity in South Africa, till every other means had been tried. But while rejecting Rhodes's advice for the time being he persuaded him to accept a seat on a commission to decide on claims for compensation by loyal Basutos; he also sent for Colonel Gordon from his "barracks and drains" at Mauritius to reorganize the colonial forces and in the hope that he would finish the business without bloodshed or heavy expense.

Rhodes, for his part, was quite willing to go to Basutoland to study the problem at first hand and did his work on the commission thoroughly. Five months were spent in taking evidence at Maseru, Leribe, Mafeteng and other places; Rhodes made a special report dissenting from his colleagues, who wished to extend the compensation to two white traders, on the ground that such a claim had never been recognized by any government. "Even England," he argued, "with all her wealth, did not compensate her loyal subjects in India for the losses sustained in the recent mutiny," and he protested "against this recommendation for compensation to be paid out of the public funds of a poor and embarrassed Colony on principles which are not founded on the practice and precedent of the older and richer countries of the world." Though he was in a minority of one, his arguments on this point prevailed.

While he was in Basutoland one of those rare meetings, of which the scanty records are so tantalizing to the historian, took place; when two outstanding men of a generation come face to face and then pass on. Rhodes and Gordon had longer and more interesting talk than Wellington and Nelson on that one historic occasion in the Secretary of State's waiting-room; but afterwards they went their ways never to meet again. Characteristic too of the British Empire was this meeting of two such men, called from the ends of the earth and thrown together for a brief space in a barbarous corner of South Africa—Gordon, who had taken it all in the day's work, as a major in the Engineers, to organize and command the forces of the great Chinese Empire, to rule with absolute sway the Soudan and equatorial Africa, to make a flying trip to Ireland, between two terms of duty, to ascertain the merits of the Irish question, to build barracks in Mauritius or to bring hope and a prospect in life to the boys of the ragged schools of Woolwich; and Rhodes, the rough diamond-digger, with all his yet unrealized dreams for the advance of the British race in Africa and throughout the world. To Gordon, the practical mystic convinced of his mission humbly to work out the will of God, Rhodes in these communings under the African sky may well have unbosomed himself of his clumsy philosophy and his fifty per cent God and all his dreams; for the older man, though surer in his convictions, would have understood. Strange as it may seem, Rhodes, the younger by twenty years, appears in practical matters to have taken the mentor's part. He it was who explained to Gordon how foolish he was not to accept the Chinese treasure, and told him not to talk to the Basutos as if he were their supreme lord, but to remember that he was only the servant of Sauer, the Minister for native affairs; and Gordon took the reproof meekly and went next day to explain this to the natives, adding, in an aside to Rhodes, "I did it because it was the right thing, but it was hard, very hard." At any rate Gordon believed in the young man, and on parting begged him to stay and work with him; but Rhodes had to be about his own business and must needs go. "There are few men in the world," replied Gordon, " to whom I would make such an offer, but of course you will have your own way. I never met a man so strong for his own opinion; you think your views are always right." So they parted. Once more Rhodes heard from him; when Gordon was starting on his last journey, he telegraphed to Rhodes to join him; and Rhodes once more had to refuse, for he was just about to join the Cape Ministry. But when, little more than two years after these meetings in Basutoland, he heard of the tragedy of Khartoum, he was deeply moved and kept on repeating sadly: " I am sorry I was not with him; I am sorry I was not with him."

By 1883 the Imperial solution for the Basuto imbroglio, which Rhodes had seen to be inevitable, was at last accepted. His friend Merriman, a member of Scanlen's Ministry, arranged the terms in London, and Scanlen proposed in the Cape Parliament the re-transfer of the country to the Home Government. The only opponents left to the proposal were Hofmeyr and his followers; so great was the Dutchman's distrust of the Imperial factor in South African affairs that he had a plan for joint action with the Free State to bring the Basutos to submission. Unfortunately for him, President Brand was quite content that the Imperial power alone should do the police work on his eastern border, and rejected Hofmeyr's scheme. In the debate in the House, Rhodes took a leading part on behalf of the Government. He had already won a considerable position for himself as a politician. At first his rather nervous, excitable manner of speaking, his squeaky voice, his jerky utterance, and his uncouth gestures had told against him; but as the hearers of Chatham had felt, so men had begun to feel, in a lesser degree, about Rhodes that " the man was infinitely greater than his words." In his second session he was already recognized as the leader of the powerful contingent from the Diamond Fields, though he had always proclaimed his indifference to party ties or local prejudices, because, in his own words, " localism is the curse of South Africa." He had made approaches to Hofmeyr by a sympathetic attitude to his proposal to allow the Dutch language to be used in debate, and a well-turned compliment to him on the terms of the loyal address he had drawn up on the conclusion of peace with the Transvaal. But in this debate on Basutoland he took occasion to make plain where he differed from Hofmeyr on methods of securing South African union.

Hofmeyr during this and the preceding year had been carrying on his great fight to capture the Afrikander Bond. Its founder, the Rev. S. J. du Toit, who afterwards became one of Rhodes's most devoted adherents, had frankly stated in his paper that " the one hindrance to Confederation is the English flag. Let them take that away, and within a year the Confederation under the free African flag would be established." Hofmeyr was alarmed at such a doctrine, for he, like Rhodes, believed the only hope of union to lie in full co-operation between English and Dutch, and, as he said, " five Englishmen in the Bond would help South African unity more than a hundred Boers " ; but such a doctrine would naturally keep off any Englishman. On the advice, therefore, of a friend, he himself joined the Bond, and by ceaseless negotiation and persuasive talk, of which he was a past-master, brought round the majority to drop the disloyal part of their programme ; still, to secure that end, he thought it prudent to admit that South Africa might one day be independent, though he never regarded the eventuality as within the practical politics of the next fifty years. At any rate, Hofmeyr, by joining a body which had once expressed such sentiments about the British flag, had become suspect to Rhodes ; and in this speech he determined to have it out with him.

At the outset he easily disposed of Hofmeyr's plan for joint action with the Free State in Basutoland by pointing out that the Free State itself did not welcome the suggestion : " that people are surely the best judges of the question, and they say they want to be protected by the Imperial Government." Then turning to the wider question of union, " I would like to hear," he added, " what Mr. Hofmeyr is reported to have said about a United States of South Africa under its own flag. . . . I have my own views as to the future of South Africa, and I believe in a United States of South Africa, but as a portion of the

British Empire. I believe that confederated states in a colony under responsible government would each be practically an independent republic, but I think we should also have all the privileges of the tie with the Empire. Possibly there is not a very great divergence between myself and the honourable member for Stellenbosch, excepting always the question of the flag." In a later speech Rhodes crystallized his view in the phrase: "the government of South Africa by the people of South Africa with the Imperial Flag for defence."

Hofmeyr was able to answer this question satisfactorily, for Rhodes's formula exactly corresponded with his own view of South African union; of which he gave ample proofs, when later he attended two colonial conferences as a delegate for the Cape. In the following month Rhodes welcomed his assurances and praised the "high aim . . . of the honourable member for Stellenbosch. His aspirations are for the union of South Africa." Thus early in his parliamentary career Rhodes laid down the guiding principle of his South African policy, and found, as he had hoped, that for this policy he could work in hearty co-operation with the leader of his Dutch fellow-colonists.

CHAPTER VIII

THE FIRST STEP NORTHWARDS—BECHUANALAND

RHODES was the more willing to admit the "meddlesome Home Government" into Basutoland, because he felt that a call would soon be made on all the colony's resources to deal with the more vital problem of Bechuanaland. In this territory, he believed, the future not only of the Cape but of all South Africa was involved.

Bechuanaland, bounded on the east by the Transvaal and by Damaraland and Namaqualand on the west, forms the isthmus leading from Griqualand West to the interior of Africa. The trackless Kalahari desert makes a great part of it uninhabitable, except by a few wandering Bushmen, but on the east, close to the Transvaal border, there is a strip of good land where the Bechuana tribes congregated in their villages, Taungs, Mafeking, Kanye and Shoshong. Along this strip, always hugging the Transvaal border, was the well-marked track by which explorers, hunters, missionaries and traders travelled into the interior, and which was the main approach to the Tati Gold Fields, opened in 1869, Matabeleland and the hunting grounds of the Zambesi.[1] Made famous by men like Livingstone and Moffat, Baines, Mauch, Gordon Cumming and Selous, the track was known as the English road or the Missionaries' road. Its proximity, however, to the Transvaal border had not been without its dangers. During the 'fifties the Boers used to raid the border villages

[1] A petition from Kimberley in 1884, which shows the inspiration of Rhodes, describes it as "the great trade route to the interior, well known to the English people through the narratives of Livingstone and Moffat . . . along it the trade and commerce of the interior have for years passed unmolested."

of the natives and interfere with European travellers on the road. Thus in 1852 they sacked Livingstone's mission station at Shoshong and later told Moffat that he must obtain leave from their Government to travel to his own headquarters in Bechuanaland. Sir George Grey and other governors protested against these aggressions; the Keate award of 1871 and the Pretoria Convention ten years later definitely excluded the republic from interfering in Bechuanaland. But the Boers never ceased to regard this borderland as coming naturally within their sphere, and were likely to continue doing so until it had been placed under some more powerful government than that of the native chiefs.

Several Englishmen before Rhodes had come to the conclusion that the only way of safeguarding this approach to the interior was to bring it within the British dominions. In 1871 the missionary Mackenzie had advocated this; Southey had always contemplated an advance beyond Griqualand West; in 1878 Sir Bartle Frere had urged the Colonial Secretary to proclaim a protectorate over Bechuanaland as far north as Lake Ngami, not far short of the Zambesi; and long before these Livingstone had boasted—not idly: "The Boers resolved to shut up the interior and I determined to open the country; and we shall see who have been most successful in resolution, they or I." Rhodes had come to the problem afresh, with special opportunities for understanding its importance. Living at Kimberley, the starting-point of the up-country trade, he knew well the value of this trade to Cape Colony; in one year alone, he told the House, a single Kimberley firm had done business in Bechuanaland of the value of £100,000. At Kimberley he was constantly seeing hunters or missionaries setting forth along the road or returning with the booty of the chase, and with tales of the country and natives of the far interior. He himself had travelled along part of the road in his trek with Herbert and again with Warren's expedition against the Korannas. As a result of endless talks with Merriman, Pickering, Jameson and other friends, and no doubt with Warren and his staff in 1879, he had long formed the conviction that Bechuanaland, the key to the interior, must be secured. But he differed in two points from others who had previously held this view. First, he believed that the Cape itself, as the dominant state in South Africa, should undertake the task, instead of calling upon the Imperial Government to proclaim a protectorate. Secondly, he believed that the question could be raised above a contention on racial lines, and that English and Dutch might be induced to co-operate in forwarding a South African policy. In a word, he believed that the extension of British influence could only be worked in accordance with the sentiment of South Africans and with the help of the Cape politicians, English and Dutch.

In his second session, when for the first time he called attention publicly to the question, the southern part of Bechuanaland was in a hopeless state of confusion and anarchy. Native troubles on the border had given the usual opportunity for the designs of needy European adventurers. Mankoroane, the Batlapin chieftain at Taungs, just beyond the Griqualand West border, had a feud with Massouw, his neighbour within Transvaal territory; and farther north, at Mafeking, Montsioa was at war with Moshette, a rival chief of the Barolongs. Mankoroane and Montsioa were regarded as friendly by the English; the cause of their antagonists was favoured by the Boers. Both sides in the two disputes made large promises of land to any white volunteers who should come to their help, and it may be imagined what a disorderly crew of shady adventurers, cattle and horse thieves and land sharks had been attracted to the four camps by this bait; in fact, the whole borderland of Griqualand West and the south-west Transvaal had become a veritable Alsatia. Both Mankoroane and Montsioa, the chiefs with English leanings, got the worst of it, and by the end of 1882 had been obliged to cede considerable portions of their territory to satisfy the claims of their rivals' white mercenaries, mostly Boers. These Boer volunteers, as they were called, proclaimed independent republics over the territory they had thus acquired. Stellaland was the name given to the republic formed on Mankoroane's lands, with its capital at Vryburg, and Van Niekerk, a Transvaal farmer, as the administrator; the other, in Montsioa's country, was called Land of Goshen, and was administered by one Gey Van Pittius, with his seat of government at Rooigrond, close to Mafeking. But the establishment of these republics brought no peace; the defeated chieftains were always on the look out for their revenge; cattle and horse thefts, raids and reprisals went on as before. The Transvaal Government, naturally disturbed at the unsettled state of their border, urged the Imperial Government to make some arrangement by which peace could be maintained. But the Imperial Government would not hear of accepting any further responsibility north of the present border, nor would they allow the Transvaal to encroach beyond the boundaries laid down by the London Convention.

The danger, as it appeared to Rhodes, in this chaotic state of affairs lay chiefly in these new republics of Stellaland and Goshen, both of which lay right athwart the road into the interior. Whether they remained independent or, as seemed more probable, were absorbed by their neighbour the Transvaal, they were a standing menace to communications with all the country up to the Zambesi. Already there were reports of natives returning home from the Kimberley mines being robbed and impeded on their way through the new republics, and the fear of high tariffs and other obstacles to trade and travel through them was, to judge by the example of the Transvaal customs duties, no visionary danger. So, after uttering his preliminary warning in 1882, in the following year he got himself appointed on a commission to investigate some dispute about the boundaries of Griqualand West. Interpreting his instructions largely, he took occasion to visit Mankoroane at Taungs as well as Van Niekerk at Vryburg. From the former he obtained a long catalogue of his grievances against the Stellaland volunteers and an offer to cede his country to the Cape. At Vryburg he found intrigues afoot for the annexation of the new republic by the Transvaal, but secured a petition from a considerable minority of the settlers, requesting annexation by the Cape Government. He found nobody who wanted to be taken over by the Imperial Government.

The occasion was critical, for the Transvaal deputation was soon starting on its way to London to press for modifications of the Pretoria Convention, especially in relation to the republic's south-western boundary, and Merriman was already there to discuss preliminaries with the Colonial Office. So impressed was Rhodes with the need for immediate action that he at once got into communication over the telegraph wires with the Prime Minister, Scanlen. For the next month animated conversations between the two were carried on by this means, Rhodes pointing out that unless prompt action were taken hostilities would break out afresh, urging that Merriman should be instructed to protest against "an inch more territory" being handed over to the Transvaal; "part with the interior road," he added, "and you are driven into the desert"; and that the only statesmanlike course was to meet the Cape Parliament with a proposal to accept Mankoroane's offer and the petition he had obtained in Stellaland for annexation to the Cape. "For goodness' sake," he implored, "meet Parliament with *some* policy. . . . I put it to you, if you have to go out, is it not better to go out on what is a real policy?"

But Rhodes's prayers and taunts were unavailing. Scanlen was too much afraid of the Dutch vote to propose annexation and would give only non-committal answers. So on his return to Cape Town Rhodes himself proposed in Parliament that a resident commissioner should be sent to Mankoroane, as a preliminary to the annexation of Stellaland, and tried to arouse the House "to the supreme importance of this question of Bechuanaland . . . a question upon the proper treatment of which depends the whole future of this colony. . . . I look upon this Bechuanaland territory," he continued, "as the Suez Canal of the trade of this country, the key of its road to the interior. . . . The question before us really is this, whether this colony is to be confined to its present borders, or whether it is to become the dominant state in South Africa—whether, in fact, it is to spread its civilization over the interior." Some said, he went on, turning with a compliment to Hofmeyr and his followers, that it would be just as good for their purposes if Bechuanaland fell to the Transvaal; but would it be so? Already the Transvaal was making it difficult for Cape traders by high tariffs; if then the Transvaal was allowed to close the only door to the interior by similar tariffs it would mean ruin to the Cape trade. He said that from no animus against the Dutch as a race; on the contrary, he would confirm the titles of the Dutch settlers in Stellaland, only they should be brought under the jurisdiction of the dominant state in South Africa.

This appeal fell unheeded from his lips. Hofmeyr, with the recollection of the annexation of the Transvaal fresh in his mind, thought then that the only way of maintaining the Dutch cause was to support the Transvaal through thick and thin; he also felt with some reason that these border quarrels concerned the Transvaal more intimately than Cape Colony, and that the Imperial Government's policy of refusing to intervene, while not allowing the Transvaal to do so, was like that of the dog in the manger. Apart from the Dutch, the question at that time interested very few of the Cape colonists. It required pressure from an unexpected quarter to arouse the feeling which Rhodes and his Kimberley friends had been unable to stimulate. The action of Germany now, and not for the last time, helped him in a difficulty.

The scramble for Africa had just begun when Rhodes entered public life. In 1879 Stanley inaugurated King Leopold's Congo Association and began to mark out territory for that philanthropic society; M. de Brazza soon followed suit for the French in the same region; other French explorers started annexing territory farther up on the west coast; and the Republic obtained a free hand in Tunis. Italy turned longing eyes on Tripoli and on the Red Sea littoral. Portugal began to revive claims on the east and west coasts of Africa that had lain dormant for nearly three centuries. Germany also determined to have her share. Hitherto, under Bismarck's influence, she had confined herself to Europe and planted no colonies; "for us," said the great chancellor, when pressed to expand overseas, "it would be just like the silken sables in the noble families of Poland, who have no shirts to their backs"; and he had no desire to compete on this score with France and England, then the chief colonizing powers. England's fleet rendered rivalry hopeless there, while France was encouraged by him to devote her energies to Tunis and Tonkin to divert her from Alsace-Lorraine and other unpleasant memories of 1870. But even before 1870 there had been a colonial party in Germany; and the success of that war had strengthened it. German missionaries and traders and a few explorers had long been active in South and East Africa; the great merchants and shippers of Bremen and Hamburg had founded colonization societies; a widely read article by E. von Weber in 1879, advocating the establishment of German influence in Delagoa Bay, the Transvaal and Matabeleland, "to pave the way for the foundation of a German African empire of the future," had stimulated the popular imagination. In 1882 Bismarck himself yielded to the growing feeling and began to take a hand in the scramble. He went warily to work, leaving France and other countries to their own devices, and picking out those parts of Africa in which England alone was interested, because at that time England had become involved in the Egyptian morass, whereby she had alienated France, and was prepared to pay a heavy price in other quarters for Germany's support. Besides, it was thought that her opposition could be discounted, for though she had long enjoyed free scope for her trade and political influence on the Zanzibar coast, in South Africa and on the Gold Coast, and though most of the discoveries in Central Africa had been made by her explorers, she had hitherto been averse to declaring protectorates or annexing territory, even when pressed to do so by the native chiefs. Gladstone, too, was in power, and he had already expressed his apprehensions of African adventure. "Our first site acquired in Egypt," he had written in 1877,[1] ". . . will be the almost certain egg of a North African Empire that will grow and grow . . . till we finally join hands across the Equator with Natal and Cape Town, to say nothing of the Transvaal and Orange River on the south, or of Abyssinia or Zanzibar

[1] *Nineteenth Century* for August 1877.

to be swallowed by way of *viaticum* on our journey": a curious forecast of Rhodes's own projects and of the opposition which he would have to meet.

The first point of German attack, in south-west Africa, was well chosen. The native territories of Damaraland and Namaqualand, extending from the Orange River to the Portuguese claims in Angola and from the Atlantic to Bechuanaland on the east, had always been regarded as within the Cape sphere of interest, but had never been formally annexed. Ever since 1867 various suggestions for the annexation of the country had been put before the Home Government by the Cape Ministries, by Sir Bartle Frere and even by the German Government, who desired protection for the Rhenish missionaries established among the natives. In 1878 Lord Carnarvon had grudgingly agreed to take over Walfisch Bay, the only good harbour on the coast; but this was the limit of concession; and in 1880 Sir Hercules Robinson had been explicitly instructed by Lord Kimberley that "the Government will not give its support to plans for extending British jurisdiction over Great Namaqua and Damaraland." When, therefore, on May 1, 1883, the German flag was hoisted at Angra Pequeña on the coast of Namaqualand, the English had only themselves to blame. Bismarck even went so far as to enquire whether England would protect the factory to be set up there by the Bremen merchant Lüderitz, before he declared a German protectorate; and added that he had "not the least design to establish any footing in South Africa." But when the German flag had once been hoisted he insisted on his rights, and a British ship sent from the Cape to Angra Pequeña was warned off by a German gun-boat.

For some months afterwards animated discussions went on between the English and German Foreign Offices about the German claim to this territory. Too late, our Foreign Minister, Lord Granville, and Lord Derby, his colleague at the Colonial Office, saw the danger of this intrusion by a foreign power into South Africa. Derby sent urgent messages to the Cape Ministry for arguments to rebut the German contention that we had no rights there. Unfortunately Scanlen's Ministry was then preoccupied with its own precarious position and apparently did not realize the importance of haste. Lord Derby's telegrams were left unanswered, and the proof, for what it was worth, of a virtual administration of the territory in Sir Bartle Frere's time was never produced. Rhodes himself is not exempt from blame in this matter, for during the seven weeks before Scanlen's fall he was occupying the post of Treasurer-General in the Ministry. Apparently he and Merriman knew the danger of delay, for, as Rhodes himself related afterwards, they used to say daily to one another, "We must have Damaraland," but they were unable to impress their zeal upon the rest of the Cabinet, before it went out ingloriously "on the question of a bug," in other words, on some trivial agricultural matter. On April 24, 1884, Bismarck had formally announced a German protectorate over Damaraland and Namaqualand, which, in spite of the belated protest of Scanlen's successor, was recognized by Lord Granville on June 22.

This move by Germany had one good result, however, in reinforcing Rhodes's arguments for keeping a way open through Bechuanaland. The position in South Africa was now somewhat similar to that of the English and French in America at the beginning of the Seven Years' War. The English on the American sea-board were then in danger of being cut off from the interior by the efforts of the French to connect their colonies of Canada and Louisiana by a series of posts immediately behind the English settlements. Once more the English appeared to be in danger of losing their chance of expansion into the interior by an understanding between Germany and the Transvaal about closing the way through Bechuanaland, or even, as Rhodes suggested, by further aggression on Germany's part. "Do you think," he asked, "that if the Transvaal had Bechuanaland, it would be allowed to keep it? Would not Bismarck have some quarrel with the Transvaal, and without resources, without men, what could they do? Germany would come across from her colony of Angra Pequeña. There would be some excuse to pick a quarrel—some question of brandy or guns or something—and then Germany would stretch from Angra Pequeña to Delagoa Bay. I was never more satisfied with my own views than when I saw the recent development of the policy of Germany. What was the bar in Germany's way? Bechuanaland. . . . If we were to stop at Griqualand West, the ambitious projects of Germany would be attained." These fears of Rhodes were not lessened by the extraordinary marks of favour with which the Transvaal delegation, then in Europe, was received in Berlin.

Fortunately for Rhodes's views, the Imperial Government had left the question of Bechuanaland open by the London Convention of February 1884. The Transvaal delegation had urged strongly their claims for a rectification of the border which would put the republics of Stellaland and Goshen and the southern part of the missionaries' road under their control. But feeling in England, as well as in the Cape, had been awakened to this question of Bechuanaland, partly by the German advance, partly owing to the reaction from Gladstone's surrender of 1881. The missionary Mackenzie had been stirring up interest at home by public meetings and newspaper articles, and by his tales of Boer oppression of the natives had enlisted the support of powerful bodies like the Aborigines Protection Society, and such men as Sir T. Fowell Buxton and W. E. Forster. Sir Hercules Robinson, called home to advise the Colonial Office, was strongly against the Boer claims, and though Scanlen, representing the Cape Ministry, was weak, he was kept up to the mark by his colleague Merriman's messages from Cape Town, as well as by Rhodes. In the end, Lord Derby had excluded Stellaland and Goshen as well as the trade route from the Transvaal, and had received from Scanlen a promise to contribute to the expenses of a protectorate over Bechuanaland.

But even so, the Imperial Government did not grasp the nettle firmly and declare a protectorate at once. Various agents were sent up to investigate affairs and exercise an ill-defined authority without clear instructions as to their proceedings. First came Captain Graham Bower to report; he reported that the Stellalanders were an orderly community and was favourably impressed by Van Niekerk. Next, in April 1884, the Rev. John Mackenzie was sent as deputy-commissioner. No worse choice could have been made, for though he had done good work in directing public attention to the country, and during his twenty years as a missionary there had won the confidence of the natives, he was singularly wanting in tact and was hated by every Dutchman in South Africa for his virulent attacks on that race. He went up with the fixed ideas that the settlers in Goshen and Stellaland were rascals and freebooters who must be dislodged, that the imperial might of England must be displayed, and that annexation by the Cape was a solution to be avoided at all costs, owing to the large Dutch element in that colony. His actions were in keeping with his prejudices. In Land Goshen he made no attempt to conciliate the settlers and made no protest against a surprise attack by Montsioa on their capital Rooigrond; in Stellaland he quarrelled with Van Niekerk and attempted to divide his followers; he raised the British standard there without any authority to do so, demanded a large force of police to overawe all malcontents, and countenanced some of the worst rascals at Mankoroane's headquarters. In fact, as Rhodes, who from Kimberley was keeping an eye on his proceedings, telegraphed to the High Commissioner, he seemed to be working for "a split on race lines: if true, this certainly means trouble."

While Mackenzie was acting in this high-handed way in Bechuanaland, Rhodes had an opportunity of again defining his policy. It was on the introduction of a bill for annexing southern Bechuanaland to the Cape by the new Prime Minister, Upington. Opinion had thus advanced considerably since the preceding year; now, not only the Ministry but the leading members of the late Government were in favour of the proposal; then Rhodes had stood almost alone. Again he took a leading part in the debate, with the delicate task of steering a middle course between those who, like Mackenzie, demanded the intervention of the Imperial Government, and the followers of Hofmeyr, who wished the country to fall into the hands of the Transvaal. Turning first to the latter, "Was this House," he asked, " prepared to say after the debt we had incurred, that we should allow these republics to form a wall across our trade route ? The railways had been constructed with a view to the trade of the interior. He was not exactly a follower of Sir Bartle Frere, who wanted to jump immediately to the Zambesi, but he believed that the colony would gradually extend in that direction, and that the civilization of Africa would be from the colony of the Cape of Good Hope. Were we to allow a neighbouring state to acquire the whole of the interior . . . a state which imposed a hostile tariff of 33 per cent against our goods ? We must look to the development of the north, not only in the interest of the merchants, but also in the interest of our farmers. Bechuanaland was the neck of the whole territories up to the Zambesi, and we must secure it, unless we were prepared to see the whole of the north pass out of our hands." He was equally severe on Mackenzie and his school. Mackenzie with all his sympathy for the natives had little for the whites of South Africa, and had already estranged the settlers who had petitioned for annexation to the Cape. For this was the true solution ; the responsibility was the Cape's, the chief interest was the Cape's, and the Cape alone without interference from the Imperial Government could settle the matter amicably with the Transvaal. " If the Cape did not act," he continued, " the Imperial Government would interfere ; and possibly the interference of the Imperial Government might lead to a repetition of those unfortunate occurrences which they had had in connection with the Transvaal. . . . We must not have the Imperial factor in Bechuanaland. . . . They should at once negotiate with the Imperial Government and with the people of the Transvaal [with a view to annexation to the Cape], and foremost they should try and remove the Imperial factor from the situation."

The motion, which was also supported by Scanlen and Merriman, was carried ; and Rhodes, the real protagonist, leapt into sudden notoriety by his attack on the " Imperial factor." He was no great speaker, but he had a happy knack of coining phrases, often in the form of blazing indiscretions, which curtly expressed a popular opinion.

His claim to dispense with the Imperial factor in the situation caught the fancy of Englishmen as well as Dutchmen in South Africa, tired of the meddling of Exeter Hall and Downing Street. It was received with the same rapturous applause as, five years later, the cautious Governor's sudden indiscretion in attacking "the amateur meddling of irresponsible and ill-advised persons in England, which makes every resident in the Republics, English as well as Dutch, rejoice in their independence and converts many a Colonist from an Imperialist into a Republican." Rhodes's phrase meant no more than what he expressed in a later speech: "Gentlemen, I have ever held one view: *i.e.* the government of South Africa by the people of South Africa, with the Imperial flag for defence"; and so it was understood in South Africa. But in England it was regarded as an attack on the Imperial connection generally: he was spoken of as a dangerous politician prepared to "cut the painter"; and it was many years before he completely lived down the reputation he had acquired in the English press for disloyalty to the Mother Country.

Less than a fortnight after this speech he was called upon to act on his professions. Mackenzie had set the whole country by the ears; and both the Transvaal and the Cape Ministry represented that he was a danger to peace, Rhodes and a considerable section of the opposition agreeing with them. So Robinson recalled him and in August sent up, the third agent in succession since March, Rhodes himself, with the title of Deputy-Commissioner, to try another line. He had no more definite instructions than his predecessor, so he framed his own programme. He found that Van Niekerk and his party in Stellaland, though preferring to come under the Transvaal, were quite willing to accept the dominion of the Cape if their land-titles were not interfered with; but that in Goshen Van Pittius, a regular swashbuckler, had no intention of coming to terms; on the contrary was preparing fresh attacks on Montsioa. "My policy, if it can be called one," he thereupon telegraphed to Sir Hercules, "is contained in a few words, viz. to try and effect a reconciliation with the

Niekerk party and obtain their co-operation in dealing with Rooigrond. . . . I know exactly the object I am working for; to stop, if possible, a collision between our police and the Boers and to prevent a general war, which must necessitate British troops, and the revival in an intensified form of the old race feelings, which I am still in hopes are dying out." He first went to see Van Niekerk and his chief lieutenant, "Groot" Adriaan De la Rey, a huge uncouth Boer from the backveld with a sinister reputation for violence. "I shall never forget our meeting," said Rhodes, describing it some years later. "When I spoke to De la Rey, his answer was, 'Blood must flow,' to which I remember making the retort: 'No, give me my breakfast, and then we can talk about blood.' Well, I stayed with him a week. I became godfather to his grandchild and we made a settlement." This settlement, ratified by Rhodes and Van Niekerk in September, stipulated that the settlers should recognize a British protectorate before the end of the year, but that they might administer the government of Stellaland, subject to the British Commissioner's approval; that their land-titles should be recognized, and that all Mackenzie's proceedings should be declared void. The visit to Rooigrond was not so successful. Here he found the Transvaal border Commissioner, General Joubert, and characteristically plunged into a discussion with him on South African federation over their first luncheon. But Van Pittius was surly and insolent and actually pressed forward an attack on Montsioa at Mafeking in Rhodes's presence, an attack in which the British agent Bethell was killed. Rhodes was powerless to restrain him, as he had not even an escort with him; he therefore returned forthwith to Stellaland. Montsioa was compelled to sign a treaty giving up most of his territory to the Goshenites, and much to Rhodes's indignation the treaty was confirmed by Joubert. A few weeks later Kruger, prompted by Du Toit, the founder of the Bond, who had accepted office in the Transvaal, violated the London Convention he had recently signed by proclaiming Montsioa's territory under his Government's protection. This was too much for all but the most bigoted supporters of the Transvaal in Cape Colony and for English public opinion. It was felt that this was a good opportunity to show Germany as well as the Transvaal that England was not yet a negligible factor in South Africa. Lord Derby instructed Robinson to make stern representations to Kruger; and resolutions of protest came from all parts of the colony. Kruger saw he had gone too far, and within a month recalled the obnoxious proclamation.

Rhodes himself was now one of the first to propose the introduction of the Imperial factor. Upington's Ministry, dependent on the support of the Bond, were still haggling over the terms of annexation with the Home Government and it looked as if the country would be lost unless that authority stepped in: moreover, a salutary lesson was needed to Van Pittius and the Transvaal Government, and indirectly to Germany. He therefore urged that an expeditionary force should be sent from England to enforce the Convention and establish a protectorate over Bechuanaland; and suggested that Sir Charles Warren, whom he had known in Griqualand West, should take command. Both Sir Hercules and Lord Derby agreed. The expedition was sent out with remarkable despatch, and by Christmas 1884 Sir Charles Warren had 4000 well-equipped troops on the borders of Stellaland. Before that a fourth set of emissaries from Cape Town, no less than the Prime Minister Upington and his Treasurer, Sprigg, had gone to Goshen to attempt one more settlement: their settlement practically yielded all Van Pittius's demands and was promptly repudiated by Robinson; while Sprigg and Upington were burned in effigy at Cape Town. Thus the coast was clear for Warren, the fifth within a year to attempt a settlement of the Bechuanaland question.

Warren settled it after a fashion, but not to Rhodes's satisfaction and not without creating as much bad blood as Mackenzie himself. He began well, shortly after landing at Cape Town, by confirming Rhodes's agreement with Van Niekerk; but soon repented of that concession. For he evidently came out with the determination to ride roughshod over the country and to make the most of his imposing military force. He gave an early taste of his quality by insisting that Mackenzie should accompany him as adviser, in spite of the High Commissioner's representations that Mackenzie was distrusted by the Cape as well as the Transvaal Governments and had done no good in Stellaland. He consented to see Rhodes also, on Robinson's recommendation of him as " clear-headed, honest and quite disinterested, as well as fresh from Stellaland," but from the outset neglected his advice.

One of Warren's first acts was to arrange a meeting with President Kruger at Fourteen Streams on the Vaal, to discuss the beaconing off of the Transvaal border and other points of difference. This very meeting was made the excuse for an imposing display of military strength, which gave great offence. Whereas Kruger came with a few artillerymen as a guard of honour, Warren, professing to fear a hostile ambush, sent forward two hundred dragoons and yeomanry to scour the country beforehand. He also came attended by the obnoxious Mackenzie, as well as Rhodes. The occasion, however, is chiefly interesting as the first meeting between Rhodes and the only opponent worthy of his steel that he was destined to encounter.

Paul Kruger was then sixty, nearly twice Rhodes's age, and had memories extending back to the Boers' first movement of revolt against British domination. As a boy of ten he had accompanied his parents on the great trek from Cape Colony to the then unknown country beyond the Vaal. A rough rude upbringing he had amongst savages and wild beasts and was soon depending for his livelihood on his own exertions. " I have not had much schooling," he once confided to a Bloemfontein audience, " in the ordinary acceptation of the term. When I was ten years old I had to begin fighting for my life in my country and since then I have always been busy with few intervals. That has been my only schooling. But I have learned one thing, to distinguish friends from foes." One book, however, he did know well, his Bible, and from its teaching and the teaching of his own experiences had culled his cunning in statecraft and his philosophy of life. He knew personally every burgher in his republic and had known most of their parents, and among them had acquired a legendary reputation for courage and slimness. Tales were told of many a feat: how he had hacked off his own thumb when he found it mortifying from a wound; how he went alone to beard a rebel chieftain in his kraal with all his savage warriors; how in one memorable day he had started running at dawn, gone home to drink a cup of coffee at mid-day and been soundly thrashed there by his father for disobedience, then resuming his race had shot a lion by the way, and finally at sunset had out-distanced the fleetest Kaffir runners, against whom he had been running for a wager: these were household tales in the Transvaal. Added to these his more solid achievements in negotiating his country's independence in 1881 and in obtaining still better terms for her in the recent London Convention account for his wonderful prestige with his burghers. He regarded himself more as a prophet than a statesman, a prophet chosen by God to guide a chosen people into the ways of righteousness and safety. He never forgot his early trek, when he had been taught that he and his people were fleeing from bondage to the ungodly English; and his recent experiences did but confirm his belief that his chief duty was to circumvent that ungodly race. Some of the ungodly race had already invaded his land, to prospect for gold at Barberton in the low veld and the De Kaap goldfields in the mountains; but they had been few and comparatively unsuccessful, so did not seem likely to bring many more in their train or interfere with his burghers' secluded existence: for his strength and his trust lay in his country's isolation. It was a broad and pleasant land with plenty of healthy high veld for the summer grazing and of well-watered low veld for the winter pastures and the lazy form of agriculture affected by his people; broad enough for every burgher to have his own farm-house, remote, as he loved it, from every other dwelling-place, and with all the land within sight for his own domain. Even so there was a fly in his ointment. With all their present elbow-room his Boers never felt quite happy without illimitable spaces into which to roam when the trek fever was upon them. But the south was already taken up by their cousins of the Free State, in the east the Portuguese and Swaziland cut off their access to the sea, in the north the savage Matabeles forbade further access towards the Zambesi, and now in the west the ungodly race and that newly arisen adventurer of theirs, Rhodes, were seeking to confine them strictly within their allotted borders. A stiff-necked old gentleman Kruger already was when he first met Rhodes in January 1885, and he became more stubborn with increasing age; immovable in his old traditions and prejudices, giving way on details only as a last resort, but never yielding in his determination to keep his country inviolate and his people untouched by any change in the plan of life which they had brought into the country fifty years before.

In the interview at Fourteen Streams Rhodes was over-shadowed by the martial Warren and took little part in the proceedings, confining himself to a discussion on the land-titles and cattle-thefts in Stellaland and complaints of Joubert's conduct at Rooigrond. Kruger in his own Memoirs, dictated long afterwards, says that he reproved Rhodes for abusing an absent man; but the statement of Mackenzie, who had no love for Rhodes, seems more probable, that the President did not seem altogether displeased at the attack on his own rival for the presidency. Rhodes at least went away from this first interview with a great respect for the sturdy old President. If he was a fanatic on the subject of his own country, well, so was Rhodes himself on England's mission to civilize the rest of the world. He spoke of him afterwards as "one of the most remarkable men in South Africa," and expressed a fellow-feeling for "that extraordinary man," whose one dream, when he had not a sixpence in his treasury, was the same as his own, "to extend his country over the whole of the northern interior." He certainly realized now and henceforward that he was an opponent to be dealt with warily. Kruger, on his side, returned the compliment by admitting the capacity of his youthful antagonist to make himself unpleasant: it was not for nothing that he had "learned one thing, to distinguish friends from foes"; and he is reported to have said to his friends: "That young man will cause me trouble if he does not leave politics alone and turn to something else. Well, the race-horse is swifter than the ox, but the ox can draw the greater loads. We shall see."

It became apparent by this interview that no further danger was to be apprehended from the Transvaal. But both Rhodes and Warren were still nervous about Germany's intentions, and were supported by the Home Government and the Cape in their determination to prove England's intention of retaining the corridor to the interior through Bechuanaland.[1] But the two men differed fundamentally as to method. Rhodes's idea was to secure the co-operation of Van Niekerk and the Stellaland burghers, avoid all further friction with the Dutch, and make it easy for the Bond party to agree to annexation by the Cape of the southern part of Bechuanaland, with a loose Imperial protectorate of the northern part: in this way the Cape colonists, who were chiefly concerned, would have an interest in maintaining the open door to the interior. Warren for his part, influenced by Mackenzie, was opposed to extending the Cape borders: he desired to establish the Imperial authority throughout Bechuanaland, and by his provocative conduct succeeded in making it impossible for any Cape Ministry to assume responsibility for any part of the country. Rhodes was plainly given to understand that his occupation as Deputy-Commissioner was gone. His advice was unheeded and he was left with nothing to do but to sit in his hut at headquarters and discuss with young Currey and Ralph Williams, a friend on Warren's staff, day-dreams about the advance of British power to the great Central Lakes and the confusion of Germany. Finally, after a month of this, when Warren disowned Rhodes's arrangement with Kruger's Attorney-General about compensation for cattle-thefts, repudiated his agreement with Van Niekerk about the status of Stellaland and the recognition of land-titles, an agreement which he himself had confirmed at Cape Town, and even arrested Van Niekerk on an utterly untenable charge of murder, Rhodes felt himself in honour bound to resign and leave the country. Warren, after a

[1] Germany had expressed some alarm at Warren's expedition, but had been reassured by Granville, who disclaimed any intention of interfering with Namaqualand and Damaraland (Transvaal, 1885, C. 4310).

parting insult to him as a "danger to the peace," then felt free to act as he chose. He proclaimed martial law in southern Bechuanaland, visited Land Goshen, whence he found that Van Pittius and all his volunteers had fled, and then proceeded with his army on progress with Mackenzie through northern Bechuanaland. Here he did his best to stimulate a native war by accepting from Khama, chief of the Bamangwatos, a concession over country which really belonged not to Khama but to his neighbour Lo Bengula, king of the Matabeles, and to arouse all the bitterest feelings of race hatred in South Africa by proposing that only settlers of pure British origin, to the exclusion of the Dutch, should be admitted into Bechuanaland. In all these proceedings he disregarded not only the advice of Rhodes and the Cape Ministry, whom he insulted, but also the High Commissioner himself. In August 1885 he was hastily recalled; but the harm was then done. In one respect his mission had been successful, in making plain both to the Transvaal and to Germany that England had no intention of abdicating her position as the paramount power in South Africa. But he had made co-operation with the Cape impossible for the time being. The Dutch party, after seeing the Governor ignored, the Rhodes agreement with Van Niekerk repudiated, and Mackenzie allowed to dictate an anti-Dutch policy, washed their hands of the whole business. The Cape Government, dependent on the Dutch, refused to relieve the Imperial Government of any part of its burden in Bechuanaland; consequently in September it was decided to establish Crown Colony government over the country as far north as the Molopo River, so as to include Montsioa's and Mankoroane's territory, as well as Stellaland and Goshen. The Crown Colony was given the name of British Bechuanaland, to distinguish it from the Protectorate established over the northern part up to Lo Bengula's borders.

When the Cape Parliament met in June Rhodes took occasion to express the bitter humiliation he felt, as an Englishman, at Warren's proceedings. "I remember," he said, "when a youngster, reading in my English history of the supremacy of my country and its annexations and that there were two cardinal axioms: that the word of the nation when once pledged was never broken, and that when a man accepted the citizenship of the British Empire, there was no distinction of races. It has been my misfortune in one year to meet with the breach of the one and the proposed breach of the other. The result will be that when the troops are gone we shall have to deal with sullen feeling, discontent and hostility. . . . The breach of solemn pledges and the introduction of race distinctions must result in bringing calamity on this country, and if such a policy is pursued it will endanger the whole of our social relationships with colonists of Dutch descent and endanger the supremacy of Her Majesty in this country."

He was naturally sore for public and personal reasons at the outcome of his endeavours.[1] He had been personally insulted by Warren and practically driven out of the country; and he had seen all his efforts to draw English and Dutch together for the first step northwards made unavailing; while in return he had only reaped abuse and insinuations from his fellow-countrymen for daring to say a good word for the Dutch. But he could at least have consoled himself with the reflection that his exertions and his influence had played no small part in the Imperial Government's decision to checkmate any designs by the Transvaal or Germany on Bechuanaland; and within ten years he was to persuade the Cape to annex the Crown Colony with the Crown's full consent. Above all his efforts to unite Dutch and English in one policy, though unsuccessful for the moment, stood him in good stead afterwards, for they were not forgotten. It was felt that he was justified when he said in the same speech in which he attacked Warren: "I can at least appeal to the House from the fact that I have for the last three years been trying to deal with the question, not with the idea of stirring up difficulties with neighbouring South African states, not with any desire to embroil ourselves with colonists of Dutch descent,

[1] For his work as Deputy-Commissioner Rhodes was offered some small decoration. This he refused, but said he would appreciate a formal letter of thanks from the Secretary of State. Such a request was unprecedented and caused some fluttering in the Colonial Office dove-cotes; however, it was eventually sent.

but with a real feeling that in Bechuanaland lies the future of South Africa, and that with our right dealing with this question will depend the union in the future of South Africa." [1]

[1] The controversy between Rhodes and Warren died hard. In 1885 (Sir) Ralph Williams published *The British Lion in Bechuanaland*, defending Rhodes and attacking Warren and Mackenzie. Both sides of the dispute were put forward in the "*Transvaal*" bluebooks of the same year, Warren's by himself and Rhodes's, with evident approbation, by Sir Hercules Robinson. *Austral Africa*, a long-winded pamphlet in two volumes, appeared from Mackenzie's pen in 1887, in defence of Warren and himself, and against Rhodes and Sir Hercules. The two main disputants also engaged in a long controversy in *The Times* during November and December 1885. Rhodes's letter, which opens the ball on November 11, probably constitutes a record for length in the correspondence columns of that paper, for it occupies close on four columns of small print. On November 17 and 26 Warren rejoins in large print. On December 2 Rhodes comes out with another letter nearly two columns in length (small print again); on December 14 Warren concludes with a final letter in large print. The comparative value then attached by *The Times* to the two men, by the fount assigned to their letters, is interesting.

For his first letter Rhodes had gone to an hotel in Chester, where he thought he should be quiet, and he was helped to concoct it by his friend Ralph Williams: the finished production was then shown to Mr. R. Maguire for further suggestions. According to Sir R. Williams, he was the scribe, while Rhodes stalked up and down the room without a coat, rubbing his hands together or ruffling his hair and ejaculating suggestions which Williams would put into consecutive English. At intervals Rhodes would call a halt, "to look at it from Warren's point of view," and state what he imagined to be Warren's case, in order to be certain that his own arguments covered the whole ground.

CHAPTER IX

GOLD AND DIAMONDS

" Put money in thy purse. . . . Put money in thy purse. . . . Make all the money thou canst " : this seems to have been the chief lesson learned by Rhodes after the comparative failure of his first great adventure in politics. He had tried the Cape Government, he had tried the Imperial factor, and they had both failed him, or at any rate he had not got what he wanted done as he wanted. For the future he felt that he must take his own course. Most men with original ideas have had to make a similar resolution and have sought to attain their objects by their eloquence in the Senate, by conquests on the battlefield, or by their power of imparting sparks from their own burning convictions to their fellows. Rhodes did not neglect these means, but he was singular in this that he attached enormous importance to the influence of wealth in securing public objects. If one has ideas, as he told General Gordon, one cannot carry them out without wealth to back them: "I have therefore tried," he added in narrating this incident, " to combine the commercial with the imaginative." He did not, as so many others have done, regard wealth as an end in itself, but as a preliminary to success he believed it to be essential, and was unflinching in putting his theory into practice. For three years after the Bechuanaland episode he gave himself up almost entirely to the pursuit of wealth. He kept in touch with politics, but only took part in them incidentally when a question directly affecting his interests cropped up: on his main conception of a further advance northwards he was biding his time silently till the day when he could come forward to crush all opposition by his financial power.

I

During the five years that he had been devoting his energies chiefly to affairs of state in Basutoland and Bechuanaland or at Cape Town, he had not lost sight of his De Beers Mining Company. Since its incorporation in 1880 with a capital of only £200,000 it had prospered exceedingly, largely owing to the vigilance of Rhodes himself, who was secretary of the Company till 1883 and then chairman. He was always on the look out for improved and more economical methods of working. In the middle of his election campaign he writes to his friend Rudd that "the expenses are simply damnable" and that the extravagance of the new engineer must be curbed, and two years later is quite ready to have a committee of the directors to consider further economies. He also seized every opportunity of buying up and incorporating other claims and companies. By 1885 the De Beers Company was already the chief owner in that mine, and its capital had increased from the original £200,000 to £841,550. But this was not enough: he was determined to clear out all rivals and make his company the sole proprietor of his "nice little mine." Before starting operations at Kimberley, and soon after his final fling at Warren in the Cape Parliament, he went home to England to raise funds and conciliate interests and then returned to devote himself to the process of amalgamation.

But if Rhodes was bent on amalgamation at De Beers, so were others in the other mines. In fact a closer amalgamation of interests had become a necessity if the diamond industry was to survive at all. Owing to the conditions of mining at Kimberley, the small digger of the early days, content to work for what he could find on one claim or even a quarter or an eighth of a claim 31 feet by 31 feet, had long found it impossible to make a living. The cost of pumping out the water from the mines had been the first serious tax on these men's resources and had driven most of them away: their claims had been bought up by various companies, but in their turn only the strongest of the companies could survive the next and more serious disaster to the industry. The reef, which formed a casing round the "yellow" and "blue" ground, began gradually to fall in, as its support was cut away, and finally, early in the 'eighties, millions of cubic feet of reef collapsed, burying in some mines half the diamond claims that were being worked. Futile efforts by mining boards and the richer companies were at first made to remove the reef and expose the claims again, but that was soon found to be a hopeless method: the only resource left, and that an expensive one, was to sink shafts beneath the fallen reef and start underground mining on the buried claims. These successive calamities, the increased cost of production, and the reduction in the price of diamonds had been hastening on in the other mines the same process of amalgamation to which Rhodes was devoting himself at De Beers; for only the strongest companies found it possible to survive. Thus by the end of 1885 the original 3600 claims, into which the four Kimberley mines had been divided, had all been concentrated into the hands of ninety-eight owners; of these, there were thirty and thirty-seven respectively in the Bultfontein and Dutoitspan, which had hitherto suffered least from landslides, but only ten in De Beers, and nineteen in the Kimberley Mine, the original New Rush, where Rhodes had worked his first claim. But even this reduction in the number of claim-holders did not solve all difficulties. There was still a great deal of waste involved in the attempt by ninety-eight separate owners to exploit an area of only seventy acres in the aggregate; and the new system of underground working introduced another element of confusion. Instead of one main shaft for each mine, each company had to have its own, and the tunnelling gave rise to constant disputes about encroachments between rival claim-holders. Barnato afterwards described the resulting confusion at De Beers. "Why," he asked, "was the underground system not a success in this case? Because one company was working against another; that is to say, if one company was on the five hundred feet level, the opposing company could go and eat into each other's boundary walls and pillars to such a dangerous extent that the entire mine was in a condition which threatened collapse at any moment." Similar considerations in the other mines were making the need of amalgamation self-evident.

Rhodes, however, was the first to succeed. By 1887 he had bought up all the remaining claims at De Beers and thus made his company the sole owner of the mine. This amalgamation of interests helped him considerably in cutting the costs of working. He chose his engineers and officials well, and could afford to pay them good salaries, finding his profit in this policy. They introduced the best engines and labour-saving appliances, which amply repaid the heavy initial outlay. Between 1882 and 1888 the cost of winning a carat had been reduced from 16s. 6d. to 7s. 2d., while the reserve of "blue" on the drying grounds had increased from 3000 to 300,000 loads. Great savings, too, had been effected by the introduction, largely on Rhodes's initiative, of compounds for the native workers. Hitherto it had been very difficult to prevent thefts of diamonds by these natives, who abstracted them from the workings and secretly sold them to illicit diamond buyers (I.D.B.): in one year alone, it was estimated, claim-holders had lost diamonds to the value of £725,000 by these thefts. But when the natives were confined, during the whole of their term of service, in compounds, they could be properly watched and searched and had no means of communicating with unlicensed dealers; thus by this system the losses by thefts became almost negligible. These compounds were also of advantage to the natives themselves, for they were well cared for in them, well fed at a low cost, and prevented from touching liquor, on which they used previously to waste most of their earnings. Thus in spite of the great reduction in the price of diamonds from 30s. to 18s. 5½d. per carat within six years and the great increase in capital by all the accretions of claims and companies, the De Beers Mining Company, which had paid only 3 per cent on the original £200,000 in 1882, in 1888 paid 25 per cent on a capital of no less than £2,332,170.

Meanwhile Barnato, at the Kimberley Mine, had been pursuing much the same policy. He also had been acquiring all the claims he could lay his hands on, and by the time Rhodes had amalgamated the De Beers Mine had made his own Central Company the strongest in the Kimberley Mine. But he still had some competitors, the most considerable of which was the French Company; in time he had hopes of absorbing that and then he would be in a better position than Rhodes, for his mine was the most productive and the richest on the Diamond Fields. Rhodes saw the danger. It was brought home to him in this way. In 1887 he sunk a shaft in his mine, whereby 2500 loads a day could be raised and the total output of the mine had increased to 1,000,000 carats a year: at the same time he found that the Kimberley Mine could do as well if not better, for in an incredibly short time the Central Company had sunk a similar shaft, and another company in the same mine was following its example. Already, owing to over-production, the price of diamonds had sunk and was still sinking; if it came to a cut-throat competition between the two mines, profits would disappear altogether, and then the weaker mine would have to succumb. Now Rhodes used to calculate that, taking one year with another, young men engaged to be married and others were prepared to spend £4,000,000 a year, no more and no less, in the purchase of diamonds for their sweethearts and wives: if the price of diamonds was high, they bought fewer stones, if low, they bought more, but never, on an average, more than were worth the £4,000,000. The problem to his mind, therefore, was how to limit the annual output of diamonds for the market that the £4,000,000 they fetched should show a clear profit to the diamond mining companies: the amalgamation of interests in one mine only was no remedy for this state of things as long as there were rival companies elsewhere. The only solution he saw was to amalgamate all the diamond mines under one control, and so regulate production and prices to suit the interests of the industry. Others before him, his friend Merriman for one, had conceived this idea of one gigantic diamond corporation, but had failed to bring it off.

But this did not daunt Rhodes, he remembered the Umkomanzi valley and the cotton: so he resolved to make one more attempt. This resolution brought him into direct antagonism with Barney Barnato.

Before 1887 there had been no such rivalry; each had been too busy looking after his own mine. But on this question of fixing prices and eliminating competition the two kings of the diamond industry took diametrically opposite views. Rhodes's idea of a huge corporation, of which he would naturally be the guiding spirit, to control the four mines and regulate prices, did not suit Barnato at all. He was equally convinced that over-production must be checked, but he proposed to secure that end either by a working agreement between equals, or by breaking all his competitors, including De Beers, and so making the Kimberley Mine supreme. On one thing he was quite determined, not to allow his holdings to be sunk in the gulf of De Beers: and, if it came to a fight, he was quite prepared for it, for he had an immense belief in the Kimberley Mine as capable of producing diamonds of better quality, in larger numbers, and more cheaply than De Beers. When, therefore, in May 1887 Rhodes opened the offensive, he readily took up the challenge.

The two champions in the great contest for the autocracy of the Diamond Fields were fairly matched. If anything, the opinion of Kimberley inclined slightly in favour of Barnato's chances. Both were rich; Rhodes told a friend in 1885 that he was worth about £50,000 a year, but Barnato was richer and seemed the more adventurous of the two. Besides his large holding in his own mine, he had spread his net over every other undertaking in Kimberley which seemed to him at all promising. His London house, Barnato Brothers, gave him a footing in the city and enabled him to float and finance new companies more readily than Rhodes; and as a buyer he was in close touch with the diamond market. One characteristic the two men had in common, a knowledge of the diamond mines unrivalled in the fields: in other respects the contrast between the two men was striking. Even in their method of acquiring this knowledge the contrast was apparent.

Rhodes, slow and methodical, trusted mainly to his own great power of observation and his familiarity with every practical detail of the Kimberley workings, but he did not disdain the learning of others. " Please send me all books dealing with the custom of other countries, especially colonies, as to minerals. . . . the Colonial Institute might help you. . . . Please attend to this ; you know exactly what I require," he writes to Rudd on the eve of his election ; and, though not normally a great reader, when he wanted to get up a subject he read voraciously and had a retentive memory for what he noted as valuable. Barnato, on the other hand, never read books and only occasionally skimmed newspapers, finding it, as he said, " cheaper to pay a man to pick out what I want than to waste time myself in looking for it " ; but he made up for this by his extraordinary nimbleness of mind. Unlike Rhodes, who was reserved and difficult of approach except to his intimates, Barnato was like a piece of quicksilver, darting about with irrepressible good humour in bars and on racecourses, at the street corner or on the boards of the theatre, where he was the most popular amateur actor of Kimberley, never taking a rebuff, but always with an eye to business and ready to pick up any hint that would put him on the track of a " good thing." His wild speculations were a byword, but they were not so wild as they appeared ; for his rashness was always tempered with a strong element of Jewish caution. As in his first venture, so always, he was ready to stake his last guinea, but always with the expectation that it would bring him in thirty shillings. Indeed his quickness and acumen in financial calculations amounted to genius : he boasted, and with reason, that he had never engaged in a speculation which proved a failure.

But against Barnato's brilliant gifts and his rapid success Rhodes had certain solid advantages. Barnato's was in a sense a bubble reputation, depending solely on his financial acumen : had this failed him, he would have sunk, hardly regretted. Though admired, he was not respected in Kimberley, where strange stories, probably untrue, were hinted about the origin of his wealth : at any rate, owing perhaps to his inveterate habit of combining business with pleasure, he could not obtain admission to the not very exclusive Kimberley Club. But Rhodes was respected even where he was not liked. He always had a purpose, which he pursued with persistence, sometimes even with ruthlessness; for he was not tender with those who came across his path and he rarely forgot an injury;[1] thus he was a dangerous enemy. On the other hand, and in this lay his principal strength, he was noted for straightforward dealing. In a community where crooked and underhand methods were not uncommon, Rhodes, taking a leaf from the English diplomatist's notebook, always played with his cards on the table: "I find in life it is far better to tell the town-crier exactly what you are going to do and then you have no trouble," he once declared in a telegram to Beit. When he dealt with a man he told him frankly what he wanted and what he was prepared to give, and he was never a defaulter. Besides the respect of the community, he had firm friends, who loved him for himself alone and would have stuck to him had all his financial schemes gone awry. They loved him for a boyish and uncalculating enthusiasm for better things than money-making, the kind of enthusiasm which led him, while on a visit to London in 1885, impetuously to jump into a hansom and drive to Holloway Gaol, just to see Stead. "Here is the man I want," he exclaimed, when he heard of Stead's imprisonment for the *Maiden Tribute to Modern Babylon*, "one who has not only the right principles, but is more anxious to promote them than to save his own skin"; and being denied admission to the prison, he went to Exeter Hall, for the first and only time in his life, to protest against the treatment given to Stead. Then, apart altogether from his position at Kimberley, he had already gained a standing by his political work, at home as well as in South Africa; and this was useful even in financial transactions. During that same visit to England he found himself no longer the "cypher" that Lord Randolph Churchill had

[1] He long retained a curious prejudice against banks and bankers, because he had not found them accommodating when he was struggling for funds.

spoken of only the year before. His speech about the "Imperial factor" had given him notoriety and his action in Bechuanaland had fixed the more serious attention of persons interested in South Africa; even *The Times* had opened its columns to him. His Oxford friends brought him forward, and, at the suggestion of one of them, the Conservative Whips asked him to stand as a candidate for Bristol, an offer which he refused, partly because he was not sure that he was a Conservative, partly because he felt that his work lay in South Africa. In this decision Rhodes was undoubtedly right. His genius for financial organisation, for which Kimberley and Johannesburg gave him full scope, would have been comparatively wasted in England; as for his bluff methods and crude ideas of statesmanship, they were more suited to a new country, where problems and politics are simpler, than to the complicated machinery of European affairs.[1]

Barnato had a weak spot in his armour, the presence of rivals in the Kimberley mine itself; and Rhodes was quick to take advantage of this weakness. His policy was to obtain such a control over the Kimberley Mine that Barnato, no longer master in his own house, would have to yield at discretion. His first move, in May 1887, was to bid for a large block of claims in the Kimberley Mine known as W. A. Hall's, but in this he failed, being overbid by a syndicate headed by Sir Donald Currie, who also had schemes of his own for amalgamation. Thereupon he sent off two friends to join the ship which was carrying Sir Donald home, in the hope of persuading him to re-sell. Sir Donald, half-tempted by Rhodes's offer, called at Lisbon to learn the market value of the shares, and, finding it was higher than Rhodes's price, turned on the emissaries: "You young thieves, had I listened to you, I should have sold at a loss," and would have nothing more to say to them. But they had also taken advantage of the call at Lisbon to telegraph Currie's decision to Rhodes, who thereupon beared the market so successfully that when the

[1] Sir Charles Dilke said of him acutely that "he had none of the knowledge or the mode of concealing want of knowledge, one or other of which is required for English public work."

ship reached Plymouth Currie's shares were no longer worth what Rhodes had offered. Currie had his lesson: he recognized that he had come up against an antagonist whom it would be dangerous to cross and dropped out of the competition. Rhodes then flew at higher game. His plan was no less than to buy up the French Company, Barnato's chief rivals in the mine, lock, stock and barrel. For this ambitious project he required more capital than he could himself command, so in July he sailed for England to see if help was to be had from the Rothschilds. Mr. Gardner Williams, the new general manager of De Beers, had connections with that firm, and when Rhodes came to discuss the matter with Lord Rothschild, he found him favourably disposed; indeed so good an impression did Rhodes make on this pillar of British credit, that for the rest of his career Lord Rothschild remained his friend and a staunch if sometimes puzzled and anxious ally. If, said the cautious financier, as they parted, the French Company were willing to sell, the firm would "see if they could raise" the £1,000,000 required. This was good enough for Rhodes, who that same evening went off to Paris to negotiate with the French directors. Their price was £1,400,000. To meet this Rhodes took up a loan of £750,000 from Rothschilds, and issued 50,000 De Beers shares at £15 through a Hamburg syndicate, on the understanding that De Beers and the syndicate should share equally in any profit from the rise in value of these shares. As they soon rose to £22, each party made the handsome profit of £100,000 on the transaction.

So far all had gone well, but Barnato was not the man to allow such an invasion of his mine without a fight. The agreement with the directors of the French Company had still to be confirmed by the shareholders, and before the general meeting Barnato had bettered Rhodes's offer by £300,000. Then came Rhodes's most surprising move in the game. To all appearance he retired from the contest, went to Barnato and said it would be a pity to waste money in cutting one another's throats, and offered to let him have the French Company for the price he had himself agreed to pay for it: nor did he require cash; all he asked was the equivalent of the purchase price in newly-issued shares of Barnato's Kimberley Central. Barnato, delighted, closed with the offer, perhaps not seeing the trap into which he was falling, or, more probably, confident that his control of his own mine would remain unimpaired. There he miscalculated: though the shares in the Kimberley Central to be handed to his rival amounted to only one-fifth of the increased capital, this fifth gave Rhodes the footing he required in the mine; and once established in a position he was a difficult man to budge.

For the moment, however, the victory appeared to be Barnato's. He was still able to out-vote Rhodes at the Kimberley Central, and he never relaxed his policy of crushing the competition of De Beers. He went on producing diamonds at a greater rate than his rival and put them on the market at such a price that it hardly covered the cost of working. Rhodes then realized there was nothing for it but war to the knife: "We saw this," he told his De Beers shareholders, "that you could never deal with obstinate people until you get the whip-hand of them, and that the only thing we had to do to secure the success of our industry was to get the control of the Kimberley Mine." To do this, however, some £2,000,000 was required and he anxiously inquired of his friend Beit where the money was to come from. "Oh," answered Beit, no less eager than himself, "we shall get the money, if we can only get the shares"; and the money somehow was forthcoming. Then began a rare game of beggar-my-neighbour. Rhodes, supported by Beit, bought Kimberley Central shares right and left, with the natural result of forcing up the price. Barnato in his turn bought up shares with equal recklessness, and prices soared still higher with the competition. Barnato did not mind, for he was convinced his mine was worth two of De Beers, and he still went on buying. So did De Beers, and prices leapt up further. But then Barnato found that he had traitors in the camp. While Rhodes's supporters generally stuck to their shares,[1]

[1] This was not universally the case. The story goes that Beit, who had been buying Kimberley shares recklessly, went in some trepidation to confess himself to Wernher, the cautious head of the firm. "Oh,

many of Barnato's shareholders, tempted by the huge profits, parted with theirs. At last, when diamonds were selling almost at a loss and Central shares were fetching a higher price than even Barnato thought them worth, he saw that the game was up. He had fought well and gallantly and, when he saw himself beaten, surrendered in a generous spirit. In March 1888 he loyally accepted terms which gave Rhodes complete control of the Kimberley Mine: he himself gave up Central in exchange for De Beers shares, and the De Beers holding in Kimberley Centrals was raised to 11,000 out of a total of 17,000 shares. After this settlement the two rivals exchanged courtesies. At Barnato's request Rhodes took him to lunch at the Kimberley Club, which he had never before entered, and then, turning to him, said, "Well, you've had your whim; I should like to have mine, which you alone in Kimberley can satisfy. I have always wanted to see a bucketful of diamonds; will you produce one?" Barnato, much flattered, shovelled all his available diamonds into a bucket into which Rhodes plunged his hands, lifted out handfuls of the glittering gems and luxuriously let them stream back through his fingers like water.

Rhodes could be ruthless and unscrupulous for an object, but no doubt he excused the means to himself by the importance he attached to the object. As soon as he had secured his victory for amalgamation, he reverted, in the deed of association, to his underlying purpose of securing means to carry out his Imperial policy. A corporation entitled the De Beers Consolidated Mines was formed with the modest capital of £100,000 in £5 shares. All these shares, except twenty-five, were held by four men, Rhodes, Barnato, Beit, and Philipson Stow, who constituted themselves life-governors of the Corporation and reserved to themselves the power of issuing further shares, to be exchanged in the first instance for those of the Old De Beers Company and of the Kimberley Central on amalgamation. But the critical meeting to decide on the terms of the Corporation's trust deed was put off by

---

that's all right," said Wernher, "I found the firm was getting more Kimberley shares than I liked, so I have sold a lot at excellent prices."

Rhodes from time to time, while he gave up everything to watch by the bedside of his dearest friend, Pickering, who lay dying. On this trust deed all depended, for with it he designed to forge the instrument for his political ends. At last the meeting was held in Jameson's little cottage at Kimberley, the parties present being Rhodes and Beit on the one side, and on the other Barnato and his nephew Woolf Joel. Barnato wanted a company concerned solely with diamonds, Rhodes a company so constituted that its profits could be devoted to his scheme of northern expansion or other projects for the benefit of the Empire. All day they argued and through the night, Rhodes bringing out his maps and discoursing on his plans, Beit alone showing sympathy, Barnato and Joel caring only for the strictly business aspect and left cold by Rhodes's enthusiasm. At last, as the light of dawn was beginning to show, wearied and overborne by his persistence, influenced too, maybe, by Rhodes's cynical promise that he should become member for Kimberley, Barnato yielded. "Some people," he said with a shrug, "have a fancy for one thing, some for another. You want the means to go north, if possible, so I suppose we must give it you." No wonder Barnato used in after days to avoid meeting Rhodes when he differed from him, "for," he declared, "when you have been with him half an hour you not only agree with him, but come to believe you have always held his opinion. . . . No one else in the world could have induced me to go into this partnership. But Rhodes has an extraordinary ascendancy over men: he tied me up, as he ties up everybody. It is his way. You can't resist him: you must be with him."

How different the new trust deed was from the prospectus of an ordinary company and how wide-spread were its objects became apparent from a singular law-suit caused by its provisions. At the general meeting of the Kimberley Central Company, held to ratify the amalgamation with De Beers, an overwhelming majority were for the agreement. But a few shareholders stood out and brought an action to prevent amalgamation on the ground that under their deed of association they could only unite with "a similar company." Their counsel had light work in showing that the De Beers Consolidated Mines was not "similar" to the Central Company, of which the sole business was "to dig for diamonds in the Kimberley Mine," whereas the new corporation could "take steps for the good government of any territory . . . they would be empowered to annex a portion of territory in Central Africa, raise and maintain a standing army and undertake warlike operations"; and he compared its powers with those of the old East India Company. The Court took the same view and declared for the recalcitrant shareholders. "Diamond mining," said Sir Henry de Villiers in delivering judgement, "forms an insignificant portion of the powers which may be exercised by the Company. The Company can undertake financial obligations for foreign governments, and may carry on diamond mining, coal mining or gold mining in any part of the world. It can carry on banking in Africa or elsewhere, and can become a water-company in this colony or elsewhere. . . . The powers of the Company are as extensive as those of any Company that ever existed."

This judgement did not seriously interfere with Rhodes's plans. Acting on a hint conveyed by the judge, he and Barnato used their majority in the Kimberley Central Company to put it into liquidation and then bought up its assets on behalf of the De Beers Consolidated Mines, paying in a cheque for £5,338,650 to the liquidators. Thus before the end of 1888 the amalgamation of the two most powerful mines in Kimberley was consummated. Dutoitspan and Bultfontein still stood out, but "being poorer mines on the margin of cultivation they would have to accept our offers," said Rhodes, "or fight us on two grounds, larger output and lower rates." The inevitable fall of reef occurred in both mines in 1888. Rhodes was lunching at the club when one of the chief owners of Bultfontein came in to announce the disaster to his mine: the party immediately rushed off in a cab to view the scene. For an hour Rhodes sat brooding on the edge of the mine, undisturbed by the crowd of sight-seers, and then had his proposal for amalgamation ready. De Beers bought up the chief interests in both mines and was able to regulate their output by securing a perpetual lease of the workings. A new mine, the Wesselton or Premier, discovered in 1891, also fell into the clutches of De Beers, in spite of the clamour raised at the time that it should be thrown open by the Government for small diggers: the Corporation also had a large interest in the solitary Free State Mine at Jagersfontein. Hence until the discovery of the other Premier Mine, in the Transvaal, after Rhodes's death, his company had complete control of all South African diamonds, ninety per cent of the whole world's production.

From the shareholders' point of view this consolidation was a great advantage. Competition being abolished, attention could be concentrated on economy in administration and working. Development was chiefly confined to the richer mines, and large reserves of "blue" could be maintained. Mr. Gardner Williams, writing in 1902, says that four million truck-loads of "blue" are sometimes washed in one year alone, a mass which would form a cube of 430 feet, higher than St. Paul's, while the diamonds extracted from it would be contained in a box two feet nine inches square. Working expenses were kept at 10s. a carat and the price of diamonds maintained at 30s., by restricting the output and by an agreement between the Company and a syndicate of buyers, to whom the whole output was allotted. The value of the De Beers properties was estimated at £14,500,000 in 1890, but the capital was kept down to £3,950,000, the rest being paid for by debentures. Owing to the conservative system of finance, introduced by Rhodes and his colleagues, these debentures have been rapidly paid off and a large reserve in Consols and other gilt-edged securities built up, without interfering with the payment of good dividends to the shareholders. The employees of the Company also gained by the amalgamation. The 2000 white miners were paid wages varying from 16s. 8d. to £1 a day. They were well and cheaply housed in the model village of Kenilworth, carefully planned by Rhodes, with houses rented at £2 : 10s. to £5 a month, and a club-house, where single men could get their meals for 25s. a week; its streets were planted with avenues of trees, a refreshing sight in that dusty, wind-swept country, and the Company kept up a great orchard filled with vines and all manner of fruit trees. Rhodes took no less interest in the 20,000 natives housed in the De Beers compounds: he frequently visited them and looked to their comfort; and he loved to have long gossips with them as to their affairs. One Christmas Eve, however, he had a more turbulent experience with them: he was suddenly summoned to deal with a serious strike in the compound, which the managers were unable to quell. In spite of the natives' threatening attitude, he parleyed with them for an hour, and only called in fifteen policemen to arrest the ringleaders when every other means of pacification had been tried.

There was, however, another side to amalgamation. The business of the private digger, who light-heartedly took the sporting chance of a fortune or bankruptcy, was extinguished; even the old tailings, in which finds were occasionally made, were successfully claimed by the all-absorbing Corporation; and the hope of open diggings, temporarily aroused for the adventurous prospector by the discovery of the Wesselton Mine, was soon extinguished by the refusal of the Cape Parliament to interfere with the De Beers monopoly. Working economies threw many men out of their jobs; the diamond buyer outside the ring patronized by the Company had no occupation left; and the shopkeeper lost his most lucrative trade by the ring fence established round the compounds and the directors' practice of selling all goods direct to their native workmen. It is true that after prolonged agitation and a debate in the House De Beers was compelled to earmark profits from these sales for a fund administered by Rhodes himself in the interests of the community, but this brought small comfort to the individual tradesmen. Although Kimberley has since adjusted itself to the huge monopoly which now dominates it, the immediate result of the amalgamation was great hardship and distress in the town. Discontent led to violence and outrages, encouraged by the Knights of Labour, a revolutionary organization, who in their manifesto attributed the universal stagnation of business to the "existence and domination of one great Monopoly, one giant Corporation, as well as to the overweening greed and ambition of one wealthy, overestimated, disappointing politician." The wealthy, overestimated, disappointing politician was Prime Minister at the time of this outburst, and the committee appointed to investigate the causes of distress in Kimberley suggested no heroic measures of relief. But Rhodes himself personally helped to alleviate the hardship inevitable in the period of transition and he had a good answer to complaints about the monopoly. Without it the whole diamond industry would soon have been ruined by cut-throat competition, and in this ruin not only the actual sufferers but all the Europeans and natives still employed by De Beers would have been involved.

II

Diamonds alone did not occupy Rhodes's attention during the years spent in establishing his fortune; he was also one of the pioneers of the gold industry of the Witwatersrand, an enterprise which proved as profitable and very much easier than his amalgamation at Kimberley.

Long before the great discovery of reefs on the Witwatersrand in 1886 it had been known, through reports of the explorers Baines, Mauch and Hartley, that South Africa contained gold. As far back as 1867 an English company had been formed to exploit the Tati goldfields in Matabeleland, and a few years later the report of gold discoveries in the Lydenburg district of the Transvaal had led Herbert and Cecil Rhodes thither during their long trek northwards. The opening of the Pioneer reef in 1883, and later of the Sheba, had brought a rush to the De Kaap district, where Barberton was founded in 1885. But this district was soon thrown completely into the shade by wonderful tales of the wealth to be found on the Witwatersrand, the lofty ridge south of Pretoria, which divides the waters of the Vaal flowing south and the Limpopo flowing north. Here since 1883 the brothers Struben had been carrying on exhaustive experiments, first with the quartz rock, then with some peculiar layers of conglomerate occurring at intervals in the rock formation and composed of pebbles embedded in a cement matrix, not unlike almond rock in appearance, and since famous under the name of Banket. For three years the results were disappointing, but at length, in the spring of 1886, Walker, one of the workmen, struck the layer, afterwards known as the Main Reef Leader, on the farm Langlaagte. A sample of the reef was sent for assay to Kimberley, its extraordinary richness in gold was soon bruited abroad and all the prominent men of the diamond fields were suddenly seized with a gold fever. The first to go were J. B. Robinson, one of the pioneers of the old river-diggings, and Hans Sauer, a friend of Rhodes; the regular Barberton coach took them only as far as Potchefstroon; thence they travelled in a country cart to the Witwatersrand. On arriving at the spot where the city of Johannesburg with its great buildings and vast population now stands, the centre of a line of mine chimneys many miles in length, the travellers saw nothing but bleak undulating veld with a few Boer home-steads in the dips and a small group of prospectors' tents on the ridge. But Hans Sauer saw that it was good and returned to fetch Rhodes and his partner Rudd; Alfred Beit and his partner Porges, Knight and many others followed.

The gold-bearing reefs on the Witwatersrand are quite peculiar. Whereas in other parts of South Africa the gold occurs in massive beds of quartzite or thin bands of quartz, here the best gold is contained in reefs of the Banket conglomerate. These reefs are found in layers of varying thickness and at varying distances apart. The Main Reef, for example, has six main layers, one of them being the Main Reef Leader, which vary in thickness from one to forty inches: some are only a few inches, others as much as eight or nine feet apart. The outcrop of the Main Reef is found in a continuous line for thirty miles along the summit of the ridge and can be traced at intervals for a much longer distance. From their outcrop the reefs dip into the ground towards the south at different angles, sometimes almost vertically, but, as they extend southwards, the dip invariably becomes flatter. Naturally mining operations were first carried on where the outcrop appeared, but had they been confined to this area the results would have been comparatively poor: owing, however, to this fortunate tendency of the dip to flatten, shafts could be sunk at considerable distances from the outcrop with a prospect of picking up the reef again for deep-level workings. Those, therefore, who were wise in the early days took up claims over a considerable distance south of the outcrop. Another peculiarity of the gold present in the Banket formation is its close chemical association with the cement of the conglomerate, so close indeed that it does not readily yield itself to the ordinary process of passing the crushed ore over plates coated with mercury. But by a fortunate coincidence the remedy for this was discovered almost as soon as mining operations began. In 1887 the McArthur Forrest process of treating tailings by the cyanide process was perfected; and thereby most of the gold still in solution could be easily extracted. Coal, too, an absolute necessity for gold mining, was discovered in abundance at Boksburg on the Rand itself: had it not been so the industry might have been brought to a standstill by the prohibitive cost of importing coal from overseas or from Cape Colony. Thus Robinson, Rhodes and the other pioneers, who believed in the marvellous wealth to be obtained from the Strubens' discovery, were soon justified. Within a year the mining camp had been turned into the beginnings of Johannesburg; and by 1892 the gold production of South Africa, which was valued at less than half a million for the three years 1885–87, had risen in value to four and a half millions for one year, all but a sixth of it coming from the Witwatersrand.

But in the early stages considerable faith was needed to invest heavily in the Rand, for there was then no certainty that the reefs would prove so prolific. Of the optimists Rhodes and Robinson were the foremost: Barnato, deterred by an agent's adverse report, hung back. Robinson, being first in the field, picked up some of the best properties. Between the July when he came up and the following November he bought the farms Langlaagte, where Walker had struck gold, and Turffontein, where the famous Robinson Mine was opened, for £26,000. People talked derisively of "Robinson's cabbage patch," bought at such an extravagant price, but they no longer laughed when these same properties were valued at eighteen millions and in five years' time had paid over a million in dividends to the shareholders. Rhodes did not do badly either, though, owing to mistaken advice given to him about the value of East Rand properties, he missed some good things. He and Rudd took their bearings in the August of 1886; then Rudd went to England to raise capital and Rhodes began buying on a large scale in December. "The opinion is steadily growing," he writes, "that the Rand is the biggest thing the world has seen," owing to its "wonderful climate, its facilities for work and its enormous auriferous deposits: [it has] plenty of good things awaiting hard work and development." He is constantly jostling up with Robinson, Porges, Beit and other speculators; he offers to go shares with Robinson, but Robinson thinks he can do better alone; as he can sometimes. For once, while Rhodes was in the orchard trying to bargain in bad Dutch with the farmer for his property, Robinson came round into the kitchen and bought it out of hand from the farmer's wife by his readier arguments in fluent Dutch and a display of golden sovereigns. The simple Dutch farmers soon began to realize the value of their barren lands and to ask prices which made Kruger think the English purchasers were mad. Rhodes had to pay £40,000 in cash and £30,000 in scrip to farmer Van Wyk for a block called Botha's Reef, of which he had great hopes, and when he wanted the farmer to throw in as pit-props some poplar poles he saw on the ground, "Ik zal nit verkoopne" (I will not sell them) was the only answer he could get. Most of his purchases were made on the West Rand, with a few on the East; he also went farther afield and bought gold-bearing properties at Klerksdorp and Malmani near the western border of the Transvaal. It is perhaps hardly surprising that with his slight experience of gold-mining his judgement was sometimes at fault in these purchases: indeed one enlightened critic wondered whether "this clever speculator had not ventured too much on surface indications." After purchase Rudd and he floated companies to work most of the properties: one of these companies he called after his old college, Oriel; others were the Banket, Botha's Reef, May, Aurora, and Witkopje Estate.

But his principal venture was The Gold Fields of South Africa, Limited, founded in 1887 with a capital of £125,000. He handed over to it all his gold interests and shares in other companies at cost price, reserving, however, for himself and Rudd three-fifteenths of the net profits in respect of founders' shares, besides two-fifteenths as managing directors. The capital was eagerly taken up and had been increased to £1,250,000 by 1892, when it was renamed The Consolidated Gold Fields of South Africa. By that time it had given up the direct working of nearly all its properties and become a huge share trust company in Rand mines, especially deep-levels, to which Rhodes, at first incredulous, had become thoroughly converted. Its shareholders' interests were guarded by the full control it exercised over the gold-mining companies subsidiary to it; and the management, for which Rhodes was largely responsible, gave excellent results. In 1892 the dividend was 10 per cent, in 1893–94 15 per cent, and in 1894–95 no less than 50 per cent. Rhodes himself made enormous profits from the Gold Fields: for several years he drew £300,000 to £400,000 from it annually, and when, in concession to the outcry against his percentage rights on founders' shares he gave them up, he received in exchange ordinary shares valued at £1,300,000 to £1,400,000. Thus he secured his own interests; but he also thought of his wider schemes. As in the case of De Beers, so with the Gold Fields, he took power by the trust deed to be able to invest in other enterprises besides Rand mines, a provision from which he derived much support for his political designs.

During his visits to the Transvaal in 1886 and 1887 Rhodes had two more meetings with Kruger. Once he went on a deputation to the President and made a speech representing grievances of the miners: it was apparently not a very tactful speech, and at the end Kruger, pointing the stem of his pipe towards Rhodes, said in Dutch: "Tell him I have heard all these stories before. I am here to protect my burghers as well as the Rand people. I know what I have to do and I will do what I consider is right." On the second occasion he proposed Kruger's health at a luncheon given to him at Johannesburg. Kruger, in spite of the wealth brought into an almost bankrupt country by the new adventurers, was by no means happy at their sudden invasion in such large numbers. He foresaw the danger to the independence of the Transvaal from the population of aliens, who would demand rights and responsibility. Had it rested with him, he would no doubt have refrained from proclaiming the goldfields; but at any rate he meant to resist any further demands from the strangers. In his difficulty he consulted wise old President Brand of the Free State, who advised him to make friends with the miners by offering them every possible concession: but this was not Kruger's way. His policy, decided upon in 1886, was to restrict their power to the utmost, to allow them no freehold interest in any land, and to maintain the ruling aristocracy of Boer landowners, with himself as supreme arbiter. At the luncheon in Johannesburg in February 1887 he showed that he fully understood the diggers' position, explaining their grievances about the gold regulation better than they could themselves, and promising certain reforms; but on the subject of political rights he was adamant. Commenting afterwards on the newcomers' claim to the franchise, he denied that they had any right to it, and continued characteristically: "Wealth cannot break laws. Though a man has a million pounds he cannot alter the law. . . . Is it a good man who wants to be master of the country, when others have been suffering for twenty years to conduct its affairs? . . . It is the unthankful people to whom I have given protection that are always dissatisfied, and, what is more, they would actually want me to alter my laws to suit them." There was sound common sense in Kruger's apprehensions, for within a few years the "Uitlanders," as they were called, outnumbered his burghers, and it is easy to understand his desire to prevent the "cursed English" regaining political control over his beloved country. Rhodes to some extent sympathized with Kruger's alarm. In his speech at the luncheon he admitted that it could not be a matter of complaint if the Transvaal viewed the new population with some suspicion. But Kruger's methods were less prudent than his fears were justified. By his obstinate opposition even to such reasonable demands as municipal freedom for Johannesburg, by his hardly veiled contempt for the Uitlanders, and by the encouragement he gave to disreputable concession-hunters, of every nationality except the English, to make profits from the diggers' needs, he himself helped to bring the cataclysm on his country. At any rate there was no mistaking his policy, for though crafty in his methods he was open as to his aims; and Rhodes at these meetings had full warning of the long struggle before him with the obstinate old representative of a past order.

By the enterprises he had thus set going, both at Kimberley and at Johannesburg, during the three years 1885 to 1888, Rhodes was now master of the financial resources he thought necessary for his political aims. How rich he actually was it is impossible to tell and, probably, he himself hardly knew. He used to keep running accounts with various firms, Wernher Beit's principally, but also in later days with the Chartered Company, at the Standard Bank and elsewhere. These firms used to buy and sell shares for him, crediting or debiting him with the balances, besides acting for him as paymasters of current accounts, and periodically sent him in statements showing his financial position. He was constantly changing his investments, and had complicated arrangements with many individuals and firms as to the division of the proceeds of shares. The marvel is that he appears to have had such a good grasp of his most important transactions on the money market and in company promoting, and a very clear memory of his chief commitments. For months he gave public and frequent expression to his resentment against a prominent financier, who had not allotted him scrip to which he thought himself entitled, and he carried on long controversies with De Beers and the Gold Fields about his percentage rights in the profits of those corporations. His income was derived principally from those two undertakings. He admitted to Labouchere in 1897 that he got between three and four hundred thousand a year from the Gold Fields. In De Beers he had the profits of two life-governorships, for he had bought out one of the original four in 1892; and when Barnato died the proceeds of his went to the two survivors Rhodes and Beit; at any rate he received close on £200,000 a year from this source. From the numerous other companies in which he was interested, he must every year, either by dividends or by sales of shares at a profit, have obtained enough to bring his total income at least up to the million.

Nor can the value to him of all these undertakings be measured only or even principally in money. They also gave him enormous and almost uncontrolled power, if he chose to use it. At first, when he was in his full vigour, he was the absolute dictator of De Beers and the Gold Fields, with all their ramifications throughout South Africa, even, one may say, throughout the world. He could and did make them spend their money on such various objects as securing large tracts of Africa for the Empire, promoting fruit farms, breeding horses or encouraging education. His position at the head of the diamond industry gave him even the excuse for interfering in the politics of the United States. At the time of the McKinley tariff he appears to have kept an agent in America to lobby against excessive duties on imported diamonds, and a suggestion was put about that diamonds should be admitted free "in return for some support of the silver cause in the U.S.A." He was also enabled, with more justification, to promote his political views in home politics by contributions to the party chests of the Liberals and the Home Rulers; and in one general election at the Cape he spent very large sums on organizing his party.

The power given to a few men by such a huge monopoly as De Beers or such a wealthy corporation as the Gold Fields is not good for any country, even when the power is wielded by a man with such public-spirited views as Rhodes. It tends to destroy public spirit in others, and to introduce low and mercenary motives for political action even in the lifetime of the great man; and when he is gone the canker remains without his alleviating influence. Nor was such power an unmixed blessing for Rhodes himself. In his involved transactions in company promoting and diamond amalgamation he was forced to add to his band of old and tried friends a horde of satellites, whose fortune he made by judicious hints as to the probable issue of his negotiations. Such followers, not too nice in their methods, he came to regard as necessary for some of the work he had in hand, and though he never respected them or gave them the confidence he gave to the true friends, and though he always kept a chamber in his mind swept and garnished for ideas they could never understand, he became insensibly tainted by their constant presence.

Still, for good or ill, the Great Amalgamator, as he was now called, had in these three years won for himself the kind of power which he thought essential for his greater projects. To these he could now devote himself.

CHAPTER X

THE CHARTER

At Christmas time in the year 1887 the High Commissioner, Sir Hercules Robinson, was quietly occupied at Grahamstown with ceremonial duties and entertainments on the occasion of an Exhibition held in that loyal town to celebrate the jubilee of Her late Majesty Queen Victoria. The festivities followed the usual course; dances, banquets, and pony racing: the pony racing is remembered for the mild excitement over the change of ownership of a promising pony, and the importance of the celebration was marked by the due quota of innocuous speeches. An expert staff of polite aide-de-camps and secretaries was in attendance to lighten the Governor's labours, to ensure that no jarring note should mar the smoothness of the proceedings and to provide for the comfort of the vice-regal party. Suddenly Cecil Rhodes, hot foot from Kimberley, burst in upon this pleasant assembly, bringing with him Sir Sidney Shippard, administrator of the new Crown Colony of British Bechuanaland. Rhodes had not come to listen to speeches or attend dances and pony races; he was too busy for that with his gold companies and his diamond amalgamation; but he had just heard news from the north which gave him such serious concern that he felt it necessary to interrupt his own occupations and the Governor's junketings for a serious talk on the situation. For nothing short of immediate action would, he believed, preserve England's power of advancing into the interior. Now Sir Hercules was a man of patriotic feeling and of sound common sense, who sympathized sincerely with Rhodes's views; he had indeed risked much by his support of the unconventional young diamond-digger against Mackenzie, the idol of Exeter Hall, Warren, the chosen agent of the British Government, and his own Cape Ministry. But after all he was merely a governor dependent on a Secretary of State distrustful of further responsibility in South Africa; he had before him a lesson against unlicensed adventure in the fate of his predecessor, Sir Bartle Frere; and he had done as much as could be expected of any one governor by his acquisition of Bechuanaland. Here now was Rhodes, sweeping down like a whirlwind upon the happy Grahamstown party, full of schemes for further "spheres of influence" and evidently bent on securing an immediate decision. He can hardly have been entirely welcome. Still Sir Hercules was a conscientious governor; he had a liking and a great admiration for Rhodes; so he resigned himself to the spell of his masterful visitor.

The message which had disturbed Rhodes had come from his friend Ralph Williams, the confidant of his schemes in the days of the Warren expedition, and at this time British agent at Pretoria. He had heard that a treaty had either been concluded or was about to be concluded between the South African Republic and Lo Bengula, king of the Matabeles, and had sent word to Rhodes that if it were ratified it would preclude all British enterprise north of Bechuanaland. This was a serious matter to Rhodes, who had always regarded Matabeleland, with its dependency Mashonaland, as the next stepping-stone to the Central Lakes, the northern limit of his dreams of empire in Africa. The country had so far not been brought within the sphere of influence of any European power, and, if the Transvaal got beforehand with him, his plans would be brought to naught and all his labour on Bechuanaland, a mere "Suez Canal to the interior," wasted. The sudden visit to Grahamstown was to prevent this catastrophe.

The Matabeles were an offshoot of the Zulus, who had broken away from the parent tribe under the leadership of Moselikatze, one of the Zulu King Chaka's captains, about the same time as the Boers of Cape Colony began their great trek. Beaten off by the Basutos, the Matabeles swarmed through the Free State and thence across the Vaal to the western districts of the Transvaal, leaving a track of desolation wherever they passed. Here they came into collision with Boer emigrants into the same district, one of them being Kruger himself, who told a Matabele delegation in 1887 that he did not speak from hearsay of those encounters; "for I myself was present and, although then very young, I could handle a gun and shoot. Potgieter was my chief. We then came for the second time and drove away Moselikatze." After this defeat the chief led his savage warriors across the Limpopo to the broad pasture-lands north of Bechuanaland, and soon reduced to vassalage the Mahololo and Mashonas, then inhabiting a large tract of country south of the Zambesi. In 1868 Moselikatze died and was succeeded by his son Lo Bengula, a tyrant as bloodthirsty as his father. The sole object of the Matabele organisation was war. The young males of the tribe and those of the subject races captured in childhood were fed almost entirely on beef, a diet which killed the weaklings of dysentery and made the remainder very stout and fierce. In due time they were drafted into one or other of the regiments, into which the whole manhood was divided. Here the strictest discipline was maintained, and no youth was allowed to marry until he had reached the age of thirty-five and had blooded himself in fight; so, to give the would-be bridegrooms their chance, hostile raids on neighbouring kraals were a yearly occurrence. The fighting spirit of the race was also excited by periodical war-dances, in which the soldiers of the different regiments took part, attired in their gorgeous and terrifying trappings, plumes and capes of ostrich-feathers, otter-skin bands on their foreheads, ox-tails round their arms and legs, and kilts of wild-cat skin. After the destruction of the Zulu power in 1879 the Matabeles were the most formidable fighting race left in South Africa. But since their early conflicts with the Boers they had not molested Europeans.[1] Both Moselikatze and Lo Bengula, though firm in maintaining their right to "refuse the road" through their territory to any European they chose, were friendly to the few they

[1] A story is told of Englishmen done to death by the Matabeles in 1878, but the guilt was never brought home to Lo Bengula himself.

admitted. The great missionary Moffat had been allowed to establish a mission station at Inyati, and the hunters Baines, Hartley, Viljoen and Selous were always well received; a few traders, too, were permitted to set up stores near the royal kraal.

The Transvaal Boers had long cast covetous eyes on this country. In 1868, on the discovery of the Tati Gold Fields, President Pretorius had proclaimed it a Transvaal possession, but, on Sir Philip Wodehouse's protest, had taken no further steps. Again, after Majuba, Joubert had written to Lo Bengula urging him to ally himself with the Boers rather than the English, for, "when an Englishman once has your property in his hand, then he is like a monkey that has its hands full of pumpkin seeds;—if you don't beat him to death he will never let go"; and in the succeeding years various parties of Boers had talked of trekking into Matabeleland or Mashonaland. Kruger, however, never looked favourably on his rival Joubert's policy of expansion northwards. Since his rebuff in Bechuanaland his chief aim had been to obtain Swaziland on the east and access to the sea, in order to have a free port of his own; and he had no wish to complicate the issue by quarrelling with England about the north. Still even Kruger was sometimes obliged to yield to public opinion, and in 1887 he consented to the despatch of one Grobler to negotiate with Lo Bengula a treaty of protection. There seems little doubt that in July 1887 Grobler obtained a document purporting to give the Transvaal wide powers of jurisdiction over their own subjects settled in Matabeleland, and to keep a consul in residence at the king's kraal. In fact, when Ralph Williams sent his message to Rhodes, Grobler was on the point of starting to take up his post as consul. Whether Lo Bengula regarded the treaty as anything more than a vague renewal of friendship is doubtful. At any rate the republic was founding on it much greater claims than its words implied; for Rhodes had received independent evidence in a letter from Pretoria that the Transvaal had already assumed the right of determining on concessions to Europeans in Matabeleland.

Rhodes submitted his evidence to the Governor at

Grahamstown, and urged him at all costs to prevent the country falling under the control of the Transvaal. Instant action was necessary, or it would be too late, foı Grobler was already on his way, and it might be impossible to dislodge him when once he had established his influence. Sir Hercules was impressed by the danger, but Rhodes was in too much of a hurry: precipitate action might not be approved of at home and the risk was great. But Rhodes had made up his mind, and when that was so, as Barnato had observed, "he ties you up and you cannot resist him." So the Governor was tied up. Six years later Rhodes, in anecdotal mood, described to a Cape Town audience his methods of persuading Sir Hercules. The occasion referred to was not this interview, but the arguments were probably similar, for Rhodes's methods of arguing were all his own and did not vary much. Bechuanaland had been secured, and, "I remember so well," said Rhodes, "that in my discussions with your late Governor he was good enough to say, 'Well, I think that is enough,' and, Mr. Mayor, the only reply I made to him was, 'Do come with me and look at the block-house on Table Mountain.' I used that expression to him, and then I said, 'Those good old people, two hundred years ago, thought that block-house on Table Mountain was the limit of their ideas, but now let us face it to-day. Where are we? We are considerably beyond the Vaal River, and supposing that those good people were to come to life again to-day, what would they think of it and their block-house?' Then I said, 'Sir, will you consider, during the period you have been the representative of Her Majesty in this colony, what you have done? We are now on latitude 22°.' It was amusing when he said to me, 'And what a trouble it has been!' He said to me, 'But where will you stop?' and I replied, 'I will stop where the country has not been claimed.' Your old Governor said, 'Let us look at the map,' and I showed him that it was the southern border of Tanganyika. He was a little upset. I said that the Great Powers at home marked the map and did nothing: adding, 'Let us try to mark the map, and we know that we shall do something.' 'Well,' said Sir Hercules Robinson, 'I think you should be satisfied with the Zambesi as a boundary.' [He was already getting tied up.] I replied, 'Let us take a piece of notepaper, and let us measure from the block-house to the Vaal River; that is the individual effort of the people. Now,' I said, 'let us measure what you have done in your temporary existence, and then we will finish by measuring up my imaginations.' We took a piece of notepaper and measured the efforts of the country since the Dutch occupied and founded it. We measured what he had done in his life, and then we measured my imaginations; and his Excellency, who is no longer with us, said, 'I will leave you alone.'" ["You cannot resist him!"]

By such simple, child-like persistence Rhodes, reinforced by Shippard, a convinced partisan of his views, won over Sir Hercules. On Boxing Day Shippard was empowered to write a despatch to his assistant commissioner, J. S. Moffat, then on a visit to Lo Bengula, bidding him inquire about the bargain with the Transvaal and persuade the king to sign a treaty recognizing the exclusive influence of Great Britain in his country. Rhodes then returned to his business at Kimberley; and a messenger was sent with such urgent instructions for haste that after a journey of 700 miles he brought the despatch to Moffat before the end of January. Moffat, the son of Livingstone's father-in-law, who had founded the Inyati mission in Moselikatze's time, was a good agent for the purpose, as he had tact and was trusted by Lo Bengula. Going quietly to work, he got the king to admit that the Transvaal had no right to interfere in his country, that he had no wish to receive Grobler as consul, and within a fortnight, on February 11, 1888, had persuaded him to sign a treaty of perpetual amity with the Queen, whereby he engaged himself not to part with any territory or sign a treaty with any other power without the High Commissioner's sanction.

Thanks to the despised "Imperial factor," Rhodes had now obtained what in mining practice might be termed an option on Matabeleland. His next business was to convert this option into firm possession. Neither the Cape nor the Home Government could be looked to for further assistance at this stage; the Cape was not yet ready to absorb even

Bechuanaland, while the High Commissioner had gone to the utmost limits of his power. Private enterprise was the only resource left: so Rhodes determined on private enterprise; and, if he could obtain the sanction of the state for his private enterprise, so much the better. He could look to a long line of illustrious chartered companies as his models. Starting from the days of the Tudors there had been the Levant and Russia Companies for purely trading purposes, the Company of Adventurers of London trading to Africa, and the Hudson's Bay and East India Companies with their territorial and administrative rights. These ancient corporations had by this time either disappeared or lost their special privileges, but a similar form of chartered company had recently been revived in the British North Borneo Company of 1881 and the Royal Niger Company of 1886, while for the Imperial British East Africa Company also Sir William Mackinnon was shortly to obtain the royal charter. At a time when the values of territory in Africa were still but little known, and yet every nation was scrambling for power there, the advantage to the state of such semi-official companies to exploit new ground was manifest. "If the results are good," said a cynical writer, "they can be made the property of the state. If the value be little, the company can be left to its own devices and its work be ignored." On the other hand, the attraction to the private venturer was the chance of large profits. So Rhodes, following these examples, decided to obtain speculative concessions in the new country and protect them by a royal charter. His own main object was to preserve as much as possible of Africa for British civilization, to his mind the greatest blessing in the world; but to make converts he did not rely on this lure alone. "Pure philanthropy is all very well in its way," as he said, "but philanthropy plus 5 per cent is a good deal better." The marvellous discovery of gold on the Rand had disposed the public to look favourably on the reports of gold to be found in Lo Bengula's dominions brought by every traveller of repute. So gold was to be the bait to attract the public to his projects of northern expansion. By the beginning of 1888 all things were ready: he had founded the Gold

Fields and was on the eve of amalgamating the diamond mines; so he had no anxiety about finance and was prepared to start forthwith.

Immediately on his return from Grahamstown, even before the Moffat treaty had been signed, he and Beit sent up a trader, Fry, to obtain a gold-mining concession from Lo Bengula. Fry fell ill and returned without accomplishing anything. Rhodes then paid a flying visit to England, and there heard that he had serious rivals in the field. Two allied companies, the Bechuanaland Exploration Company and the Exploring Company, were in process of formation to obtain and exploit concessions in the Protectorate and Matabeleland, and the promoters had already informed the Colonial Office of their plans. Rhodes also went to sound Lord Knutsford, who, without committing himself, seemed impressed by Rhodes's ideas, whereupon he hurried back to South Africa, convinced that operations must be conducted on a larger scale. For the new mission to Lo Bengula he had some difficulty in finding the right men; but finally pitched upon Rudd, his partner, who for sixteen years had been hand in glove with him in all his ventures; F. R. Thompson, who had helped him with the Kimberley compounds, and from the age of twelve had been learning native languages and customs; and lastly, his old Oxford friend, Rochfort Maguire, the fellow of All Souls. Rudd's son, a fine strapping youth much admired by the natives, accompanied his father; no expense was spared on equipment, and there was an imposing retinue of Kaffir drivers and attendants, all under the direction of Rhodes's personal servant William. None of the party had been to Matabeleland before, but two of them spoke the language, while the third, Maguire, had that imperturbable Oxford demeanour which no difficulties or hardships could ruffle. The mission was well calculated to impress the king and his councillors with the importance of the man they represented.

Rudd, Maguire and Thompson arrived at Buluwayo, the king's principal kraal, in the latter half of 1888, having previously announced their business in a letter drawn up by the fellow of All Souls. Lo Bengula was an imposing personage, with considerable powers of attraction to

Europeans. Sir Sidney Shippard, who also visited him this year, thus describes his appearance as he came out of his royal waggon: "A few minutes after I had taken my seat near his waggon a curtain was drawn aside, and the great man appeared and deliberately stepped over the front box and sat down on the board before the driver's seat. He was completely naked save for a very long piece of dark blue cloth, rolled very small and wound round his body, which it no wise concealed, and a monkey skin worn as a small apron and about the size of a Highland sporan. In person he is rather tall . . . and very stout, though by no means unwieldy. . . . His colour is a fine bronze, and he evidently takes great care of his person and is scrupulously clean. He wears the leathern ring over his forehead as a matter of course. Altogether he is a very fine-looking man, and in spite of his obesity has a most majestic carriage. Like all the Matabele warriors, who despise a stooping gait in a man, Lo Bengula walks quite erect with his head thrown somewhat back and his broad chest expanded, and as he marches along at a slow pace with his long staff in his right hand, while all the men around shout his praises, he looks his part to perfection." Like other absolute monarchs in more civilized countries, he had to work hard for his living, and to consult his people's wishes. He spent much time in painting himself up for rain-making, and, though less bellicose than his warriors, was unable to resist their unceasing demands for raids on Mashonas and other tribes. He was hospitable and well disposed to the Europeans he knew, but much troubled with the many concession-hunters, who, as he pathetically remarked to the High Commissioner, "come in here like wolves without my permission and make roads into my country." Many of his young bloods would have been quite ready to make short work of the intruders, but he had the political instinct to see that this would be fatal to his tribe; besides, he had a regal sense of hospitality even to intruders in his country.

When Rudd and his friends arrived they found plenty of Europeans before them. The most influential was the missionary Helm, who generally interpreted in important negotiations and was trusted by the king; Fairbairn and

Usher, the two resident traders, were also privileged persons, being regarded as members of the tribe. Fairbairn was the custodian of the chief's great elephant seal, without which treaties and concessions had no validity, and with another old resident, Sam Edwards, had the mining rights in the Tati district, with authority to make laws "for keeping the peace and order." These traders, who made great profits by their monopoly, had no wish to see others invading their preserves. Two rival syndicates, Wood, Francis and Chapman, and Johnson and Heany, were each claiming the mining concession in some territory disputed between Lo Bengula and his southern neighbour Khama, having each obtained a grant from one of the two rival disputants. Maund, already in high favour at Buluwayo, was there for the Exploring Company, "guinea-pigs" Rhodes called them, seeking as wide powers as Rhodes himself; Phillips, Leask and Tainton were also on the look out for concessions, and there were Boers and Germans as well, hungrily waiting for what they could pick up. With all these rivals in the field, with Moffat and Shippard on the one side and Grobler on the other recommending their respective countries for special favours, with the English bishop of Bloemfontein, in company with a German count, choosing the same moment to inspect his mission stations in Mashonaland, no wonder Lo Bengula was worried and his young men straining at the leash. Grobler, the Transvaal emissary, was the first to fall out, for in passing through Bechuanaland he was waylaid and murdered by an impi sent by Khama, who had a grievance against him for some horse-coping transaction.[1] But enough rivals remained to make it likely that Matabeleland would be reduced to the horrible state of confusion of which Swaziland was already an example. Here the chief had been persuaded to give away concessions right and left to Boer and English speculators, who quarrelled among themselves and made the

[1] By order of the High Commissioner an inquiry was held by Shippard into the facts, and in spite of Shippard's prejudiced report against Grobler, Khama was ordered by the British Government to pay an annuity to Grobler's widow. There is no ground for the suggestion made by some Boers at the time that English officials had any connection with the murder.

country a land of strife and turbulence, while the chief was steadily drinking himself to death with the champagne, which represented his particular mess of pottage. As Rhodes had convinced Sir Hercules, the only possible remedies were either to proclaim a protectorate or establish one strong company with a monopoly of all concessions.

In their attempt to get this monopoly Rhodes's agents had a good deal of indirect support from the favour with which he was known to be regarded by Shippard and Moffat as well as the High Commissioner. Nevertheless, they had no light task. For three months or more they were kept waiting on Lo Bengula's good pleasure, with the uncomfortable prospect of being massacred at any time by the young warriors. If they bathed or washed their teeth they were accused of bewitching the water, and were always unwittingly transgressing some tribal law; once they were warned of an instant attack and decided to sell their lives dearly. However, Lo Bengula always managed to protect them, and at last, after an indaba of two days, consented, on October 30, 1888, to grant the desired concession. Even then there was a hitch about signing, for Lo Bengula thought his royal word should be enough; but in the end his mark and the elephant seal were affixed to a document granting to Rudd and the others "exclusive power over all metals and minerals situated and contained in his kingdoms, principalities and dominions," with licence to win the same and enjoy all profits therefrom; and further, Lo Bengula, "having been much molested of late by divers persons seeking and desiring to obtain grants and cessions of land and mining rights in his territories," authority was given them to exclude all such persons from his dominions. In return, the beneficiaries bound themselves to pay the chief £100 a month and to deliver to him 1000 rifles, 100,000 rounds of ammunition, and an armed steamer on the Zambesi, the last a happy afterthought of Rhodes: "same," he wrote to Rudd, "as Stanley put on Upper Congo."

Hardly won, the concession was nearly lost. Rhodes had instructed Rudd to bring it away as soon as it was completed. Rudd "obtained the road" from Lo Bengula, who parted with him on most friendly terms, gave him a large firkin of beer, and told him to bring up his "big brother Rhodes" next time. But on his journey through the Bechuana desert, with one Kaffir driver, Rudd found all the water-holes he had counted on dried up, and had to abandon the horses and make the best of his way on foot; finally, overcome with thirst and almost dying, he just managed to hide his precious document in an ant-bear hole before he fell down insensible. In this state he was discovered by some kindly Bechuanas, who gave him water and brought him back to life; afterwards he was picked up by Sir Sidney Shippard's escort, to which his son had been attached, and, having recovered the concession from the ant-bear hole, was brought with it safely to Kimberley.

For more than a year after he had received the concession Rhodes was busy making it water-tight. His first anxiety was about Lo Bengula; he knew that every kind of pressure would be put on the chief by rival speculators to induce him to withdraw his promise or give other concessions incompatible with it, and in all his instructions to Rudd he had insisted that "if we get anything we must always have some one resident or they will intrigue to upset us," for "nature," he kept repeating, "abhors a vacuum." So on Rudd's departure Thompson and Maguire were left behind to fill the vacuum. At first they retained their influence. They persuaded Lo Bengula to give public notice that the concession had been granted and was a bar to all others, and at the end of the year Maguire was put in command of an impi to warn off Haggard and other agents of the Austral Africa Company, who had come into the country to ask for a concession. But at the beginning of 1889 there was an ominous change. Maund, the capable agent of the Exploring Company, regained control. Another public notice was issued, this time denying on Lo Bengula's behalf that Rudd had been granted all mineral rights in the country; and a deputation of indunas was sent to England under Maund's charge to interview "the great white Queen." Maund and the Exploring Company, as will appear, were disposed of by Rhodes himself; but that was not the end of the trouble with Lo Bengula. Fairbairn, keeper of the elephant seal, so worked upon the chief that he got him to send a letter to the Colonial Office saying that he had signed the Rudd concession under a misapprehension. But Rhodes's means were not exhausted. His friend Jameson, who on a hunting trip in Matabeleland had earned the king's gratitude by curing him of gout, was still in reserve; so Jameson and another Kimberley doctor, Rutherfoord Harris, were sent up to try their powers of persuasion, and for the time being succeeded. But no sooner were their backs turned than Lo Bengula changed round again. He no longer needed the promptings of disappointed traders and speculators to influence him against the concession. His own fears and the anger of his warriors kept him up to the mark. He professed ignorance of what he had signed and demanded back the original document for verification; and he wrote to the Queen declaring that "the white people are troubling me much about gold. If the Queen hears that I have given away the whole country, it is not so. I do not understand where the dispute is, because I have no knowledge of writing." To his indignant indunas and warriors he offered as a scapegoat his chief adviser, Lotchi, who, he said, had "blinded" him and induced him to sign the document. Lotchi walked out of the council a doomed man, to make his last preparations. He warned all his people to escape, and said to the missionary Helm, "I am a dead man." And so it proved. A detachment of the Imbesu or Royal Regiment came to his kraal, carried off the young children and cattle, and killed Lotchi and all the others who had not fled. The position of Maguire and Thompson had become almost as precarious, and, though the king did all he could to protect them, they were virtually hostages. The first to flee the country was Maguire, in April 1889, and a month or so later Thompson made his escape. Thus the "vacuum" so much abhorred by Rhodes was created. But before this the centre of interest had shifted from Lo Bengula's kraal to Cape Town or London or wherever Rhodes happened to be.

His policy with rivals who claimed concessions from Lo Bengula was the same as with rivals on the diamond fields: to make a deal with them if possible, and only fight them in the last resort. He himself afterwards said that his worst difficulty in acquiring Matabeleland for the Empire was the settlement of some of the outrageous claims set up against him. One man, who had never left England, actually demanded compensation because he had not been able to carry out his intention of seeking a mining licence in Matabeleland owing to Rhodes's previous concession. Rhodes did not compensate him, but he did others with claims hardly less preposterous. When he heard that Haggard and Wallop had been warned off by Maguire and his impi, fearing "a literary campaign against us," he proposed to indemnify them. More than a dozen claimants of concessions were handsomely paid to drop them or merge them with his own, and no questions asked about their validity; and many a South African was long afterwards drawing a steady income of £600 or more from this source. The only rivals he seriously feared were the two allied Bechuanaland Exploration and Exploring Companies. After sounding the Colonial Office in the summer of 1888, in the following January their principal directors, Mr. George Cawston and Lord Gifford, had made the explicit proposal that the two Companies should be incorporated under Charter to work all the minerals in Khama's and Lo Bengula's territories and build a railway to the Zambesi. These were very much Rhodes's own objects, only, as he put it, this interior company must be De Beers and the Gold Fields with a combined capital of thirteen millions instead of a company with a beggarly £50,000. The Companies' two agents in South Africa had soon come to the same conclusion. One of them was Sir Charles Metcalfe, the engineer and an old friend of Rhodes, who had been sent out to make surveys for the proposed railway; but as soon as he came to Kimberley he found that nothing could be done without Rhodes's help. Maund, the other agent, had made a good fight for his principals at Lo Bengula's kraal, but on his way to England in January 1889 with the Matabele indunas began to feel some doubts after a conversation with Rhodes at Kimberley. Learning from him that, if it came to a fight, money would be no object, but that there might be means of accommodation.

Maund thought it prudent for the time being to withhold certain important letters and documents in his possession. Nevertheless Rhodes soon saw that it was time to follow him to England to conclude negotiations and arrange about the Charter himself. "Our enemies," he wrote, "may bowl us out if I do not go at once to headquarters. Our concession is so gigantic, it is like giving a man the whole of Australia: and our opponents are numerous."

He reached England in March 1889 with two tasks before him: first to deal with opposition from rival syndicates, and secondly to persuade the British Government and the British public to entrust the administration and exploitation of the interior of Africa to a Chartered Company formed by himself. The first task was comparatively easy. When Rhodes and Cawston had submitted to the Colonial Office their rival proposals, Sir Robert Herbert had thrown out the hint that their objects would be more easily attained if they combined their interests; and they had immediately agreed. Within a few days of Rhodes's arrival the terms of amalgamation were settled. The Exploring Company was given a share in the Rudd concession, which was held by Rhodes, Beit, the Gold Fields and a few others, while Rhodes and Beit joined the board of the Exploring Company. The funds for developing the new country and for building the railway were to be provided by the Rudd Concession syndicate, converted first into the Central Search Association, and afterwards, when the Bechuanaland Exploration Company and other conflicting syndicates had been brought in, into the United Concessions Company, Limited. Thus all legitimate interests in the undeveloped parts of South Africa up to the Zambesi would be incorporated into one great company.

But in the political field things did not go so smoothly. His old adversary, Mackenzie, was back in England, urging the Government to part with no more power in South Africa. He was still agitating against the transfer of the Crown Colony of Bechuanaland to the Cape, which Rhodes desired, and was even more opposed to the grant of administrative powers or a commercial monopoly to any company in the Bechuanaland Protectorate or Matabeleland. Backed by the Aborigines Protection Society and the London Chamber of Commerce he bombarded Lord Knutsford with memoranda representing that direct Crown Government was the only means of securing justice for the natives, and that the existing stagnation of Kimberley was an illustration of the evils of one too powerful company. Still more influential on the same side was the South African Committee, composed of certain well-known members of Parliament and others, such as Sir T. Fowell Buxton, Albert Grey (afterwards Earl Grey), the Duke of Fife, Evelyn Ashley, Arnold Forster, and Joseph Chamberlain. In a circular sent out by this committee, they attacked the concession given to Rudd, " a Cape colonist who is believed to have received very influential support in the commercial part of his undertaking from persons in authority at the Cape. . . . A single speculator who buys for an old song the most valuable territory in South Africa." Bradlaugh, Labouchere and other free-lances in the House of Commons asked awkward questions about the favour shown by the High Commissioner to Rhodes's associates. The stipulation that Lo Bengula should receive payment in arms and ammunition was also specially fastened upon for attack. Already in South Africa the Bishop of Bloemfontein and others had commented strongly on this provision, and their protests had been re-echoed in the House by Chamberlain. The Government at first also disapproved, but then weakly accepted the Jesuitical plea, originated by Moffat and endorsed by the High Commissioner, that rifles were a less effective and less brutal means of massacre in the hands of natives than assegais. Rhodes had also alienated many of that party, to which he might naturally have looked for support in his schemes of Imperial development, by his disparaging remarks on the "Imperial factor" and by his alliance with the Bond. *The Times*, for example, persisted in identifying this organization with the extremists who demanded the dissolution of all ties with England, and solemnly warned Rhodes, now that he had "made his pile," to turn his attention seriously to patriotism.

But, though he had powerful enemies, he was an adept at winning powerful friends. It would, no doubt, have been comparatively easy for him to obtain absolution from the Unionist party then in power and to rely entirely on their support for a policy in keeping with their traditions. But he had no such inclination. Just as in South Africa he sought the co-operation of Dutch as well as English, so in England he wanted to carry all parties with him and devoted especial attention to conciliating certain sections of the opposition. This came to him the more easily as on certain questions his sympathies were rather with the Radicals than the Conservatives, especially with those Radicals who had been taught by Stead and Dilke to take an interest in colonial affairs; and, though Gladstone personally was always suspect to him, and his unfavourable impressions were only confirmed by the few conversations he had with that great statesman, he was strongly in favour of Home Rule for Ireland. He put himself into the hands of Sir Charles Mills, the Agent-General for the Cape, and by his means soon obtained the long-desired introduction to W. T. Stead, then at the height of his power as a journalist. Stead came unwillingly to the interview, for he was an ally of Mackenzie's and was not prepossessed by what he had heard of Rhodes; but after talking to him for a few hours he made the discovery that Rhodes was the man he had long been looking for to be the practical exponent of his own doctrines; while Rhodes had already discovered in the columns of the *Pall Mall Gazette* that Stead was his mentor and his prophet. From that moment the strangely assorted pair entered into a close alliance, and a friendship was born that survived even their later divergence in politics. Rhodes confided to Stead all his dreams and his plans and made him his executor; Stead, who never did things by halves, began talking and writing about Rhodes with all the force of his enthusiastic nature, and soon persuaded the British public that in him they had found a new saviour of the British Empire. Mills also introduced him to Dilke, who, though not carried away, like Stead, by sudden enthusiasms, was also impressed by the young statesman's broad-minded views on South African and Imperial politics. About the same time, probably, he also first made the acquaintance of Rothschild's son-in-law,

Lord Rosebery, whom he came to look to as the English statesman most in harmony with his general outlook.

The benevolence of the Irish party, important less for any active support they could give than for their deadly power of obstructing any cause obnoxious to them, had already been secured. In 1887 Rhodes had travelled with Mr. Swift M'Neill out to South Africa and told him of his sympathy with Home Rule; he had presided at one of his meetings in Cape Town and offered to contribute £10,000 to the Irish party funds. In the following year, in an interview with Parnell and in letters they exchanged, he had clearly defined his position and laid down certain conditions for his support. His main interest in Home Rule was in its bearing on the larger question of Imperial Federation or, as he frankly told Parnell, "because I believed that Irish Home Rule would lead to Imperial Home Rule." In his conception of Home Rule he was in advance even of Gladstone, for he had no belief in pettifogging safeguards for the judiciary and constabulary or in maintaining the fiscal dependence, "tribute" he called it, of Ireland; the settlement, he believed, should be based on absolute trust of the Irish, and he would give them as complete a form of self-government as any of the self-governing dominions. But there was one point on which he insisted for his support and contribution to the party funds, that Irish members should be retained at Westminster. Their exclusion by Gladstone's Bill of 1886 he regarded as a fatal blot on that measure, for he hoped to make the representation at Westminster of a self-governing Ireland the precedent for the admission there of representatives from all the self-governing colonies. In fact the chief importance to him of Home Rule was that it might be made the first step to a really Imperial Parliament for a federated Empire. Parnell, whom Rhodes described as "the most reasonable and sensible man I ever met," agreed to Rhodes's terms: the Irish party would not in future oppose the representation of Ireland at Westminster and would agree to a clause extending the same privilege to any colony contributing to Imperial defence. And so the bargain was concluded. One advantage of it to Rhodes was that in the subsequent discussions on his South African policy some of his warmest supporters in the House were found in the ranks of the Irish party; and room was found on their benches for his friend Maguire, who acted as a semi-official exponent of his views. No doubt Rhodes had some such *quid pro quo* in his mind when he struck his bargain with Parnell, but none the less it was entirely in accordance with his deepest convictions. No personal consideration of minor advantages deterred him two years later from expostulating with Parnell, when he appeared to have gone back on his specific pledges, and obtaining from him a renewal of his promise about Irish representation.

Rhodes needed all the extraneous support he could get, for Lord Salisbury's Government had at first been very shy of his projects and indeed of all further adventure in Africa. It is true they accepted the Moffat treaty and waived aside protests against it from the Transvaal and Germany, but in June 1888 they were quite willing to accept Portugal's extravagant claim to a continuous dominion from Angola on the west coast to Mozambique on the east. This would have entirely precluded Rhodes from securing for British enterprise the central tracts of Barotseland and Nyassaland north of the Zambesi. The Rudd concession had been looked on coldly at first, and a message was sent to Lo Bengula from the Queen advising him to scrutinize very carefully any concession he might grant, and at any rate to give away "only an ox, not his whole herd." The leader of the House, W. H. Smith, even declared that British Bechuanaland would not be handed over to the Cape, and very discouraging answers about the prospect of a Charter were given in Parliament. However, pressure from various quarters induced the Government to modify their attitude. The Cape Government protested against any surrender to Portugal on the question of free access to Central Africa, and Sir Hercules Robinson was goaded by W. H. Smith's speech and Mackenzie's memoranda to his notorious declaration about "the amateur meddling of irresponsible and ill-advised persons in England." Robinson's support for Rhodes's plan was unqualified, and no doubt had great influence on the Government. He drew a lurid picture on the one hand of the confusion in Swaziland and on the other of the evils of Crown Colony government "on the cheap," as exemplified in British Bechuanaland, where there was "a perpetual wrangle with the Treasury for the means of maintaining a decent administration"; and concluded that the only way of escape from these dangers in Lo Bengula's dominions was to establish a strong Chartered Company.

These considerations, backed by the powerful appeals of Rhodes's influential supporters, converted Lord Knutsford and the Government to Rhodes's scheme. On April 30, 1889, Lord Gifford on behalf of the Exploring Company, and Rhodes, Rudd and Beit representing the Gold Fields of South Africa, jointly applied for a Charter to a company prepared to carry out the following objects:

1. To extend the railway and telegraph northwards towards the Zambesi.
2. To encourage emigration and colonization.
3. To promote trade and commerce.
4. To develop minerals and other concessions under one powerful organization, so as to avoid conflicts between competing interests.

Lord Knutsford forwarded the proposal to Lord Salisbury with the comment that the country would thereby be saved such heavy expenses as it had incurred in British Bechuanaland and also would retain more control over a Chartered Company than it would over a Joint Stock Company. Lord Salisbury's own view was that such far-reaching objects fell properly within the province of the Government but, being convinced that the House of Commons would not vote the money, gave his blessing to the project. Rhodes and his associates were asked to draft a Charter, and were given a private intimation that it would be advisable to include in their list of directors men of social and political standing who would command more respect in England than those who like Rhodes himself, Beit, Cawston and Gifford, were merely associated with South African companies. Rhodes took the hint and consulted his friend Colonel Euan Smith on likely men. Lord Balfour of

Burleigh was first suggested as Chairman, but his connection with the Government was a bar; thereupon Rhodes persuaded the Duke of Abercorn to accept the position; and the Prince of Wales's son-in-law, the Duke of Fife, also consented to join the Board. With his sure instinct for conciliating opponents Rhodes then approached Albert Grey, one of the most distinguished members of the South African Committee and, with the Duke of Fife, a signatory of the Circular directed against his concession. Grey hardly knew Rhodes and first consulted Lord Salisbury, being inclined like him to think that the Company's objects ought to be secured by direct Government action. Reassured on this score by Salisbury's own view of the difficulties, he then asked Chamberlain for his advice. " Well," said Chamberlain, " I know only three things about Rhodes and they all put me against him : (i.) he has made an enormous fortune very rapidly, (ii.) he is an Afrikander (*i.e.* not an Imperialist), (iii.) he gave £10,000 to Parnell." Grey assured him that he believed Rhodes to be a single-minded patriot : " Well, I have given you my advice," retorted Chamberlain, " you must decide for yourself." Grey did decide to cast in his lot with Rhodes, and, having once done so, ever afterwards supported him through thick and thin, and came to love him with all the chivalry of his warm-hearted nature. To have gained Grey, " the Paladin of his generation," as Courtney called him, was one of the best bits of work Rhodes ever did for himself and his great ideas; for in after days, when doubts arose about Rhodes's motives, the staunchness to his cause of such a transparently honest man reassured many; and his sweet companionship was a solace in some of Rhodes's darkest days.

The question of the directors once satisfactorily settled, the remaining stages before the issue of the Charter were merely a matter of slow and solemn formality. The petition and draft had to be considered by the Colonial and Foreign Offices, a Committee of the Privy Council and the Privy Council itself, before the Letters Patent granting a Royal Charter of Incorporation to the British South Africa Company were signed by the Queen on October 29, 1889. Long before this Rhodes had returned to South Africa. Being a man who did not like idleness in London, as his friend and solicitor Hawksley described him, he said, "I have done all I can, and I will leave you to have the formalities settled." Before leaving, however, he gave a taste of his impetuous methods to the Colonial Office. To save time, he writes on June 1, he is prepared to pay the Government £30,000 immediately for a telegraph line from Mafeking, as he would be bound to do under the Charter, and a further £4000 a year for the upkeep of a British resident at Buluwayo to advise Lo Bengula and "give to the Company moral support as far as this can be done without entailing on H.M. Government any responsibility or expense." A fortnight later comes the answer from the Colonial Office agreeing in principle to these proposals. "To whom shall I make the payments?" asks Rhodes by return. "Not so fast," replies the Colonial Office a week later, "you must wait till the Charter is granted." Rhodes did not wait, and on his return to South Africa cabled to the Colonial Office for 250 miles of telegraph wire, No. 8 Siemens, and a corresponding quantity of telegraph poles. But it was not till a week after the Charter had been approved that his money was accepted and the wire and poles despatched.

The power granted by Charter to the British South Africa Company was, as Rhodes had said of the Rudd concession, "gigantic." Certain clauses were inserted for the protection of native rights, freedom of religion, trade and previous concessions; the Secretary of State had limited rights of supervising the Company's operations; and after twenty-five years, or earlier, if the Company's privileges were misused, the Charter might be revoked. Otherwise they had almost unfettered freedom of action. The Company's "principal field of operations" was all South Africa north of the new Crown Colony and the Transvaal and west of the Portuguese possessions in East Africa: thus it included the Bechuanaland Protectorate and had no limit northwards, for Rhodes, "not satisfied with the Zambesi as a boundary," had had his way. In this vast territory the Company was given power to make treaties, promulgate laws, preserve the peace, maintain a police force, and acquire new concessions: it could make roads, railways, harbours, or undertake other public works, own or charter ships, engage in mining or any other industry, establish banks, make land grants and carry on any lawful commerce, trade, pursuit or business.

The capital for this vast undertaking was fixed at a million in £1 shares. It must be admitted that the promoters took good care of their own interests, for not only did they receive 90,000 shares on account of rights and concessions handed over to the Company, but the United Concessions Company retained a half share in any profits to be hereafter made. But there was no difficulty in obtaining subscribers. Except for a few questions in the House by Labouchere and others all opposition to the grant of the Charter had died down, and the public accepted it without demur. Confidence was given to investors by a subscription from De Beers for 200,000 shares, the support of the Gold Fields and Rhodes's own large holding. But this demonstration of good faith was hardly needed, for the public were fascinated by the promise of wealth in the new country. *The Times* wrote of it: "It is rich, fabulously rich, we are told, in precious metals and a half-a-dozen others besides," a country where there was game in plenty on the uplands and cultivable ground, "only in need of scratching to smile with corn and all kinds of agricultural wealth," watered as it was by "a network of unfailing streams," beside which "the cattle fatten in peace." In this "land of Goshen," three times the size of the United Kingdom, *The Times* concluded its leader: "Whether the Company finds the wealth of Ophir in the mountains and rivers of Mashonaland or not, we cannot doubt that it will lay the basis of a great English-speaking colony in what appears to be the fairest region in Africa." With such appeals to the desire for lucre and to public spirit no wonder the shares were eagerly taken up. Rich men subscribed their thousands and small investors their modest pounds: one hears of women buying a single share merely for the privilege of attending an annual meeting of the Company, to see and hear the great adventurer who had conceived the enterprise. Rhodes himself was away in Africa when this excitement began, busy with Cape politics and with preparations for the pioneer expedition ; but the sudden curiosity about his personality, so little known to the general public, only increased with his absence. When he next returned to London, he came not a suppliant but a dispenser of favours : politicians consulted him, society worshipped him, and, what he cared for most of all, he had become the talk of the busman and the working-man.

CHAPTER XI

THE PIONEERS

VAST as were the powers sanctioned by the Charter, they had yet to be made good when Rhodes returned to South Africa in August 1889; for the Company was merely permitted to administer territories and exercise privileges it might acquire by its own exertions. Having gained the approval and support of the Imperial factor, Rhodes's next object was to carry South Africa, and especially the Dutch of South Africa, with him. This desire to associate the Dutch with his enterprise was, as we have seen, no sudden impulse, but the result of a long and consistent course of policy, dating further back even than his saying to Jameson in 1878, that the Dutch were the coming race in South Africa and that it was hopeless to run the country without them. In his Bechuanaland policy he had proved his sincerity, and since then, in his comparatively rare excursions into politics, he had drawn closer the links between himself and the Bond. Both in the House and at the Paarl, where he had been invited to address a Bond meeting, he had spoken strongly in favour of their policy of agricultural protection, and had supported a great irrigation scheme in the Hartz Valley for the benefit of the farmers. He had foreshadowed, much to their delight, his own Glen Grey policy, when on a Registration Bill he had attacked the liberality of the Cape franchise law to uneducated natives. He had spoken in favour of Hofmeyr's motions for religious education in the schools and the abolition of Sunday trains, and in return had received aid from Hofmeyr in defeating a proposal to tax the diamond industry, and a glowing eulogy from him during the election of 1888 as a staunch friend to the Dutch cause. This alliance had recently been strengthened by a passing estrangement between the Bond and the Transvaal. The era of through-railways had begun; and it had become a vital matter to the Cape farmers no less than to the merchants at the ports to have cheap and rapid transport for their goods and produce to the Johannesburg markets. But Kruger, with his desire to free himself from dependence on Cape ports and to draw all his supplies from Delagoa Bay or some port of his own on the east coast, had put every obstacle in the way of the Cape policy. He refused to allow a railway to come into his country from the south, and even persuaded the Free State to reject an agreement for a line through Bloemfontein to the Vaal; he would have nothing to do with a South African conference on railways and customs, and insisted on keeping up a high tariff on agricultural products from Cape Colony. Rhodes supported the Bond in every endeavour to conciliate Kruger and leave him every loophole for a compromise. But even the Bond became indignant at this poor return for their loyalty to Kruger's people in 1881, and passed resolutions of protest against his opposition to the Cape railway extension and his prohibitive tariff on Cape produce. The very Dutchmen at the Cape, who in 1884 had been willing to let Bechuanaland go to the Transvaal, in 1889, so the Governor reported, were quite prepared to see the British sphere extended to the Zambesi; and Hofmeyr, then most favourable to the Transvaal claims, now declared himself in favour of Rhodes's Chartered Company, whereas, "had Kruger fulfilled my expectations and fallen in with my advice, Rhodes and I might have agreed to differ."

Rhodes naturally took full advantage of these favourable dispositions. It had originally been intended that as Managing Director of the Chartered Company he should be assisted by a local board in South Africa, and he himself was very anxious to secure prominent Dutchmen to sit on this board. He offered the chairmanship in turn to Sir Henry de Villiers, the Chief Justice of the Cape, and on his refusal to Hofmeyr. At first Hofmeyr was inclined to accept, and was empowered to do so by a special resolution of the Bond, but, his ingrained distaste for public responsibility reasserting itself, he thought better of it and refused. The local board then fell to the ground and Rhodes carried on the work unaided. But he secured very wide support for the Company by getting as many South Africans as possible to take a financial interest in it: he brought out 125,000 of the shares for disposal in South Africa and found no difficulty in placing even more than these among the Dutch as well as the English colonists.

He soon reaped the first-fruits of this policy. Part of his bargain with the Home Government and an integral element in his advance northwards was the extension of the railway beyond Kimberley, and he set to work arranging for it as soon as he returned to South Africa. Using as his intermediaries Hofmeyr himself and Sivewright, a British member of the Bond, he concluded, on the very day the Charter was granted in London, a favourable agreement with the Cape Ministry, who agreed to take over and work the first section of the new line to Vryburg directly it was out of the contractors' hands. The work was put through with unexampled speed, and the Chartered Company, in addition to the increased transport facilities so valuable for their own purposes, derived some profit from this arrangement with the Cape and conferred a benefit on the colonial traders and farmers.

His next business was to arrange for the occupation of the country over which the Charter had given him such large prospective powers. His gold-digging rights under the Rudd concession extended over the whole of the vague dominions claimed by Lo Bengula, including Matabeleland itself and the territory occupied by the tributary Mashonas, the whole bounded by the Zambesi on the north and by the Portuguese possessions on the east coast. It was out of the question to venture into Matabeleland itself without a large army, but the land inhabited by the gentler Mashonas offered a more favourable field; so Mashonaland was the goal decided upon. But even for this there were still difficulties with Lo Bengula. The abhorred vacuum at his court had never been satisfactorily filled since Thompson's departure, and afforded plenty of scope for the intrigues of rivals and the chief's hesitations. When Lo Bengula gave

Rudd his concession in 1888 he never anticipated that it would be made the excuse for the ambitious undertaking conceived by Rhodes: he thought a few white men would come and dig holes in the ground for gold, not that a regular armed expedition would be sent into his country to settle in townships with all the appurtenances of European civilization; and when he found he had given away more than he bargained for he began to deny that he had given anything. Though shrewd in small matters he had little knowledge of European business methods or of the real purport of legal documents, and as Mr. Maguire said of him, " he had an extraordinary dislike to come to a definite decision upon any subject, coupled with extreme unwillingness to say No." The Grobler and the Moffat treaties and the Rudd concession, mutually exclusive as they were, were probably regarded by him merely as convenient methods of fobbing off troublesome visitors. So now he persisted in " denying the road " to any expedition proposed to carry out the Rudd concession. Once more Jameson was called upon to talk him over. Jameson arrived with Dr. Rutherfoord Harris at the same time as a deputation from the Queen, composed of a military band and the three tallest of her Life Guards to announce the Charter to Lo Bengula and advise him to put his trust in the new Company. Impressed by this magnificence the chief once more gave way. At an indaba attended by Jameson and Moffat he agreed that Rhodes's agents might enter Mashonaland to seek for gold and establish tents, stores and sheds as required, and that he would then indicate to them what land they should be entitled to occupy. But he might change his mind again, so Rhodes had every motive for haste in equipping and starting his expedition.

The only known route to Mashonaland was by the old Missionaries' road through Tati into the heart of Matabeleland and thence by Lo Bengula's " royal road " through Inyati to the Mashona hills. In the present disposition of the Matabeles it seemed foolhardy to send an expedition through their country unless it were backed by an imposing military force. But this meant an expense the Company could ill afford. Their total capital was only a million, half of which was ear-marked for railways; and the Imperial officer who was consulted said he would require 2500 men for the job and that the cost would be little short of that total capital. On the other hand, failure and a disaster at the outset, owing to an inadequate expedition, would spell ruin to the whole Chartered policy. Various other plans were discussed, but all had to be rejected as unsatisfactory; and Rhodes was almost in despair.

In this despondent mood he came into the breakfast-room of the Kimberley Club a few days before Christmas. He looked vaguely at a young man seated at a table by himself and was just passing him when he recalled his face and came to sit down beside him. The young man was Frank Johnson, then only twenty-three, who had just arrived from a seven months' trek in the north on behalf of the Bechuanaland Exploration Company and was going off that night by the mail train for Cape Town. He had previously visited Lo Bengula, against whom he had a grievance, and had some concessions in Mashonaland. Rhodes soon began to pour out his woes to Johnson, and told him of the extravagant proposal made to him for an armed force of 2500 men. "Two thousand five hundred men is absurd," said Johnson, "why, with 250 I could walk through the country." Rhodes went on eating eggs and bacon and then suddenly burst out with, "Do you mean that?" "Yes." "How much will it cost?" "Give me four hours, and I'll let you know." By noon Johnson had brought his calculations to Rhodes: 179 pioneers, a troop of police and 150 natives would do the work, and the cost of their pay, food and equipment and that of making the roads required would be £89,285 : 10s. "Good," said Rhodes, "I accept the offer, and you shall command the expedition." But to his disgust and astonishment Johnson refused point-blank to serve under the Chartered Company, and went off that evening to Cape Town. Five days later he got a telegram from Rhodes to meet him next morning at the Cape Town station. "Oh, here you are," said Rhodes, as he came off the Kimberley train, and the two drove off to the top of Adderley Street, where Johnson paid and dismissed the hansom—for Rhodes never had any money about him—and walked up and down Government Avenue. "Everybody tells me you are a lunatic," began Rhodes, "but I have an instinct you are right and can do it," and he again pressed him to take command of the expedition. Finally, on the understanding that he should not act as a servant of the Company but work as an independent contractor, Johnson agreed for a cheque down to enlist and equip the pioneers, make a road and hand over Mashonaland to a civil government in nine months' time. "That's all right," said Rhodes, "I'll give you that cheque. Now let's get some breakfast at Poole's." After breakfast Rhodes told Johnson to draw up the draft contract,—he would have no lawyers interfering—took him to his friend Sivewright to look through the draft, and gave him a cheque for £20,000 on account.

The question of expense for the Company had thus been satisfactorily settled, but the danger of disaster was not yet averted, for no alternative to the risky road through Buluwayo had been suggested. To some of Rhodes's advisers the danger of a conflict with the Matabeles was no objection: the Matabeles, they argued, would have to be suppressed sooner or later, and the sooner the better. Happily saner counsels prevailed. The proposed route became known, and several of those acquainted with the ferocity of the Matabeles pointed out the serious risks involved. Among others, Mackenzie wrote to Lord Salisbury and Lord Knutsford to say that, opposed though he had always been to the Charter, he did not wish to see a disaster befall the Company, and "could not bear to think of all those fine young Englishmen being speared some night." But the advice which finally diverted Rhodes from this foolhardy route came from one who had more claim to speak about Lo Bengula's dominions than any other European.

Frederick Selous was then a man of forty in the prime of life and vigour. For twenty years he had been a mighty hunter in Matabeleland and Mashonaland and also north of the Zambesi; in veld-lore and in knowledge of the natives he was unrivalled; he knew every track in Lo Bengula's country and was that chief's trusted friend; he shared Rhodes's love of the Dutch and throughout South Africa was famed for his chivalrous and sunny spirit His book of sport and travel had reflected this spirit, and by its attractive descriptions of Mashonaland had helped to encourage the interest at home in Rhodes's quest. He had first met Rhodes ten years before, when he came to tell him of his brother Herbert's death in Central Africa, and had then shown him quills of gold obtained from the native workings in Mashonaland. During the Charter negotiations in London he had again met him and urged him to settle the country permanently. Rhodes had said to him then, "I shall soon have a job for you," and in January 1890 summoned him to Kimberley to discuss routes. Selous at once warned him against the Buluwayo route, which would only lead to bloodshed and disaster, and suggested an alternative way, avoiding Matabeleland altogether, through Tuli on the Limpopo, and thence northwards straight up through Mashonaland itself. Dense bush at the outset and numerous rivers to cross would be a bar to rapid progress, but these disadvantages would be more than outweighed by the comparative safety of the route. Rhodes, not an obstinate man when he saw good reason against his plans, was convinced by Selous, and persuaded him to guide the expedition by the way he proposed. Selous thereupon went off on a flying visit to the Zoutpansberg, to consult an old hunter well acquainted with the country, and while there heard rumours of a project which made it more than ever imperative for Rhodes to despatch his expedition promptly.

Ever since the Grobler treaty he had dreaded being forestalled by the Boers from the Transvaal. He knew that many of them cast longing eyes northwards and that the London Convention had put no explicit obstacle to the fulfilment of this desire. In September he had already been scared by the rumour of a Boer trek into Mashonaland and had at once sent the Imperial Secretary a letter characteristic of his cavalier methods. "The report as to Boers squatting," he writes, "may of course be incorrect, but you will soon learn the correct facts and if true you must instruct the police to expel them. If not the game is up. You cannot allow a single Boer to settle across the Limpopo until our position in the north is secure." Selous's report was even more alarming. A burgher named Bowler was organizing a trek to take up a concession he claimed in north-east Mashonaland and preparations were said to be well forward. Sir Henry Loch, Robinson's successor as Governor and High Commissioner, protested to Kruger against any such plan, and went to confer with him at Blignaut's Pont in March 1890, taking Rhodes with him. The President was not in the best of tempers, for he came fresh from a stormy meeting with malcontents at Johannesburg, who had torn down and trampled on the Republican flag, and he was well aware that the policy of a trek northwards, which his rival Joubert openly favoured, was popular with many of his burghers. But he was really much more anxious to obtain control of Swaziland and thence gradually make his way to a port on the east coast, and knew that in the London Convention Loch held a trump card, as Rhodes called it, that might be used against this plan ; so he was ready for concession. On obtaining from Loch some rather vague assurances about Swaziland he promised Rhodes not to interfere with the Charter and to damp down the trek. A few months later Hofmeyr was sent up to clinch the bargain ; a formal agreement was signed recognizing the interests of the Transvaal in Swaziland, while Kruger renewed his undertaking not to interfere in Lo Bengula's dominions.

Meanwhile the pioneer expedition was getting under way. Besides Johnson's 179 pioneers destined for settling in the country, a force of British South Africa Police had to be enrolled to accompany them and keep order afterwards. Though Johnson was mainly responsible for choosing the settlers, Rhodes laid down the conditions for their recruitment as well as for that of the police, and took a personal interest in the men selected. He insisted that the ranks were to be open to Dutchmen as well as Englishmen, and that every man in both forces must be inured to hardship and adventure, amenable to discipline and ready to turn his hand to some trade or business. He himself went to Basutoland to buy ponies, and trustworthy men were commissioned to choose recruits and buy more horses in likely centres. For the pioneers Nicholson brought from Haenertsberg in the northern Transvaal men who had come from all quarters of the globe to rough it at those primitive diggings ; the Johannesburg contingent under Lieutenant Mandey included Bowden and Wimble, heroes of the cricket field, and Schermbrücker, descendant of an Eastern Province pioneer. One raw Yorkshire lad, who could not persuade any recruiter to take him, dogged Rhodes's footsteps till his persistence was rewarded. Among those from Cape Colony, Natal or the Free State were Jack Spreckley, Chester Masters, Grimmer, Inskip, a boy of nineteen who passed himself off as twenty-one and is now a director of the Company ; Bowen, Neumeyer and Coryndon, who soon showed his mettle as administrator of Barotseland ; the Burnetts, George and Ted, matchless scouts and trackers ; a couple of Nesbitts, a well-known Cape name ; Johnson's partners Heany, a Virginian, and Borrow, Hoste, a Union Line skipper, Roach, the gunner, an Irish V.C. and a naval middy, now an admiral. There were three parsons, the Jesuit father Hartmann, Canon Balfour and Surridge ; a doctor, Tabiteau, besides lawyers, builders, tailors, butchers, bakers, engineers, miners, farmers and ranchmen. Early in May this likely lot of young men, numbering 184 altogether, full of courage and the spirit of adventure, had assembled at the trysting place, Mafeking : here they were equipped with Webley revolvers and rifles, breeches and tunics of corduroy, army boots and gaiters, felt wide-awakes and waterproof overcoats. Their pay was to be 7s. 6d. a day, and at the end of the journey each was to receive fifteen gold claims and a 3000-acre farm. They were divided into three troops under Heany, skipper Hoste, and Roach, with Johnson, the dashing young contractor of twenty-three, at their head.

A twenty days' march from Mafeking, which served to weld this heterogeneous crowd into an orderly body, brought them to Macloutsie on the northern border of Bechuanaland. Here they found the British Bechuanaland Police, who were to watch the Matabele borders while they advanced, and five troops of the Chartered Company's new police who were to accompany them. The police were under the command of Col. Pennefather of the Inniskilling Dragoons, with Forbes, Heyman and Keith Falconer as troop leaders, and Sir John Willoughby of the Horse Guards as staff-officer. Rhodes was once reproached for having filled up the ranks of the police with too many Englishmen from home, and he answered that, with all his love of colonials, he had to admit they were not so good at discipline as men from a more settled country: nevertheless there was a good sprinkling of colonials, English and Dutch, in the police also. Here, too, they found 200 of Khama's natives under his brother Radikladi, to act as scouts and road-cutters, and also Selous, to guide them, Jameson, with Rhodes's power of attorney, and Colquhoun, to be the first administrator. Selous and Jameson had just returned from a final visit to Lo Bengula to ask him to renew the "promise of the road" which he had previously given; but the king had veered round once more. "I am tired," he said, "of Rhodes 'mouths' and will do nothing unless Rhodes, 'the great white king,' comes up himself to ask me." However, as Rhodes could not go, he and Jameson resolved to risk Lo Bengula's displeasure and, acting on their rights under the concession and on previous promises of "the road," to proceed with the expedition.

Lord Methuen, deputed by Sir Henry Loch to inspect the pioneer column, gave them leave to go after three weeks more drilling and preparation, and on June 27, 1890, the start was made from Macloutsie. Selous had determined on Mount Hampden in the north of Mashonaland, distant 460 miles, as his objective. As far as Tuli he had already cut the road, but there the difficulties began. For half the distance the course lay across low swampy country, thick with mopani brush, through which every yard of road had to be cut. Five rivers in succession had to be crossed, and any one of these in flood might have held up the column for months. Besides its physical difficulties, the country was most favourable to ambush from an enemy, who could easily have approached the column unperceived through the bush or taken up a commanding position on one of the numerous granite kopjes rising out of the low ground. Nor was the danger of attack remote: twice, before the pioneers had left the low country, messages came from Lo Bengula ordering them back, and his warriors were known to be eager to make an example of the intruders. In such country an attack in overwhelming numbers by the savages might have been disastrous to a force reduced to little more than 400, after detachments of police had been left behind at Macloutsie and Tuli, encumbered besides with ninety ponderous waggons and a travelling saw-mill. Fortunately the march discipline was good and precautions were duly observed at every halt, while in Selous they had a rare guide. Each day he went ahead with the Bechuana scouts and one of the three troops of pioneers to cut the road nor ever once led the column astray. But even he began to be anxious after Lo Bengula's second message, for it seemed as if the low country would never end. At last, after some six weeks of this work, riding well in advance, he descried in the distance the long-hoped-for pass leading up to the high veld. Naming it Providential Pass, he rode back with the good news, and by August 15 had brought the whole column safely on to the high open country, where with their field-guns and maxims the Europeans were more than a match for any number of savages. By September 11, without a single casualty, they had reached the site named Salisbury after the Prime Minister.[1] The goal had been attained, a good road had been made to connect Salisbury with civilization, and forts to guard the communications had been thrown up at Victoria near Providential Pass and Charter, all well within the nine months agreed upon by Johnson. Even a relay postal service was organized, the first use to which it was put being to send an express letter to Rhodes announcing the column's safe arrival, which reached Macloutsie in five days. " When at last I found that they were through to Fort Salisbury," said Rhodes, " I do not think there was a happier man in the country than myself."

[1] Salisbury is south of Mt. Hampden, Selous's objective, but he had left the column on another errand when they arrived there and decided to go no further.

Rhodes, to his great disappointment, had been unable to accompany the column. Detained by a political crisis at Cape Town, he had been gazetted Prime Minister of the Colony a few days after the pioneers left Tuli. "If I could quit that responsibility," he told the Dutchmen at the Paarl, "no man would be happier than myself, because I can then go and live with those young people, who are developing our new territories. The life is better than that of receiving deputations, whilst it has all the romance which attaches to the development of a new country." But at the end of October he escaped from Cape Town and came up country with Sir Henry Loch. At Vryburg he attended the opening of his new section of railway, only begun that year, and in his speech recalled his last visit there five years before, when Warren had called him "a danger to the peace of the country." Travelling thence by road, he paid visits to Montsioa at Mafeking and Khama at Palapye on his way to Macloutsie. True to his policy of interesting the Dutch population in the new country, he had brought with him two Cape Dutch members of the Assembly, one of whom, De Waal, has left a lively account of this and another journey he took with Rhodes. Major Leonard, then in command of the police detachment left at Macloutsie, has also written a graphic description of the impression made on him by the great man. Sitting opposite to him at lunch, writes Leonard on the first day, "I saw a substantial organism, slow in his movements, deliberate in his manner and phlegmatic in his temperament. A big, heavy-looking, carelessly dressed man, not unlike a Dutch farmer, with an awkward slouching figure and a dull rather expressionless face, who talks in a curious dreamy way, as if he was half asleep, and was taking no interest in what he was saying, but was thinking of something totally different . . . with Rhodes I made no headway, and my conclusion is that his admirers have overrated him." Next morning Rhodes hung about the camp, taking in everything, "but our conversations were only trivial commonplaces; either he would not or I could not get him to talk . . . but I am beginning to think he is very deep. For under that dull exterior, which is but a mask, he is continually taking in all around and about him . . . his command of temper and faculties wonderful." This dawning conception of Rhodes's depth was strengthened by an incident next morning, when the great man suddenly demanded the major's two best corporals to go with him to Tuli. Leonard objected that this would leave him short of N.C.O.'s. "N.C.O.'s, N.C.O.'s," murmured Rhodes vaguely. "What are N.C.O.'s ?" Leonard explained, and added that troopers would do as well for Rhodes's purpose. "No, I prefer corporals and I must have them," Rhodes snapped out in a quick decided way ; "his whole manner had changed and he was quite another man. It was only momentary, a mere flash in the pan ; then relapsing into the dreamy, dull expression and shaking his head in a semi-pathetic kind of way he turned to Lange (his secretary) and said, 'They must be good men or Leonard wouldn't be so anxious to keep them.'" In the evening Rhodes gave a taste of his oratory. After a dull official speech from the High Commissioner, "up rose the Colossus refreshed with wine or possibly by the subject nearest his heart . . . certainly he was like a man transformed. No longer that slouching gait and in place of the heavy eyes, orbs full of meaning flashing with a dangerous gleam that betrayed a fixity of purpose, strength of will and a spirit that would do or dare anything, he stood upright and erect, speaking well and to the point [about the northern expansion]. At first he talked very slowly and methodically as if he was weighing each word with a balance ; but soon warming to his subject . . . he spoke fervently and earnestly yet slowly and carefully as *the* man in authority." Finally after three days, in which they "only talked of trivial things, and I did not even once induce him to touch on present or future policy," the major sums him up as "dogged, determined to a degree and tenacious to the last gasp ; once he gets hold of an idea he will never let it go till he has attained it. In fact he is tenacious even to obstinacy and inclined to petulancy if he cannot have his way . . . powerful more than pleasant . . . sheer brute force of will and rugged genius of mind."

The unfortunate Governor had an experience of this

petulancy and obstinacy. Rhodes had made up his mind to visit his pioneers in Mashonaland in spite of all Loch's arguments that, as Prime Minister of the Cape, he had no business to go wandering off into an unknown country, where he might be massacred by savages or held up for months by swollen rivers. His reply was that he had not come on this tiresome journey merely to see the British Protectorate, but his own protectorate up north; and the utmost concession he would make was that he would reconsider the matter at Tuli: and thither he drove off in a pet at dead of night. Here he at last set foot on his own land; but the rainy season was beginning and the Governor's warning about swollen rivers bore fruit. Though "our horses," he admitted, "are fat and strong; we healthy and in sound spirits; our provisions more than enough; we must turn here," he decided, "we cross the Shashi and the Crocodile, we travel down the Transvaal *via* the Blaawbergen and Zoutpansberg, pay Oom Paul a visit and return to Cape Town."

On a journey like this Rhodes was at his best. He loved the freedom of the veld, and to gain it was ready to put up with any of the discomforts of travel. In the worst circumstances he remained cheerful, even when a lion was pursuing him in his pyjamas or when the transport had broken down, and they all seemed lost in the low country. "Well," he said on that occasion, "here we are in a dark wild world. What will it avail us now to upbraid Johnson with having deceived us with the road? What lies before us is to decide what to do, and if we don't make that decision now, the delay may result in our catching fever. . . . Come, speak your minds and let us devise a plan." Once when travelling on a crazy coasting steamer infested with beetles and cockroaches, "Well," he said, in answer to his companion's shrill complaints, "I cannot say I like them, but as I have had many a worse time than this in my life, I don't worry myself much about such minor discomforts"; and then as the grumbles still went on, "Oh, my good friend, take the world as it is. . . . How silly to be afraid of such harmless little things! Why, I treat them like flies." "Looking at the comparative," as he called this rough philosophy, enabled him to go through much worse trials than a few beetles in a steamer-cabin; and he expected those about him to take the rough with the smooth as philosophically as himself. Once, relates his Boswell, De Waal, he handed over the party's last bottle of whisky to a poor fever-stricken pioneer they found stranded by the wayside, and on De Waal's angry remonstrances added as a further gift his companion's favourite pony and professed to be astonished at De Waal's resentment. But his elephantine sense of humour at others' expense was redeemed by the saving grace of being able to see a joke against himself. "Come back; too many cooks spoil the broth," roared out Rhodes as De Waal rushed forward officiously to help a man unloading horses at Beira: but a few minutes later, when the man got into difficulties, "Nonsense," he said with a guilty smile, "go off and help him." At times, as he rode along, he would disconcert his companions by hour-long bouts of silent reflection, when they could not get a word out of him: then suddenly he would wake up from his abstraction and begin to talk, garrulous as a child, of people he had met, of his politics and his ambitions or of his vague philosophy of life, and, like a wilful child, urge and tease them into disputation and argument.

But let some affair in which he was interested crop up, and the wilful child at once vanished to give place to the shrewd, hard man of business. When he gave an order, it was sharp and there was no gainsaying it; and his sudden gusts of wrath were terrible. Once when his Cape boy had not brought round his cart in time, Leonard describes him as raging like a lunatic; the boy was to be arrested and given no food, and "he kept on alternately abusing the boy and repeating the order." Then, when the storm had had its effect, calm would succeed as suddenly. And he could interrupt any pleasant jaunt to attend to business. On this journey he stopped at Pietersburg to interview Adendorff and Barend Vorster, two Boers who claimed to have a concession from Chibe, a minor chieftain in Mashonaland, and were organizing another trek. They thought to bluff him into paying them compensation to give up their claim, but he refused to be bled and told them he would give them nothing until he had verified their rights; and, as it happened, in the following year he obtained conclusive proof from Chibe himself that the concession was worthless. He visited Johannesburg to discuss the cyanide process and his interests in the Gold Fields: "the great man's visit was a great success," reports his agent, "and I have never seen him in better form or temper" owing to the success of his trek. When he arrived at the outskirts of Pretoria he was disgusted to find a pompous reception awaiting him, with high officials in state carriages and a guard of honour to escort him into the capital. Here he took coffee with the President, but at this interview appears to have met his match. He tried, according to Kruger's version, to put into practice his theory that you can make a deal with any man, but signally failed with this wily antagonist. "We must work together," began Rhodes, so Kruger's version runs; "I know the republic wants a seaport: you must have Delagoa Bay." "But the harbour belongs to the Portuguese," objected Kruger, "and they won't hand it over." "Then we must simply take it," was the reply. "No," said the President, "I can't take away other people's property. If the Portuguese won't sell the harbour, I wouldn't take it, even if you gave it me: for ill-gotten goods are accursed." There is obviously some foundation for this account, for Rhodes had the question of Delagoa Bay much on his mind at this time,[1] and may well have sounded the President with a view to a deal: and a cynical disregard of Portuguese susceptibilities was not alien to his methods. But the old President rather overdoes his virtuous indignation, considering his readiness only six years previously to annex a portion of Bechuanaland, which he had expressly engaged not to do by the recent Convention of London. At any rate the conversation must have ranged over other subjects, though this is the only topic recorded by Kruger. He had just signed the Swaziland Convention and probably renewed to Rhodes his assurance that he would not allow his countrymen to meddle with the Charter rights. Rhodes at least professed himself well satisfied.

[1] See below, Chap. XIII. p. 198.

Kruger undoubtedly meant to fulfil his promise, but some of his burghers were difficult to restrain. Adendorff and Vorster, in spite of their talk with Rhodes, persisted in their intentions, and in March 1891 inserted advertisements in the papers inviting volunteers to found a republic in north-east Mashonaland. This Banyai trek, as it was called, alarmed the Colonial Office as well as the Chartered Company; and, after a flying visit home by Loch and Rhodes, the Queen issued a proclamation in April declaring a protectorate over Lo Bengula's dominions and warning trespassers that they would be treated as enemies. And now Rhodes began to reap the advantage of his conciliatory policy to the Cape Dutch. Du Toit, the former fire-eater of the Bond, who had instigated Kruger's abortive Bechuanaland proclamation in 1884, had been entirely won over to Rhodes's views. A few years before he had demanded " a united South Africa under its *own* flag," but now he sounded a very different note. " Let us not ignore," he wrote, " the guidance of Providence. God has given us England as a guardian, a more considerate one than Israel found in Pharaoh of old." At this juncture, with a cousin of Hofmeyr's, he was employed in organizing Dutch opinion both in Cape Colony and the Transvaal against the trek, and, as a set-off to Adendorff's scheme, enlisting Boers to settle in the new country on Rhodes's own terms. The official support of the Bond was even secured. Immediately on his return from his visit to London, during which he had been invited to Windsor Castle, Rhodes went to address the Bond Congress at Kimberley. Referring with ingenuous satisfaction to the " consideration he had received from the politicians of England and to the expression of a desire by Her Majesty herself that he should meet her and have the honour of dining with her," and pointing to the " extraordinary anomaly it would have been considered in the past, that one who possessed the complete confidence of Her Majesty herself should have been able to show that at the same time he felt most completely and entirely that the object and aspirations of the Afrikander Bond were in complete touch and concert with a fervent loyalty to Her Majesty the Queen," he drew the moral that there was nothing incompatible between his own aspirations and their ideal of a united South Africa. In another speech, and in an open letter to the secretary of the Bond, he declared that the Chartered territories were held by him merely as a trust for the Cape and South Africa generally, and that all South Africans prepared to acknowledge the Company's authority were welcome. He had already given an earnest of his freedom from race prejudice by including Dutch lads as well as English among his pioneers, and so felt justified in appealing to the old Bondsmen as fathers: "Your young men, because they are your young men, have gone up sixteen hundred miles, have slept in their boots every night, and have felt that they would be murdered at four o'clock every morning: oh, yes! every one said so, from the President of the Transvaal downwards. . . . And now what has happened? . . . Mr. Adendorff and Mr. Barend Vorster and Mr. Du Preez say they are going to take the results of the labours of your sons. . . . When these gentlemen say that they are going to take from my young men their rights and dispossess them of the results of their labours, then I confess I lose my temper; and I tell you to-night that if they continue with it, and if these people will not accept our rule and law, then there will be a difference between us." "My young men," "your young men," it was all one to Rhodes: he spoke and felt with the same affection for all the fine lads who had added more homes to England.

After the publication of a letter signed by Hofmeyr discountenancing the trek, most of the volunteers melted away, leaving only a few score hot-heads under a Colonel Ferreira to end the scheme in ridicule. At the end of June this valiant band approached the drift of the Limpopo opposite Tuli. It so happened that Jameson had just arrived there, and he knew how to deal with them. Their leader Ferreira was arrested on the Tuli side and sent back to parley with his followers: he was told to explain to them that their concession was so much waste paper, but that any of them who chose to enter the country on the Company's terms were free to do so. The raiders' bouncing spirit soon evaporated at the sight of the police maxims, and they turned to the more profitable business of selling their surplus meal, tobacco and salted horses to the troopers: some even joined the police or took farms under the Company. Ferreira and his secretary were retained as prisoners on parole, and soon induced their gaolers to take shares in the Mashonaland Agricultural and Supply Syndicate founded on the spot chiefly for the benefit of the promoters. Rhodes was never more troubled with raiders from the Transvaal, but, true to his word, did all in his power to encourage the settlement of Boer farmers. He sent up Van der Byl and several leading Dutch agriculturists to inspect and report on the country to their neighbours, and later encouraged a number of Boer families to take up a block of farms in the promising district of Melsetter in the east of Mashonaland. And he never veered from this policy. In fact, ten years later, when we were at war with the Transvaal, one of the grievances against him of an English transport rider was that he flooded the road with the waggons and spans of oxen of Boer refugees "who had been in arms against us a few weeks before."

But though all danger from the Transvaal was thus averted, things had not gone too well with the pioneers during their first year in the country. The Portuguese, whose claims must be reserved to the next chapter, had caused a good deal of anxiety; while serious transport difficulties and the enormous expense of the administration had been the source of much discontent. At first when news came of the pioneer column's success there was a rush to the new country. Intending settlers and prospectors, who had been waiting at Macloutsie and Tuli, began pouring in; transport riders began to ply their trade with waggon-loads of stores. Dr. Rutherfoord Harris, who had been given charge of the Company's transport and supply, had arranged for large reserves of food to be collected at Tuli and an energetic agent to forward them. But even in the most favourable circumstances the difficulties of transport were great. Until the disputes with Portugal were settled, Salisbury's sole base of supplies was Cape Town or Port Elizabeth, nearly 2000 miles away; and of this 2000 miles 1000 beyond railhead at Vryburg consisted of bad roads, over which all supplies had to be brought by ox-waggon at a cost of £60 to £80 a ton. And the circumstances were not favourable, for the rainy season of 1891 was one of the worst known: all the rivers were in flood and the drifts impassable for months, during which no supplies came through at all. The result was that the whole population of settlers, scattered round the country on farms or mines, were in very serious distress. They could obtain meat and a poor kind of Kaffir-corn from the natives, but flour, groceries and the commonest luxuries were almost unobtainable. A whisky and soda, for example, cost 10s. 6d. at Salisbury, and a sixpenny pot of jam sold for £3; as for agricultural implements and heavy mining machinery needed for developing the country, they were not to be had at any price. The settlers had other grievances. The farms allotted were disappointing, and the Company's mining regulations, entitling it to 50 per cent of the scrip of any newly formed company, were regarded as a strong deterrent to mining enterprise. The pioneers on the whole stood the test of hardship well, but many of the later arrivals, especially those fresh from England, were loud in their complaints. "Many of them thought," said Rhodes, "that a fortune was to be made in about a week or a month; but they found a bare country whose future must depend on the energy of its first occupants, and that a race out from home and a race back would not in any part of the world give one a quarter of a million of money."

From the Company's point of view also radical reforms were needed. Colquhoun, partly on account of the difficulties with Portugal, had raised the police force to a strength of 700, a crushing burden on an undeveloped country; and the total cost of administration for the first year came to a quarter of a million. The settlers' complaints, which gradually permeated to England, the failure to find gold in any paying quantities, and the great cost of administration were having a serious effect on the Company's credit. The directors at home were in despair and were continually imploring Rhodes to send them news of gold discoveries; £1 Chartered shares, which had started at a premium of 275 per cent, fell below par; and "then," as Rhodes said, "undoubtedly came a true period of depression. The condemnation of the home papers could only be compared to their previous undue sanguineness." One step Rhodes took at once to remedy the evils. In July 1891 he superseded Colquhoun and gave a free hand as administrator to Jameson. This was an ideal choice. Jameson had courage and driving power, devotion to Rhodes's interests, and a wonderful tact in dealing with the rough lads in the country. "He is getting more and more popular every day," wrote one of the pioneers to Rhodes. "If you had searched for twelve months I am sure you would not find a more able man and so thoroughly suited to the position. If only he had been in power from the start." He immediately reduced the police from 700 to 100, and for a small retaining fee persuaded the settlers to volunteer for service when needed, and by this and other economies soon brought down the annual expenses from the quarter of a million to £40,000. But, in spite of this improvement, it was full time for the master's eye to survey his domain, when Rhodes was at last able to visit it, a year after the pioneers had reached Salisbury.

His presence in the country was like a glorious burst of sunshine on the winter of its discontents. He came by Beira, bringing horses and natives to work in Mashonaland, in spite of objections by the Portuguese officials. Pushing through the marshy fly-belt of the Pungwe, having somehow, as it was currently reported, "found a means of squaring the tsetse-fly," he travelled on to Salisbury at his usual lightning speed, eyes and ears all open to everything. At Umtali, while his horses were resting, every grumbler of the place came to him with his tale of grievances; and though nothing was altered in the state of affairs, his sunny presence sent every one away contented. He went to the hospital, not to see the patients, for "if I were ill," he remarked, "I shouldn't like to be stared at," but to give the nurses a cheque for expenses and promise them a medical library from England, and left declaring that if these ladies could live at Umtali it was absurd for any man to grumble.

Further on the faithful De Waal is allowed to choose a site for a farm and have it measured out forthwith by the Surveyor-General. "I had just been speaking to my friends in the waggon," Rhodes tells him, "about the grandeur of the place, and I told them that I was sure you would not pass it without desiring a slice of it." At Salisbury more grumblers come to see him. Their main grievance is the dearth of provisions: "Well," says Rhodes, "I know that when the rivers were full the waggons could not cross, but I could not help that. You certainly cannot expect to be already provided with roads, telegraphs, bridges, post-carts, etc. etc., all within the short space of twelve months. But if you wanted food, you had plenty of beads, linen, etc., to change for food in the Kaffir kraals as we did on our way up. . . . No, your agitation has not arisen from want of food, but from something else; it is want of *liquor* that displeases you." He dealt in less cavalier fashion with remediable grievances, such as unsatisfactory land grants and the 50 per cent mining regulation. This last was a pet nostrum of Rhodes's, for he believed with some reason that a postponement of all charges on diggers and prospectors until they had proved their ground and could float a company, was in their interest; but he was open to argument and agreed to reduce the Company's share in hard cases. But of far more use than his promises and his lavish gifts of money to the scores of deserving and undeserving cases of distress were his straight talks, his practical advice, his intense belief in the country, and his cheery optimism, "always looking at the comparative." The settlers felt that he was one with them when he talked to them about their farms and their fencing, inspected their mines and found them good, and snubbed Lord Randolph Churchill, then touring through the country, for his doubts and his aloofness. He was specially interested in the Zimbabwe ruins as evidence of a former civilization and prosperity, made friends with the natives, and like another Joseph had storehouses erected against times of scarcity. Then, when his time was up, he posted back to Vryburg by every available means of conveyance—oxen, mules, horses—covering the last 625 miles in seven days. The whole round journey from Cape Town and back took him barely more than two months; but in that time he had restored the confidence of every one in the country. "It is quite a different Mashonaland since you came," wrote one of the pioneers, "for now every one is hopeful." Thereafter the settlers had many more trials and hardships to undergo, but in the worst times they never despaired, because they had learned that they always had their founder watching over them and ready to help. In this and succeeding visits he implanted in them that absolute trust in himself, the memory of which was still lively, when Lord Selborne travelled through the country sixteen years later and Rhodes himself was dead. In him, writes Lord Selborne, they had one "who was in complete touch and sympathy with them, who was always accessible, always kindly. . . . So long as he lived they had a friend in their midst. . . . Of his memory they always spoke in terms of deep affection."

CHAPTER XII

RHODESIA

WHEN the Charter was granted, the idea of the Government was that the philanthropists of the British South Africa Company should spend their resources on developing unexplored tracts of South Africa, while the Crown should exercise considerable control over their proceedings. Theoretically the Crown had large powers of control, for the Company could not conquer or administer any territory without its explicit consent intimated by Order in Council or proclamation of the High Commissioner, and all relations of the Company with other powers had to be conducted through the Foreign Office. But in practice the control was very slight. No provision had at first been made for an Imperial officer specially to watch and report on the Company's proceedings, and, in the absence of such supervision, the Company's officials might well embark on a course of action, from which there was no receding and for which the nation was bound to accept responsibility. The danger of such an occurrence was more than once illustrated in the first few years of the Company's existence.

One of the expedients whereby the Government hoped to retain influence over the Company broke down from the outset. The three life-directors, the Dukes of Abercorn and Fife and Mr. Albert Grey, had been insisted on for their unblemished social and political position as a guarantee against any undue preponderance of Cecil Rhodes and his South African friends on the Board. The Duke of Abercorn proved a dignified and excellent chairman, and the Duke of Fife pleased the shareholders by telling them more than once that theirs was the only company of which he had consented to be a director; Albert Grey was indeed a man of the noblest ideals, of a tact which amounted to genius and of great administrative ability: but all three, with the rest of the Board, succumbed at once and irretrievably to Rhodes's dominating personality. He was the only director who knew what he wanted and how to carry it through, and when he was not there the rest were all at sea and ready to send for him on any emergency. In fact, as long as he lived, whether on the Board or off it, Rhodes was the South Africa Company. "We are in the dark here," writes Grey to him at a crisis in the Company's fortunes, "but I have the fullest confidence in the wisdom of any move which you and Jameson may agree in thinking the right one. . . . Do whatever you think right. We will support you whatever the issue." In South Africa he was of course supreme. He was not only managing director out there, but had the Board's power of attorney to cover his actions on their behalf, and, owing to the breakdown of the negotiations with Sir Henry de Villiers and Hofmeyr,[1] the scheme of a local board, which might have exercised some check on him, fell through. The Imperial Government soon had to adjust itself to the facts and to recognize that in dealing with the Chartered Company they were dealing with Rhodes. And he was not an easy man to deal with.

The Pioneer expedition into Mashonaland, of which we have already traced the fortunes, was really only a small item in Rhodes's plans for the Chartered Company. Bechuanaland and Mashonaland, ever since the days when he had dreamed his dreams at Warren's headquarters, he looked on only as stepping-stones to the region of the Great Central Lakes, and had formed his ideal of a great British dominion through the centre of Africa stretching from Cape Town to the Mediterranean In the terms of the Charter he had taken care to leave free scope for these ambitions, for, though the Company's field of operations was limited on the south, the east, and the west, it had no boundaries on the north.

When he was arranging for the Charter he had already

[1] See Chapter XI. p. 141.

obtained a vantage ground beyond the Zambesi. Since the death of Livingstone in 1873 at Chitambo, near Lake Bangweolo, Scottish missionaries had been spreading the gospel in that region, and the African Lakes Company, in alliance with them, had established trading factories on Lake Nyassa and in the Shire Highlands. But the Arab slave raiders from Zanzibar had long regarded this region as a favourable ground for their business and were in constant conflict with the missionaries and the Company. These conflicts had almost reduced the Company to bankruptcy, and when Rhodes was in London in 1889 he was told by Major Lugard, fresh from an expedition against the raiders, that their suppression could only be secured at a much larger cost than the Company could afford. It looked as if this advance post of British enterprise would have to be abandoned, unless the Government would undertake the task of protecting the traders and missionaries ; but though Lord Salisbury was anxious that British influence should not entirely disappear from this region, he was at a loss for the funds. Rhodes, however, was ready to step into the breach. He entered into negotiations, not finally concluded till 1893, with the African Lakes Company for the purchase by the Chartered Company of their good-will and stock-in-trade. This was to give him the necessary financial and commercial interest in the development of the country. He then turned to the Government and offered, on condition a British protectorate were declared over the Lake Nyassa district and the Chartered Company were allowed to administer the rest of Central Africa, to provide for a definite period £10,000 a year for the upkeep of the protectorate. This arrangement, so favourable to the Government, was at once accepted by Lord Salisbury. A protectorate was declared over Nyassaland in 1891, and Sir Harry Johnston was sent out in the dual capacity of Government Commissioner in the protectorate and administrator in the Company's sphere. The Chartered Company paid the £10,000 for five years for the upkeep of the police, and Rhodes, out of his own pocket, contributed a further £10,000 to carry on war against a peculiarly turbulent slave-chief, Makanjira. Johnston gradually suppressed the slavers, and by a small but efficient force of Sikh police ensured security for life and property in both his spheres; steamers were placed on Lakes Nyassa and Tanganyika, British justice was administered in consular courts, and settlers were encouraged on the Shire Highlands. In 1895 the Company took over the direct administration of their districts and made very large profits by the trading business acquired from the African Lakes Company.

Rhodes also acquired a footing for the Company further west. Early in 1889 Lewanika, titular chief of Barotseland, a large undefined territory, stretching from the southern border of the Congo state to the north bank of the Zambesi, learning of the Moffat treaty with Lo Bengula, applied also to come under the Queen's protection. Lord Knutsford refused the application at the time, but in the following year a trader named Ware obtained a comprehensive concession from Lewanika over his dominions. This concession was bought up by Rhodes and subsequently confirmed by further concessions, and ultimately the Government recognized Barotseland as well as the Lakes district as within the Chartered Company's sphere.

But before the boundaries of the Company's domains in either of these districts or even in Mashonaland could be finally settled Rhodes found himself in conflict with two foreign powers, Germany and Portugal. Of these Germany was more easily disposed of. Up till 1890 the extent of German East Africa had never been clearly defined, and claims were put forward to the whole country between Lakes Nyassa and Tanganyika as far as Lake Bangweolo. Included in this tract was the Stevenson road connecting the two first-named lakes, which had a sentimental interest to the British people for its association with Livingstone, and also the tree near Lake Bangweolo where the great missionary breathed his last. In 1890, however, Lord Salisbury negotiated with Germany the treaty which was to settle once for all the points of difference between the two nations in Africa, and determine the boundaries of South-West Africa and German and British East Africa and the protectorate of Zanzibar. Lord Salisbury made the mistake of not consulting the Cape Colony as to interests which concerned them directly or indirectly in the proposed treaty, and was far more concerned in making a satisfactory deal about Heligoland and Zanzibar than with any sentimental considerations about Livingstone's grave or Stevenson's road. Rhodes not only had a real feeling for historic associations but was naturally unwilling to part with territory claimed by the Chartered Company; so he asked Grey to urge their rights on Lord Salisbury. Grey met with a cold response and telegraphed out to Rhodes that the Stevenson road was in danger. No answer came, but some weeks later an announcement appeared in the papers that the Chartered Company's agents had erected two new forts on the Stevenson road, Fort Fife and Fort Abercorn. Meeting Rhodes later Grey asked him the meaning of these mushroom forts. "Oh," said Rhodes with a chuckle, rubbing his hands together, "I knew they could not give up a fort named after a member of the royal family"; [1] and he was right. The treaty fixed the German boundary just short of the Stevenson road, leaving to the Chartered Company this vital communication between the two lakes and all the country westwards.

The Portuguese claims were more far-reaching. After their discovery of South Africa in the fifteenth century they had made sundry settlements on the east and west coasts at Angola, Delagoa Bay, Quilimane and Mozambique. These settlements had never been entirely abandoned, and a treaty was stated to have been made in the seventeenth century with a mythical Emperor of Monomatapa, on which they founded a right to Mashonaland. But this treaty was not given prominence or acted upon until after the scramble for Africa had begun in 1880, when the Portuguese, hitherto content with a few coast settlements, began to make the most extravagant claims to the interior. They not only asserted a right of continuous dominion across Africa from Angola to Mozambique, which would have included Barotseland, the Nyassa region and the whole course of the Zambesi, but also stated that their coastal territory from the mouth of the Zambesi to Delagoa Bay extended westwards to Gazaland and Manicaland and

[1] The Duke of Fife was married to a granddaughter of the Queen.

included Mashonaland itself. The former claim had actually been recognized by France and Germany in 1886 and had nearly been accepted by England two years later.[1] Acting upon it in 1889 an adventurous Portuguese Major, Serpa Pinto, had made a raid into the Shire Highlands, slaughtered some of the natives who relied upon our protection and formally annexed the country; and for a long time the Portuguese authorities put every possible obstacle in the way of the African Lakes Company, whose only access to the interior was by the Zambesi and Shire rivers. The Portuguese Government had protested at once against the Moffat treaty and the Rudd concession, and had tried to forestall Rhodes by sending roving bands under half-caste Capitãos Mors to distribute Portuguese flags and terrorize the native kraals in Manicaland, Gazaland, and on the eastern outskirts of Mashonaland. The most notorious of these buccaneering adventurers was a Goanese called Gouveia, or Manoel Antonio de Souza, who had founded a semi-independent native state to the east of Manicaland. But negotiations for a settlement had been going on during 1890, and three weeks before the pioneers reached Salisbury a convention had been signed to delimit the respective spheres of England and Portugal. It was satisfactory to England in respect to Nyassaland, where the British interests were recognized; a favourable arrangement was also made for the lease of a quay to the Lakes Company at the Chinde mouth of the Zambesi, recently discovered by Rankin, and for free navigation on the waterways; but Rhodes discovered, much to his indignation, that most of Barotseland and the whole of Manicaland were ceded to Portugal. He wrote angry letters to everybody whom he held responsible for it, bidding them "drop this wretched treaty." After a good deal of abuse of the Portuguese, "I do not think I am claiming too much from your department," he added to a Foreign Office official, "in asking you to give some consideration to my views . . . and that if you have any regard for the work I am doing, you will show it by now dropping the Anglo-Portuguese agreement." The trouble was that Rhodes, concentrating all his

[1] See Chapter X. p. 134.

attention on his own views, was apt to pay too little heed to views relevant to other parts of the Empire. It was pointed out to him on this occasion that if we were too hard on Portugal, there might be a revolution there and in Spain also, and that a Spanish Republic might render the supply of provisions for Gibraltar difficult. It had been just the same with regard to the treaty with Germany. One of those interested in British East Africa had written complaining that there was not enough co-operation between Rhodes's Company and Mackinnon's I.B.E.A., and that Germany stood to gain in the negotiations by this disunion; whereas if Rhodes could have thought of the islands of Manda and Patea, off the East African coast, as well as the Stevenson road, England might get both. But he would not see it. He could think of other parts of the Empire when he had leisure, but allowed nothing to stand in the way of his own immediate object. This impatient method had its risks, but it accounts for a great deal of Rhodes's success in getting what he wanted. He once wrote to a friend: "The story of the importunate widow is the best in the Bible."

Fortunately the Portuguese themselves relieved him of his anxiety about this convention by refusing to ratify it in an outburst of indignation at the concessions they were themselves called upon to make. So the pioneers were able to stake out further claims. In 1890 the only tangible sign of the Portuguese occupation of Manicaland was a small fort at Macequece on its eastern border. Before the pioneer column had actually reached Salisbury, Jameson, taking Colquhoun and Selous with him, had left it to view their proceedings. He found that Umtassa, the paramount chief of the country, did not recognize the Portuguese claims, and concluded with him a treaty which practically amounted to a British protectorate and a gift of all minerals to the Company. Two months later the Portuguese brought up strong reinforcements and occupied Umtassa's kraal, but were all caught napping there by Captain Forbes and thirty of the B.S.A. police, who disarmed the rank and file and took prisoners the redoubtable Gouveia and two other high Portuguese officials. The capture of Gouveia had a great effect on the minds of the natives, whom he had oppressed, and helped the Company in their peaceable settlement of the country. Selous then went off to make treaties with other chiefs further north, and Dennis Doyle, on behalf of Rhodes, was sent to get a concession from Gungunhana, the Chief of Gazaland, to the south of Manicaland. But here the Portuguese were on the alert; and when Jameson, after an adventurous journey of twenty-five days by river and jungle, came to confirm the treaty he found the Portuguese in possession and the Company's ships, sent up the coast to meet him and to convey arms to Gungunhana, under arrest. But after two more skirmishes at Umtali, the Company's new settlement founded near Umtassa's kraal, and at Macequece, in which they were beaten, the Portuguese came to terms. By the treaty of June 1891 the spheres of the two nations in Central Africa were defined as in the abortive convention of the previous year, while the Company gained Barotseland and the greater part of Manicaland, leaving Macequece and most of Gazaland to the Portuguese. Of still more importance to the Company were the transport facilities granted. The navigation of the Zambesi and Shire rivers was declared free, and the prospect of a new and much shorter access to Mashonaland was obtained by the opening of the port of Beira and the promise of the Portuguese to build a railway thence to Umtali and Salisbury, a distance of only 380 miles as compared with the 2000 miles from Cape Town. This treaty gave Rhodes all he could reasonably ask, for he had always said that he would be quite content to leave the low-lying coast districts to the Portuguese, as long as he held the healthy uplands of the interior for his people. It also restored the ancient friendship and alliance between the two nations, while in Africa the Company ever afterwards had the most cordial relations with the Portuguese.

Even after this settlement with Portugal the Company's position was still unsatisfactory in one respect. Although they had the right to dig for minerals in Mashonaland, they had no explicit power to deal with the land. It is true this had hitherto made no practical difference: farms had been allotted to the settlers and Salisbury had been cut up into stands for sale; and Rhodes had cheerily spoken of the 10,000 farms, each of 4000 acres, waiting to be taken up by Europeans. Still, the want of title was a defect, which might lead to questionings and trouble in the future. One Edward Amandus Lippert, a German financier, had observed the weak spot and resolved to make his profit thereby. He made his way with a Mr. Renny-Tailyour to Lo Bengula's kraal and found the king in a good disposition for his purpose, for he was still being worried for concessions and moreover was becoming anxious at the Company's lavish grants of land. Lippert represented himself as the disinterested friend anxious to save him trouble, and offered to take off his shoulders the burden of assigning to Europeans any land necessary for their operations, receive the rents himself and pay Lo Bengula £1000 down and a "globular sum" annually, as Rhodes described it, of £500.[1] The offer was accepted, and Lippert returned with the concession in his pocket to Pretoria to make the best use of it he could. He approached Alfred Beit, who was his cousin, with a proposal to float a company to develop it, and on his refusal hawked it round to others and, when told it was valueless by the Chartered Company's agents, spoke darkly of the support he had been promised by the German Government.

The news of this concession troubled Rhodes greatly, as it might seriously hamper the Company's freedom of action. His first inclination, after consulting Sir Henry Loch, was to dispute its validity, and he procured the arrest of Lippert's accomplice, Renny-Tailyour, as he was travelling through Bechuanaland. But on second thoughts his natural disposition to a deal reasserted itself, and he made

[1] The wording of the concession is far-reaching. "Whereas," Lo Bengula is made to say, "large numbers of white people are coming into my territories and it is desirable that I should assign land to them . . . and appoint some persons to act for me in these respects"; to Edward Amandus Lippert, in consideration of the above-mentioned payments, is assigned the sole right for a hundred years "to lay out, grant or lease for such period or periods as he may think fit, farms, townships, building plots and grazing areas; to impose and levy rents . . . for his own benefit; to give and grant certificates . . . for the occupation of any farms, townships, building plots and grazing areas."

several unsuccessful attempts through agents to bring Lippert to reasonable terms. Finally he saw the man himself and arranged that, after it had been confirmed by Lo Bengula, the concession should be bought by the Company. The price was no doubt large; still, it was cheap at any price to the Company, whose entire scheme of settlement might otherwise have been at the mercy of Lippert and a rival syndicate. Wide, however, as were the powers granted by Lo Bengula, they were nothing to the fantastic superstructure of rights subsequently built upon this document by the Company. Rhodes himself, though not quite consistent in all his utterances on the subject, generally spoke of the land as public property, for which he and the directors were merely trustees, and warned the shareholders that any profits they might make must come solely from minerals. But after his death the directors propounded the theory that all the land in Lo Bengula's dominions was the Company's private property. They had several arguments in support of this view, but based it mainly on this Lippert concession, by which at most they obtained agents' rights for a hundred years; by that time, too, Lo Bengula himself had long disappeared and his country had been conquered on behalf of the Crown. This contention, vehemently opposed by the settlers, was not finally disposed of till 1918, when the Privy Council declared the Lippert concession valueless as a title to private property in the land. But nothing in the Privy Council judgement impugned the use made of the concession at the time it was granted. Rhodes was thereby enabled to give secure titles to his settlers and also to use the proceeds of land sales to cover purely administrative costs.[1]

Lo Bengula had now granted away his minerals and land rights; the only remaining danger to the settlers was the presence of Lo Bengula himself and his savage Matabele hordes in their immediate neighbourhood. For the first three years of its existence the settlement of Europeans in

[1] In their first report the directors estimated the land at their disposal at 80,000,000 acres, which, capitalized at 3d. an acre, amply secured the shareholders' capital.

Mashonaland was a strange anomaly. By the admission of the Crown the country still belonged to Lo Bengula, and Jameson was sharply called to order by the Colonial Office for speaking of troublesome natives he had chastised as rebels: in fact, the newcomers were there only on sufferance. For Lo Bengula, being an ignorant savage, never understood the concessions he had granted in the wide sense their legal phraseology might warrant and as they were interpreted by the Company, and resented the creation of an independent state within his borders. "I thought you came to dig for gold," he wrote to the Secretary, "but it seems you have come . . . to rob me of my people as well"; and he was beginning to find confirmation of his fears expressed years before to the missionary Helm: "Did you ever see a chameleon catch a fly? The chameleon gets behind the fly and remains motionless for some time, then he advances very slowly and gently, first putting forward one leg and then another. At last, when well within reach, he darts out his tongue and the fly disappears. England is the chameleon and I am that fly." But he had no idea of giving up his rights without a struggle and continued by his own barbarous methods to assert his sovereignty over the Mashonas, among whom the settlers were living. Twice in 1892 he sent raiding bands of his warriors to punish cattle thefts and exact tribute from these unfortunate people; and the raiders carried on their depredations under the eyes of the Europeans in the neighbourhood. These raids stopped all farming and mining, for the native workers fled to their caves in the hills and even the settlers in isolated camps felt insecure. As early as 1891 it was the common talk in Mashonaland that "until the Matabeles are crushed and welded into shape the success of the country either as a mining concern or a new market and administration will never be accomplished." Other less worthy considerations also had their influence. The rough tumbled country of Mashonaland had not proved the expected El Dorado either for mining or farming, and longing eyes were cast on the more fertile uplands, where the Matabeles pastured the largest and finest herds in South Africa. Rhodes himself had long seen whither events were drifting and at Tuli in 1890 had given this answer to a Transvaal Boer who had offered to fight the Matabeles for him: "Yes, Mr. Graaff, I shall certainly some day be pressed to do as you want me to do, but you must remember that I have only the right to dig gold in that land; so long, therefore, as the Matabele do not molest my people, I cannot declare war against them and deprive them of their country, but as soon as they interfere with our rights I shall end their game; I shall then ask for your aid and be very glad to get it, and when all is over I shall grant farms to those who assisted me."

In July 1893 matters came to a head. The telegraph line had been cut near Victoria and Lo Bengula sent an impi, partly to punish the culprits, partly to recover some cattle stolen from his own kraal. The savages behaved as usual—murdering, pillaging and burning round the country-side and even within the precincts of Victoria itself. Captain Lendy,[1] the Company's officer at Victoria, remonstrated, but without avail, and Jameson came down from Salisbury to deal with the offenders. Jameson was convinced that the raiders must be given a sharp lesson; otherwise there would be no peace in the country; and, though the Company was hardly prepared for war with so formidable an enemy as the Matabeles, he had supreme confidence in himself and in Rhodes's support. He telegraphed to him saying that it might be necessary to strike a blow at once and march on Buluwayo. Rhodes was in the Cape House at the time and scribbled off the laconic answer: "Read Luke xiv. 31,"[2] to which Jameson replied that he had read the verse and that it was all right. Meanwhile he had summoned the indunas of the impi to an indaba and told them plainly that, unless they were off the commonage in an hour, he would make them go. At the end of the hour Lendy was sent after them with a troop

[1] Captain Lendy had already acquired unenviable notoriety by his brutal treatment of N'gomo, a Mashona chieftain charged with theft. He had been severely censured by the Colonial Secretary, and should have been cashiered. It was certainly unfortunate that the Matabele War was opened with this man in a responsible position.

[2] "Or what king, going to make war against another king, sitteth not down first, and consulteth whether he be able with ten thousand to meet him that cometh against him with twenty thousand?"

of police ; though they were already moving off, Lendy nevertheless fired and killed some. By this action the die was cast : Lo Bengula recalled a strong impi he had sent to Barotseland and Jameson began to make his preparations for war.

Nearly three months passed, however, before hostilities actually began. On hearing of the events at Victoria Sir Henry Loch took charge of the negotiations with Lo Bengula, made Jameson withdraw the claim he had made for compensation and enjoined him not to move without his permission. Loch was not in an enviable position with regard to Rhodes and the Chartered Company. Though he had little control over Jameson's actions in Mashonaland, his would be the responsibility, if anything went amiss. " The danger is," he complained to a friend in England, " the Company as soon as they are a little better prepared, may bring about fighting, as they can't stand long armed and waiting for events with the possible view of committing H.M.'s Government in their quarrel. So I am obliged to watch both friend and enemy." His relations with his masterful Prime Minister made his task none the easier. He had a sincere admiration for him, but was not so completely under his sway as his predecessor appears to have been : and Rhodes liked to be a dictator and resented criticism no less from a governor than from anybody else. In the previous year Rhodes had taken umbrage at a fancied attempt by Loch to curtail the Company's operations, and now he strongly objected to any interference by the Imperial authorities. To do him justice he took the brunt of the work on his own shoulders. Immediately after the Victoria incident he ordered the enrolment of men, bought up horses in the Transvaal and sent them up to Charter and Victoria ; and, to meet the expenses of campaign, sold 40,000 Chartered shares at a loss. " I was afraid," he told the South Africa Committee three years later, " the Doctor might have a bad time, and I did sell my interest in various things to provide money to carry on the war, because I felt that if there was a disaster, I was the only person to carry it through." On September 18 he sailed for Beira on his way to Mashonaland, telling Loch before he left that "the Company asked for nothing and wanted nothing."

Loch, though always made to feel in Rhodes's presence the lesser of the two kings in Brentford, stuck manfully to his rights. As an old soldier, he realized more fully than Rhodes or Jameson the formidable undertaking it might prove to conquer Lo Bengula's 15,000 savages with only 1000 Europeans, and was anxious lest the war should spread to the protectorate, for which he was directly responsible. With the full support of his chief, Lord Ripon, he insisted on satisfying himself about Jameson's preparations and plan of campaign before allowing him to stir, and, in spite of Rhodes's assurance that the Company wanted nothing, strengthened the police force in the protectorate with a view to a possible diversion against Buluwayo. At the same time he did his utmost to avert hostilities by messages to Lo Bengula. The chief himself, though he refused any further payments under the Rudd concession as "blood money," to the end seemed anxious to avoid an open rupture; but after the events of July it was impossible for him to restrain the hotheads of his tribe. Bands of his warriors still hovered about the outskirts of Victoria, and in October some of the Imperial police were fired on by Matabele scouts. The bellicose spirit of the settlers and one of its motives is equally plain from the terms of the "Victoria agreement," which the volunteers called up for service in August required Jameson to sign before they would march. By this agreement the lion's skin was carved up before he was slain: every man who invaded Matabeleland was to receive a farm of 6000 acres, valued at £1 : 10s. an acre if the Company wished to repurchase it for public purposes, twenty gold claims and an equal share of all "loot"—the famous Matabele herds.

With these dispositions on both sides war could hardly be avoided. After the firing on the police patrol Loch gave permission to Jameson to start. Within less than a month the issue was decided. Six hundred volunteers and four hundred native auxiliaries, with a good supply of maxims and field-guns, marched along the high plateau leading from Mashonaland to Buluwayo. After repelling two attacks, on the Shangani and Imbembesi Rivers, of Matabele forces numbering some 5000, the column entered Buluwayo on November 4, 1893. A diversion from the south by Goold Adams and the Imperial police materially assisted them, and Goold Adams joined them in Buluwayo a few days later. Before the volunteers arrived Lo Bengula had blown up his royal kraal, no doubt with gunpowder received in payment for concessions, and had fled northwards. Major Forbes and Captain Alan Wilson were sent with a small party in pursuit, but at the Shangani the force divided, Wilson being sent across the river to follow up the spoor. Thus isolated from the rest Alan Wilson's detachment was suddenly attacked by an overwhelming number of the king's bodyguard; Forbes, who was also engaged, could send him no help. For some time Wilson's fate was in doubt and Rhodes, already at the front, hurried up from Buluwayo with reinforcements. But it was too late. Wilson and his men, surrounded by their enemies, died where they stood like gallant Englishmen, the last man falling only when the last cartridge had been spent. Rhodes, who loved his gallant pioneers, was deeply affected by the tragedy and glory of this last stand, and erected one of his most famous memorials to their memory. Save for this, his men came almost scatheless out of the brief campaign which gave him the whole of Matabeleland.

Lo Bengula, harried as a fugitive, did not long survive the loss of his country. Two months later news came that he had died of small-pox on the Shangani. Barbarous and cruel as he was, according to the traditions of his race, all the Europeans who met him unite in testifying that he had many of the qualities of a great gentleman. To men he knew well and trusted, like Selous, he was courteous and scrupulous in his dealings. When his young men were crying out for the blood of Maguire and Thompson, he would not suffer a hair of their heads to be touched. Even when the Europeans were advancing on his capital, he set a guard to protect the four European traders who had not escaped in time; and they were found safe and sound by the Company's forces amid the ruins of the native village. It is humiliating to feel that he did not always meet with the same consideration from the Europeans. He was badgered and worried into granting concessions which he barely understood, and he vainly tried to avert the dangers he foresaw from a white settlement. Even at the last, two of his envoys to the High Commissioner were killed at the outposts in a blundering affray; and, worse still, two European troopers, to whom during his flight he had entrusted a sum of money as an earnest of his readiness to surrender, embezzled the money and kept back his message.[1] No doubt the state of society he represented was incompatible with the European civilization brought within his boundaries, and the ending of the savage Matabele system was a benefit to all Lo Bengula's subjects: nor could the raids and massacres of his tribesmen have been stopped otherwise than by military conquest. Still, in spite of these reasons to justify it, and in spite of the redeeming courage of Alan Wilson and his men, the mercenary motives that inspired many of those who took part in this war give it a sordid aspect, which does not redound to the national credit. It is satisfactory at least to know that Rhodes himself felt a twinge of compassion for the "naked old savage," as he called him, deserted by his royal regiments at the last and left to die friendless, and that he undertook at his own charge the education and support of his sons.

Before the issue of the war was known Rhodes had found a fresh cause of grievance against the Imperial Government in a message from Loch that all negotiations about the settlement of Matabeleland were to be conducted by the High Commissioner. In a peremptory telegram to the Board of Directors he required them to find out the meaning of this message, and demand that the Company, having asked nothing of the Government, should be free to settle terms with Lo Bengula, subject only to Lord Ripon's approval. "I certainly intend to settle the question on South African lines," he telegraphed to a Dutch friend at the Cape. "I had the idea and found the money and our people have had the courage to fight without

[1] It is satisfactory to know that this dastardly conduct subsequently came to light, and that the two men were sentenced to penal servitude.

help from home.[1] Surely I should have a voice in the final settlement. I feel I can reckon on the people of Cape Colony supporting me in this view." He instructed Jameson on arriving at Buluwayo to retain the management of everything in his own hands for the Company, and told him not to allow the Imperial representative to have a say. Accordingly Jameson began to allocate farms and to seize the king's cattle. But even Rhodes, after his first outburst of petulance, could hardly maintain that the Crown should have no voice in the settlement, especially when Loch and Ripon tactfully assured him that nothing should be decided without his consent. He declared Jameson's action to be merely provisional, and in a speech to the volunteers at Buluwayo warned them that all arrangements about land grants must be subject to the High Commissioner's approval. Still he could not resist a dig at the "negrophilists of Exeter Hall," and talked some arrant nonsense about the opposition to the war by a small section in England, which he spoke of as "conduct that alienates colonists from the Mother Country," and hinted that "it was in the same spirit that the Mother Country lost America," ignoring completely the wholehearted support given him throughout by the Liberal administration and the great mass of Englishmen at home. He was on surer ground when he came to giving practical advice to his settlers, and in a characteristic peroration illustrated all that was best in his own belief and practice. "Many of you," he concluded, "are going to leave, and we wish them all joy and success; but I must confess that my feelings and sympathy are most with those who are going to stay and make this their home, and to them I do heartily wish success. I would say to these that when afterwards they are alone and have afterwards possibly to deal with hardship, let them deal with such whilst considering always what I call the comparative state: 'Were I not here, where should I be and what should I be doing?' When you think of what you might have been doing elsewhere, many of you will

[1] This is hardly exact. The presence of the Imperial police on the border and their diversion of a large force of Matabeles, south of Buluwayo, materially contributed to Jameson's success.

find it is a great source of comfort that you have a great country that we know with many miles of it mineralized . . . and that there is a fair prospect of many of them being of value. Then you have, if you are inclined that way, a certain sentiment about knowing that 800 of you have created another state in South Africa, large in extent, with every prospect of being proportionately valuable, and that you have put an end to the savage rule south of the Zambesi."

In the end Rhodes had his way about Matabeleland in the agreement of May 1894 between the Company and the Crown. The whole of Lo Bengula's dominions were treated as conquered territory and assigned to the Company to govern on the lines of a Crown Colony. The appointment of the administrator and his council and of the judges was vested in the Board of Directors, subject to the Secretary of State's approval: the Board alone could impose taxes and customs duties and issue ordinances concurrently with the High Commissioner and the administrator in council. The Company was free to allocate all land as it pleased, subject to two reserves set apart for the natives; and as the successor of Lo Bengula, who claimed the ownership of all herds, it was allowed to retain all the cattle in the country, provided the natives were allowed a certain proportion for milking. The Secretary of State and the High Commissioner retained the power of veto, but an *ex post facto* veto was no great safe-guard in a country still so remote from communication. In effect Rhodes, as sole managing director of the Company, became almost absolute in the whole territory extending from Bechuanaland to the Zambesi.

In the following year, in recognition of his great work, Rhodes was made a Privy Councillor, and all the Company's sphere in South Africa, including Mashonaland, Matabeleland, Barotseland and Central Africa, received by Proclamation the title of Rhodesia, whereby formal authority was given to a name already suggested by the settlers' affection for their founder. Rhodes himself was vastly pleased at the personal distinction given to him as Privy Councillor, but still more at the title chosen for his country: as he said, in his shy boyish way, to a friend, "Well, you know, to have a bit of country named after one is one of the things a man might be proud of."

By 1895 Rhodes was at the pinnacle of success and glory. A life-time's thought, no doubt, but only six years' ostensible work had enabled him to "paint the map of Africa red" to a greater extent than had been accomplished by the labours of previous centuries. And it was no mere painting of the map. Over a large part of this great dominion, 750,000 square miles in extent, larger than Spain, France and the former German Empire put together, order and settled government had been established; no internal or external danger to its peace gave cause for apprehension. The railway was being pushed on towards Salisbury from Mafeking and from Beira; Salisbury, Buluwayo and other townships had been put in touch by the telegraph line with the outside world. The even more ambitious scheme of the African Transcontinental Telegraph Company, almost entirely a creation of Rhodes's forethought and private capital, had begun linking up the whole of Africa from Cape to Cairo and had already reached Blantyre in the distant Shire Highlands. To secure the through route he had begun negotiations with the German Government for way-leaves through German East Africa, and as a second string had obtained from Lord Rosebery's Government a treaty with the Congo State allowing him to run the telegraph along the western shore of Lake Tanganyika in exchange for the lease of the Lado Enclave.[1] In Southern Rhodesia farming, stimulated by Rhodes's encouragement and his practical help, was already giving promise, and gold production had at last taken a favourable turn. The public finances were improving and confidence in the country was shown by the rapid development of its chief centres, Salisbury, Buluwayo, Gwelo and Umtali. The climate had been proved healthy and fit for white men to work in and rear families. Already Rhodes's wish, "Homes, more homes, that is what I want," formulated as he looked over the uplands of Rhodesia and thought of the

[1] Owing to the opposition of France and Germany this treaty was never ratified.

squalid tenements General Booth and others had shown him in London, was being realized.

Rhodes's great wealth was no doubt a large factor in his success ; and there was an element of truth in the critic's envious comment that it was easy for him to attain his objects " with your armies and your gold and with all the quiet, majestic, resistless advance of an elephant through brushwood." He himself never underestimated this factor. " If we have imaginative ideas, we must have pounds, shillings and pence to carry them out," he said to Gordon. But something more was needed. Earl Grey, the friend who more than any other could pierce through Rhodes's crust of cynicism to the noblest elements in him, put his finger on one essential : public spirit. Sending him a model in gold of the first Rhodesian mine opened for working with the inscription,

εἷς οἰωνὸς ἄριστος, ἀμύνεσθαι περὶ πάτρης,

he added, " In Tudor and Plantagenet times men did things first for England, then for themselves. Some of our big wigs can't believe you act like this." And Rhodes himself knew that even with wealth and public spirit he could never have succeeded without the feeling of the people and his own persistence. In this matter of the feeling of the people he had the true instinct of the great statesman. " We went far to the north," he told a Cape Town audience ; " we occupied all short of the Zambesi ; we did it by the feeling of the people. For after all, even if you have the wealth, it is impossible to carry out a conception unless you have the feeling of the people with you ; . . . and I have found out one thing," he added, " and that is, if you have an idea and it is a good idea, if you will only stick to it, you will come out all right. . . . In those early days every one was against me. When I pointed out to the House, as an individual member, that the hinterland must be preserved, I could not get a vote, I could not get a single vote ; and one had to continue at the question in spite of every difficulty. I made the seizure of the interior a paramount thing in my politics and made everything else subordinate. . . . My paramount object weighed with me as supreme."

CHAPTER XIII

PRIME MINISTER OF THE CAPE

I

FOR the five years succeeding 1885 Rhodes had, much to the disappointment of his friends, taken very little part in the proceedings of the Cape Parliament. Sauer had urged him in 1888, as soon as his diamond amalgamation was completed, "to give some time and attention to other things than mining. I mean of course the politics of this Colony and the states adjoining—in fact the whole of South Africa." But he remained deaf to all appeals. At the general election of 1888 he had, as usual, been returned for Barkly West, but was too much absorbed by Chartered business to take his seat in the session of 1889, and for the same reason intended to be absent from his parliamentary duties during the following year. Early in June 1890, however, he suddenly changed his mind and, "without waiting to pack his portmanteau," hurried off to Cape Town, took the oath and his seat, and threw himself into the political fray.

A desperate attempt by Sir Gordon Sprigg's moribund ministry to recover popularity was the occasion of this sudden change of plans. In the recent development of railway communications attention had been mainly devoted to the great trunk lines connecting Cape Town and Port Elizabeth with the north, where the best markets for overseas goods and Cape produce were to be found. As a result the more recent port of East London and the country farmers in the western and central districts of the Colony had felt themselves neglected. To remedy this grievance

Sprigg proposed a great scheme of railway construction to tap hitherto undeveloped districts and link up existing lines at a cost to the taxpayer estimated at anything from seven to twelve millions. It was a plausible scheme, for every Dutch farmer likes to have a railway as near his front door as possible, and seemed calculated to catch votes. But it was extravagant, especially at a time when the Cape finances were none too flourishing; for many of the proposed lines would admittedly not be paying. To Rhodes this vote-catching appeal was particularly obnoxious, for he hated localism and did not want the colony's resources diverted from schemes of general utility to unremunerative lines in out-of-the-way districts. One of Sprigg's ideas was to connect the newly discovered Indwe collieries by a rambling railway with East London. Develop the Indwe collieries by all means, Rhodes argued, but develop them in the most rational way by giving them the shortest possible line to their best market, Kimberley, which would willingly take any amount of cheap colonial coal in place of English sea-borne coal at £8 : 10s. a ton. As for East London, its proper function was to be a mart for the rich grain trade of the Free State and the Eastern Province, not to compete with Port Elizabeth for long-distance traffic; "but there seems a sort of mania," he complained, "when one port has its distinct area, to let another port come in and render what by itself is profitable unprofitable when shared by two." Sprigg had over-reached himself. The Bond farmers, dearly as they would have liked their particular railways, are a frugal race and were alarmed at the cost; Sauer and Merriman, the financial watchdogs of the opposition, joined forces with Rhodes; and after several defeats in Committee Sprigg resigned on July 10.

At that time the Bond party, led by their great tactician Hofmeyr, had the deciding voice in the Cape Parliament. In 1879, when Hofmeyr entered Parliament, out of a House of seventy-four members, he could reckon on a following of about twenty; in 1884 it had increased to thirty-three, and in the last election a few more seats had been gained. This result had been attained by infinite patience and much subterranean manœuvring on the leader's part: the tenets of the party had been purged of their anti-British bias, so exasperating to colonists of Anglo-Saxon origin, and attention had been concentrated on the practical issues of Cape politics. In fact the Bond under Hofmeyr's guidance, though still drawing most of its adherents from the Dutch population, had become chiefly a country or farmers' party as opposed to the commercial interests of the towns. But, though so powerful in Parliament, Hofmeyr had never had an absolute majority, and without that had always declined to undertake the responsibility of forming a Ministry. His purpose was served equally well without that. Few of his rustic followers were fitted for administrative duties, so he was quite content to let the more politically minded Englishmen govern and to turn out their Ministries when they ceased to be agreeable to the Bond. In this way since 1881 the Scanlen, Upington and Sprigg Ministries had successively owed their tenure of office to Bond votes. Rhodes himself, though he never enrolled himself in the Bond, had been veering more and more to their point of view. On his rare visits to the House he had generally found himself in the same lobby as the Bondsmen, and during the election of 1888 had acted in close concert with Hofmeyr, using his influence to induce several of his English friends to win seats with the support of the Bond and to get English voters to support some of Hofmeyr's candidates.

On Sprigg's resignation the Governor sent for Sauer, but as he and his friend Merriman could not count on Hofmeyr's support, he gave up the attempt to form a Ministry. Rhodes was then sent for. His first step was to find out if the Bond would be with him: he even offered either to serve under Hofmeyr or to give him a place in his Cabinet. Hofmeyr declined both offers but gave his blessing to a Rhodes Ministry. His followers were equally favourable and promised to give the new Ministry fair play. Some of Rhodes's English supporters in Kimberley were not too well pleased at these parleyings with the Dutch, but he had a ready answer for the grumblers. "I think," he said, "if more pains were taken to explain matters to the Bond party, many of the cobwebs would be swept away and a much better understanding would exist between the different parties."

He had little difficulty in forming a Ministry. "There are no clear lines of political division in this country," he once told the Cape Parliament; "I do not mean it is a question of 'ins' and 'outs,' but I would ask the House to consider whether in so far as public policy is concerned there are very great lines of difference in forming a Cabinet . . . it would probably be a matter to be settled personally or socially." And for settling matters personally or socially he was without a rival. He met Parliament within a week of Sprigg's resignation with his Cabinet already formed. It contained three supporters of the Bond: himself, Faure and Sivewright, the last a clever Scotsman who had risen from the Cape telegraph service to a great position as a contractor, and had won Rhodes's confidence by his business capacity and his help in forwarding the Kimberley–Vryburg railway. The opposition members were Innes, a highly respected lawyer, now Chief Justice of the Union; Sauer, the ablest debater in the House; and, as Treasurer-General, Merriman, a rigid economist of the Gladstone school, witty and eloquent, a Rupert of debate. It was hailed as a "Cabinet of all the talents"; but, strong as it seemed, it contained within it the seeds of discord. Rhodes may have been right in asserting that there were no clear lines of political division in the country; nevertheless there were certain underlying problems which might at any moment come to the surface and create profound dissensions in the community. One of these was the native question, on which Sauer and Merriman held diametrically opposite views to the less liberal-minded Bondsmen. Another was the rivalry between English and Dutch, never entirely allayed and liable to blaze up again at any spark. For the time being, however, Rhodes, while inclined towards the Bond view on both these questions, was able to exercise a moderating influence, and his first Cabinet survived for nearly three years. Then differences, both personal and political, became so acute that it could no longer hold together.

The immediate cause of its disruption was Sivewright. Rhodes with all his capacity for conceiving great plans was growing impatient at the drudgery of working out the details, and was only too willing to hand them over to some capable subordinate. He found Sivewright, able and not too nice in his methods, just the man for this purpose, and created some jealousy among the other Ministers by the special confidence he reposed in this "brain-carrier of the Ministry," as Hofmeyr called him. At the end of 1892 Innes, Sauer and Merriman discovered that Sivewright on his own responsibility, without calling for tenders, had given away an important contract to a personal friend of his. On being informed of this Rhodes, who was away in Europe with Sivewright, cabled his consent to the repudiation of the contract, but when he found on his return that those three Ministers refused to remain in the Cabinet unless Sivewright retired, he could not bring himself to dismiss Sivewright. In his dilemma he wrote a letter to Hofmeyr that shows the close relationship between the two men: "I feel very much ashamed of myself to write to you amidst all your trouble [Hofmeyr's father had just died]; but still I will say that I have a Cabinet crisis upon me and I need greatly your calm judgment. . . . If, however, you think I should respect your sorrow and get through the difficulty by my own judgment, just say so." Hofmeyr came and advised him to send in the resignation of the whole Cabinet and then reconstruct the Ministry, and Rhodes followed his advice. He himself was anxious to give up the lead, as he felt how undesirable it was for the Prime Minister to be absent so frequently as he was bound to be with his varied calls to London and Rhodesia, and offered to serve without portfolio under De Villiers or Hofmeyr. He first made overtures to the Chief Justice, and but for a misunderstanding, this negotiation might have succeeded.[1] He was equally unsuccessful with Hofmeyr, whereupon he felt obliged to become Prime Minister again with an entirely new Cabinet. Its principal members were his own predecessor Sprigg, who took over the

[1] For the correspondence between De Villiers and Rhodes see Note at the end of the chapter.

Treasury from Merriman; another Scotsman, Laing, who succeeded Sivewright; and his friend W. P. Schreiner as Attorney-General. With this Cabinet he carried on the government until his own resignation more than two years later.

Rhodes's dictum about the absence of clear lines of political division in the country was well illustrated by the presence of Sprigg in his second Ministry. For two years they had not been on speaking terms owing to some remark dropped by Sprigg in debate and warmly resented by Rhodes. They had met over the Kimberley–Vryburg railway negotiations of 1889; but during the whole of Rhodes's first Ministry Sprigg had opposed his measures and attacked him several times for combining the incompatible duties of Prime Minister of the Cape and managing director of the Chartered Company. But, though Rhodes still retained both posts, Sprigg, an adaptable politician, made no difficulty about entering his Cabinet. Except under stress of the most violent controversies it was difficult for Cape politicians to remain irreconcilable for long. Cape Town society is comparatively small; and most of the legislators belong to one club, where they cannot avoid meeting one another on friendly terms at the bar or the luncheon-table. The Cape House lent itself to tolerance. It was a very cultivated assembly, where Latin quotations could be made and appreciated without false shame, and where the standard of debate and good breeding was high. "Up to the present," Rhodes once told his fellow-members, "we have the best men in the country in the House," and he set up as an awful warning to them "the methods of Australian and other colonies, where members indulge in vulgar personalities." Vulgar personalities were indeed singularly rare in that polite and friendly assembly, where oratory was practised as a fine art and the roughest knocks were rarely resented or, if resented, soon condoned. The members were familiar with one another's peculiarities and proud of them. For flights of oratory and debating power the Cape House could bear comparison with most British assemblies, when it could produce a Merriman or a Sauer, Upington, the Irish orator, or even Sprigg, a most adroit controversialist: Sivewright's triumphant exposition of his railway convention with the Transvaal and his defence of his own part in the contract scandal are admirable examples of lucid statement. Hofmeyr's special bent was for insinuation in the lobbies, but when he spoke in the House no one could be more conciliatory and persuasive. For comic relief there was O'Reilly, the Cape Town Irishman, who fixed on Rhodes as the special mark of his buffoonery, and Schermbrücker, the genial and swashbuckling colonel from the Eastern Province. In many respects the Cape House of Rhodes's day resembled more the House of Commons of the eighteenth century than its twentieth-century successor. For both were in essence oligarchical and undemocratic bodies. The eighteenth-century politicians in England habitually kept a certain measure in attacks on their opponents and delivered them with an air of good breeding, since all were concerned in upholding a state of society and government favourable to themselves, and had no desire, by pushing their quarrels to extremes, to give an opening to the lower classes. Both English and Dutch at the Cape had the same caste feeling of aristocracy, but in their case the lower classes were represented by the hundreds of thousands of natives, of whom they were the political masters: in their presence they felt bound in honour to maintain an attitude of Olympian superiority. Rhodes, for example, was in some respects as radical as any member of the Assembly, but he stopped short at any attempt to tamper with the aristocratic basis of government. He only expressed the thoughts of most of his fellow-members when he praised the high franchise in Prussia, "a most enormous but necessary protection against demagogues, . . . a most unpleasant people," or when he uttered the unimpeachably Tory sentiment: "I wish to preserve the landed classes of the country as a conservative element in connection with changes that are coming over the country, . . . as a bulwark against the march of legislation, . . . which is very often hurried and mischievous." This spirit of exclusiveness generally makes for good manners: and just as in America one looked to find the most gracious hospitality and the greatest courtesy in the slave-owning South, so, of all the British dominions, South Africa with its subject races is the most distinguished for these qualities.

Rhodes himself was quite in his element in the Cape House. He understood its ways and its members understood him. As an orator and a master of words he was not pre-eminent, and he was sparing in his utterances, for he never spoke unless he had something definite to say. Then he talked in a conversational strain, taking the House into his confidence and telling them "amusing" stories—not always so "amusing" to his hearers as to himself—about his own youth and adventures. So, despite his awkward manner and his disjointed style, he was always listened to willingly for the thought he was laboriously contriving to express. During his speeches he was never troubled by the buzz of talk of which some members ingenuously complained. To these he once administered a grim reproof. "If a member," he drily observed, "has anything to say that is worth saying and worth listening to, every one listens to it. . . . When a member gets on his feet and hears a buzz in the House, he should say to himself that it is clear that what he is conveying to the House is not of much importance, and he should then either proceed to his facts or sit down," an utterance which recalls Chatham's terse word of advice to a flustered opponent: "Whenever that member *means* nothing, I advise him to *say* nothing." Rhodes, in his utterances, was certainly never guilty of "meaning nothing," though their connection with the subject under discussion was not always obvious. Sometimes in debate he would interpose a long rambling speech entirely off the point to convey some quite irrelevant idea, on which he had been reflecting and which he desired to make known to his audience. In 1892, for example, Sprigg had made a strong case against him for not having yet carried out his engagement to extend the line from Vryburg to Mafeking: in his reply he almost ignored the charge and devoted himself to a detailed vindication of his northern policy since 1880 and of his recent occupation of Mashonaland, concluding with the amusing piece of intelligence that "the honourable gentleman has put the motion on a very suitable day. It happens to be my birthday." So engaging a plea naturally proved irresistible; and the House celebrated the auspicious anniversary by rejecting Sprigg's motion. They were indeed very proud of their Prime Minister: proud of his business capacity as the "great amalgamator," proud of his Imperial vision and his care, in all his African schemes, to put the Cape first; flattered too by the glory reflected on the Colony from the deference paid at home to their leading statesman. His personal disinterestedness in Cape politics also earned their respect. After he had been in office three years it was discovered that he and his secretaries between them had cost the Colony no more than £527 : 5s. during the whole period. "The country is never likely to have another Prime Minister in exactly the same position as Mr. Rhodes," said Merriman, then speaking from the opposition benches, "for there is not a man in the Government who takes less out of the pockets of the country and is more modest in his demands." And he was liked because he always remained one of themselves, simple in his address and mindful of his fellow-citizens' chief interests as farmers, miners or traders. Above all, he was the first statesman among them to merge the divergent views of English and Dutch into one common outlook as Cape Colonists and South Africans.

This friendly atmosphere in the Cape Parliament facilitated Rhodes's special methods of government. He was once attacked in the House for telling a London audience that he proposed running his trans-African telegraph through the Mahdi's territories, and expected no difficulty about it, "for I have not found in life any one I could not deal with." Far from expressing shame at the sentiment, he repeated it and further explained his theory: "I have invariably found in life that you could either quarrel or deal with men; *i.e.* you could sit down and argue with a man and reason with him or quarrel with him; but if you sit down and reason with men you would invariably find that you could settle with people or arrange with people." He consistently followed this principle of "sitting down and arguing with a man," and was well rewarded by his immunity from serious opposition during his five and a half years of office. The arguments took different forms according to the man he was sitting down with. Barnato, as we have seen, he placated by a luncheon at the Club and a seat in the House; Sir Thomas Upington, one of his most eloquent opponents, was persuaded to take a judgeship in 1892; next year Sprigg and Laing were brought into the Cabinet; Theron, a Bondsman who had opposed the Charter, was talked over by Rhodes and in 1894 proposed as chairman of committees in opposition to his former chief, Sir Thomas Scanlen. Scanlen in his turn was given an important post in Rhodesia. Some members were helped out of their difficulties by Rhodes, and by the distribution of Chartered shares others were attached to his interests. Of conscious bribery he was no doubt quite guiltless, but his wealth and his manifold activities as chairman of De Beers and the Gold Fields, as managing director of the Chartered Company, and as Prime Minister of the Colony inevitably tended to rivet many connections and incline a large number of Cape politicians to regard his tenure of power as indispensable. He also had a keen eye to the value of the press and exercised considerable control over a group of South African newspapers: not that he dictated their policy, but he was at any rate secure of their general support. His general attitude on this question is well illustrated by his remark to Garrett, the editor of the *Cape Times*: "I have never inspired an article in your paper, or requested that a given line should be taken, but you might at least be careful about facts." In Parliament he preferred to settle controversial subjects behind the scenes rather than in open debate, and he certainly laid himself open to Merriman's charge that: "Parliament was being demoralized by the practice of underhand agreement, lobbying and caucuses . . . he preferred to stand up and take his fighting in the House; the Premier preferred to take it in the lobby." His chief adviser and ally in this practice of lobbying was Hofmeyr, a past-master in the art; and Rhodes always looked to Hofmeyr to keep him in touch with the Dutch party he was so anxious to conciliate. The two men saw one another almost daily during the session, riding out in the early morning over the Cape flats and the mountain slopes, or meeting for consultation in Camp Street or Groote Schuur. Attacked in the House for his understanding with Hofmeyr Rhodes admitted and gloried in the charge. "I will take the House into my secrets," he replied. "I *did* consult the honourable member for Stellenbosch. I consulted him in the first place because he represents a large section of the people of this country; in the second place because I find his sound judgement of enormous assistance to me." As an outcome of this alliance and of these preliminary parleyings Rhodes in presenting to the House most of his important measures, the Scab Act, the Franchise and Ballot Act and the Glen Grey Act, could count beforehand on the support of the Bondsmen, whose extreme limits of concession he had already sounded and allowed for. It was assuredly from no ignoble desire to retain power that he pursued this policy: "You and some of your friends think I am too subservient to the country party," he once told an English supporter, "but I have great sympathy with the Dutch; they have needs and experiences, which we are all, I sincerely think, apt to overlook. I help them as far as I can, instead of opposing them. Is not that the better way? It pleases them and it pleases me."

The Dutch farmers certainly never had a Prime Minister so solicitous for their interests. To their great delight three of the Ministers in his first Cabinet could answer their members in their own language. Soon after taking office he declared that he would not, like most previous governments, confine his attention to the ports and the carrying trade of the colony, but make the prosperity of the farmers and the development of the country's natural resources his chief care. He created a Ministry of Agriculture and took great pains to improve the methods of that hitherto neglected industry. In place of Sprigg's extravagant scheme of railway construction he put forward a well-thought-out programme for connecting the central farming districts with their markets at small cost to the taxpayer.[1] The colony's orange groves, that were being ravaged by insect pests, he saved by the introduction of the American ladybird, and he made a beginning of the scientific fruit culture, which has since proved so profitable to the Cape, by bringing over experts from the fruit farms of California to give instruction in the best methods of fruit-growing and packing the fruit for export. He improved the breed of Cape horses by importing Arab stallions and developed the export trade of horses to India. He saved the colony's flocks and revived the wool trade by the drastic provisions of his Scab Act; and, when on a visit to Constantinople in 1894, he persuaded the Sultan to let him have some goats of the precious Angora breed to cross with the Cape stock, and so improve the quality of the goats'-hair, which the colony already exported to the value of half a million annually. The wine industry, which was being ruined by the phylloxera, gave him especial concern; for it was one of the most important in the Cape: in fact about a third of the members of the House represented vine-growing districts. American vines believed to be immune were distributed to the farmers; and Rhodes himself studied wine-culture in France and imparted to them the results of his experiences. He also tried to improve their export trade. Ever since Cobden's agreement with France and the lowering of the duties on French wines the Cape wines had lost their market in England. To redress the balance Rhodes enlisted the support of Gilbey, the wine importer, and tried to persuade Harcourt to give a preference to colonial wines, both Cape and Australian. But Harcourt, though sympathetic with his difficulties, gave no hope of acceding to his request: he could not afford the loss to the budget, or the risk of antagonizing France, and saw no prospect of a *quid pro quo* in any modification to England's interest of the high Australian tariff. Rhodes for his part had no fear of protection for farmers. He objected to bolstering up "bastard industries," as he called them, not suited to the country, and refused to consider tariffs such as Australia

[1] Instead of Sprigg's seven or eight millions the three railways he proposed in 1895 were to cost the taxpayer only £700,000.

had adopted for this purpose. But tariffs to make the country self-supporting and to encourage farming seemed to him perfectly legitimate. It was a policy, too, that exactly suited the wishes of his Bond supporters.

But with all his desire to carry the Bond with him he never compromised on questions of principle. The Scab Act, which took up most of the 1894 session, introduced a system of compulsory isolation for flocks infected with scab, especially obnoxious to the independent Boer farmers. But Rhodes saw that it must be insisted on, if the wool industry was to be saved, and though he made many concessions on details he stuck to his compulsory clauses and carried them. On education also he had strong views, which often ran counter to accepted views in South Africa and gave him some trouble with the Bond. The university system in the Cape was very defective, with its isolated colleges for Dutchmen and Englishmen and a purely examining body to grant degrees. The racial question was the chief obstacle to reform; for the Dutchmen clung to their special college at Stellenbosch and dreaded amalgamation. Rhodes's project was to create a real teaching and degree-giving university at Cape Town, drawing its students from both races and from all states or colonies of South Africa: the advantage of such an institution would, he believed, be far-reaching, not least when the students returned to their homes, "tied to one another by the strongest feelings that can be created, because the period in your life when you indulge in friendships which are seldom broken is from the age of eighteen to twenty-one; and they would go forth into all parts of South Africa prepared to make the country; and in their hands this great question of union could safely be left." In this instance vested rights and racial feeling proved too strong for him; and, though he gave and collected large sums for the scheme, he did not live to see it fulfilled. He was more successful in introducing a welcome change from the arid system of judging men's work purely by examination results. When a mining school was opened at Kimberley, he and Beit offered scholarships for students there, and he insisted that the course should include practical experience in the mines. "I am entirely sick," he said, "of these theoretical things, which end in a flourish of trumpets. I want this mining-school to be such that when a lad has been there he will go home, not simply with a piece of paper in his pocket, but with an offer from a manager of a mine for a good situation." He was equally determined to allow no political influences to interfere with the proper administration of the public education. On a vacancy for the post of superintendent-general he chose the best man he could obtain from Scotland, and, when urged by the Bond to appoint an unsuitable candidate of their own, replied, "I would rather throw up my position than let a man, whom I do not think qualified, educate the young, however much I may be urged by local people."

Even in his dealings with the Transvaal, Rhodes, helped partly by Kruger's foolish policy on railway and tariff questions, partly by his own skill in diplomacy, was gradually bringing the Bond to his view that the Cape must be the dominant state in South Africa. He had persuaded the Bond to cry "hands off" to the Transvaal and pledged them to his own policy in Rhodesia, and, when Sprigg, Laing and O'Reilly attacked him for his dual position in the Cape and Rhodesia, he found his warmest supporters among their members. Hofmeyr went so far as to declare that, though "he had hoped that the North could be developed in the old Boer fashion, this was proved impossible before the Charter. If a man such as the Premier had not started the Company, the country would have been colonized in a manner very different from what they would like. They should not, therefore, place difficulties in the Company's way. If the interests of the Company and the Colony clashed, the Premier would retire from the Government, and he was right in this." Where Sprigg had failed he succeeded in obtaining from the Free State in 1891 the long desired permission to extend the Cape railway through Bloemfontein to the Vaal, and in the following year, by means of Sivewright, overcame Kruger's long-rooted objection to the further extension to Johannesburg and Pretoria. As for Kruger, by his prohibitive tariffs on Cape wine, brandy, cattle, corn, fruit and butter he was driving the

Dutch farmers of the Cape to look to Rhodes rather than himself as their chief ally. Rhodes even played the moderating part when the Bond members raised their voice in angry protest against these tariffs. "Do not let us lose our tempers," he said, "but maintain a statesmanlike and dignified attitude"; and he assured them that, if they would but have patience, Kruger was bound ultimately to yield.

II

In certain quarters, where Rhodes's "Imperial factor" speech had not been forgotten, this strait alliance with the Bond was looked on with some misgivings. *The Times*, converted to a belief in Rhodes's good intentions by the Charter policy, was still afraid that he might be a dupe. "Mr. Rhodes," it stated, "continually asserts his belief that it will be a British union within the Empire. Mr. Hofmeyr intends that it shall be a Dutch union outside the Empire . . . he is the older, perhaps the cooler, certainly the more experienced of the two. He has been giving points ever since Mr. Rhodes's return from England. . . . He asks for the equivalent now." But Rhodes was certainly not the dupe. He was even gradually weaning the Bond from its provincialism and converting it, with the other Cape Colonists, to take an interest in the wider questions for which he chiefly cared. In fact, he found a good ally for this policy in Hofmeyr, always a cautious and enlightened supporter of the Imperial connection. But where Hofmeyr worked with delicate insinuations Rhodes played his part with dramatic directness. Previous Prime Ministers had sometimes had occasion to make respectful representations to the Colonial Office on the colony's affairs, none before Rhodes had ventured, with the almost unanimous approval of his fellow-colonists, to assert the right of interfering in the general concerns of the Empire. He had not been in office a fortnight before he brought up for the consideration of the House the treaty just signed by Lord Salisbury with Germany for settling African boundary questions,[1] and carried what was virtually a vote of censure on the Home Government

[1] See Chap. XII. pp. 166-7.

for signing such a treaty without consulting the Cape. He claimed by this resolution that, as the "dominant state in South Africa," the Cape was entitled to a voice in any future agreement concerning territory south of the Zambesi, and supported it by a reference to his own successful stratagem in forcing the hands of the Government by the creation of Forts Fife and Abercorn: "I obtained," he said, "an arrangement of boundaries, which seemed almost impossible, but which showed what could be done by making one's voice heard." He set a new precedent, which pleased the Dutch, in proposing that the House should send a vote of condolence to the Queen of Holland on her husband's death. He even undertook to purchase for the colony a large tract of territory from a foreign power. In 1891 the Portuguese were in difficulties owing to the claim of an American, M'Murdo, for compensation for the forcible seizure of a railway he had constructed from Delagoa Bay to the Transvaal border. Kruger was especially interested in this railway, as it was the link which was to connect his own line from Pretoria with the port at Delagoa Bay; and he hoped, when his own line was completed, to have the whip hand of the Cape by controlling a shorter railway connected with a nearer port than Cape Town or Port Elizabeth for the Johannesburg traffic. Rhodes, however, in 1891 conceived the ambitious idea of buying up the whole province of Lourenço Marques from Portugal on behalf of the Cape, which would have put this railway and all the cards in his own hands. The Portuguese finances were not then in a flourishing condition and it was hoped that the price might prove a temptation. Mr. Maguire, Sivewright and other agents carried on the negotiations for several years, and it was no doubt with these negotiations in his mind that, when he saw Kruger in 1891, Rhodes suggested to him that an arrangement might be made between them about Delagoa Bay.[1] Ultimately, however, the Portuguese, whose national pride was engaged in retaining their ancient possession, definitely refused all offers.

Still more remarkable was his attempt to establish

[1] See above, Chap. XI. p. 155, and cp. Michell ii. 94.

direct relations between the self-governing colonies without the intervention of the Colonial Office. In May 1891 he addressed private letters to Sir Henry Parkes and Sir John Macdonald, the Prime Ministers of New South Wales and Canada, suggesting that they should all three agree on a common fiscal policy. Writing to Macdonald he congratulates him on the result of the Canadian elections, which had turned on the question whether fiscal relations should be made closer with the United States or the Mother Country, and then goes on, " between us we must invent some tie with our Mother Country that will prevent separation . . . a practical one, for future generations will not be born in England. The curse is that English politicians cannot see the future." In a postscript he modestly explains : " You might not know who I am, so I will say I am the Prime Minister of this Colony—that is Cape Colony," and expresses a wish to meet him " before stern fate claims us." This wish remained unfulfilled, for Macdonald died before the letter reached him. But it bore fruit. In the following year the High Commissioner for Canada sent him, " as one desirous of the unity of the Empire," the resolution of the Canadian Parliament in favour of colonial preference, and invited him to pass a similar resolution at the Cape ; and four years later Rhodes met Macdonald's successor in London and tried to arrange a reciprocal reduction of duties on Canadian timber and Cape wines as a preliminary to a more general policy of preference. When the Canadian Government issued invitations for the inter-colonial conference at Ottawa, he accepted eagerly on behalf of the Cape, and secured the interest of the Dutch by persuading Sir Henry de Villiers and Hofmeyr to represent the colony. In his instructions to them he laid down that they were (1) to show a friendly feeling with the other colonies, (2) to discuss Imperial cable routes, (3) to obtain a measure of inter-colonial trade, (4) to consider the payment by the colonies of subsidies to the Imperial Navy. At the conference Hofmeyr served him well and gave a very practical turn to the discussion on cable routes and colonial contributions to the Navy. Always with the same idea of drawing closer the ties of kinship with the other colonies, in 1893 this most unconventional of Prime Ministers used Cape Government balances to relieve the financial depression in Australia. He bought £200,000 worth of Victoria and New South Wales stock, then standing at 82 per cent, as a cheap and safe investment and "as a public means of showing confidence in the two colonies," and easily persuaded the House to endorse his action.

"The future government of the world is a question of tariffs" was an opinion Rhodes was fond of repeating; for he had a great belief in the power of tariffs as an element in a bargain. A good illustration of his methods is his treatment of the customs at Walfisch Bay. This Cape port formed an enclave in German South West Africa and was the Germans' most convenient outlet for trade. The Cape had always waived the collection of duties there, partly for reasons of international courtesy, partly to preserve the port as an outlet for German trade, and partly, in Rhodes's time, as he admitted, for an ulterior motive. He was anxious to obtain favourable terms from the German Government for the extension of his Trans-African telegraph through their province of East Africa to Uganda and hoped by customs concessions in South-West Africa to dispose them to entertain his request. But he had no success. "Without putting on these duties at Walfisch Bay," he indignantly told the House, "I have been refused to let the telegraph go through their territory to civilize Africa." "Clap the duties on," shouted Merriman, interrupting him. "For two years," continued Rhodes, "they have refused for the most paltry reasons, they have refused to allow the telegraph to go through their East African possessions. They have refused over and over again, so that they are not entitled to the slightest consideration."

He does not seem to have been more successful in a singular attempt to influence the fiscal policy of the United States. The M'Kinley tariff recently passed in the States caused him serious apprehension for its possible effects on British trade, and in 1894 he apparently conceived the strange idea of communicating his sentiments to the President of the Senate. His letter is unfortunately not extant, but its tenor is apparent from the answer it called forth from Senator Lodge and thirty-three other senators. They turned the tables completely on their rash correspondent, for, after remarking on "the recent rather astonishing communication to the President of the Senate from the Premier of Cape Colony," they are moved by the nature of its author's business "to suggest another proper exercise of this legitimate discrimination. Since the discovery of the Kimberley diamond fields less than a quarter century ago, diamonds to the value of $175,000,000 have been imported into the United States. . . . It is estimated that the country now absorbs from a third to a half of the annual product of these South African diamond mines, which are controlled by English investors, who have limited the output, created a trust and practically control the price of the diamonds of the world." To break down these high prices and also as a lever to induce the British Government to adopt a more conciliatory attitude on the silver question then agitating the States, these senators propose a 30 per cent tax on diamonds, which would "check consumption and reduce the excessive and artificial prices for these stones which now prevail and might induce people of Cape Colony to believe that the present attitude of Great Britain in relation to silver is not only unfair and unjust but is also injurious to the interests of that colony." A very pretty Roland for Rhodes's Oliver!

Nevertheless the M'Kinley tariff made him all the more anxious to create "the practical tie" of colonial preference. He feared that, unless retaliatory measures were adopted, America's protective policy would starve England out of the world markets and reduce her industrial labourers to distress. But these very retaliatory measures would, he felt, give the Mother Country her opportunity of discriminating in favour of the natural products of her colonies and of receiving from them a preference for her manufactured articles; and so the whole Empire would be drawn closer together by trade interests. To the Dutch farmer this policy offered an immediate advantage in better prices on the English market for wool and wine and a prospect even for wheat. But to Harcourt and most of the English statesmen of the time the prospect was not so attractive.

Harcourt bluntly called Rhodes a protectionist, much to his indignation, for like all tariff-reformers he was convinced that he and his school alone possessed the true secret of free trade. He was not a very clear thinker and in his anxiety to relieve the English industrial labourer, forgot that a preference to colonial products would imply higher prices for all foodstuffs and raw material, and raise the price of living and the cost of manufacture in England. However, it must be admitted that he was so convinced of his case that he was willing to give where he did not receive. When he was negotiating with the Colonial Office for the settlement after the Matabele War, he tried to get a preference clause into the new constitution so framed that, without any return from England, it should be impossible to increase the existing low tariff on British imports into Rhodesia or to put any duty at all on goods sent from states in the South African Customs Union. The provision was harmless enough and in no way violated the principles of free trade, but Harcourt and his colleagues rejected it on the ground that it might interfere with the treaty rights of other powers. In the Cape Parliament the Cape farmers expressed bitter disappointment at the loss of free trade with Rhodesia and were pacified by Rhodes, as best he could, by the promise not to let the question rest. Four years later he had better success with Lord Salisbury's Government and had the clause inserted in the Rhodesian Constitution.

By his vehement methods of asserting Cape Colony's solidarity with other parts of the Empire Rhodes succeeded, to a greater extent even than Macdonald in Canada, in demonstrating the practical possibility of a closer union between England and her colonies. Men like Seeley, Sir George Grey, Dilke and Stead had long been preaching this doctrine; what was needed to make it a living force was proof that the Mother Country would not thereby increase her heavy responsibilities or the colonies lose their precious independence in internal affairs. Macdonald afforded this proof for Canada and Rhodes for South Africa. Before he came into public life complete independence or humiliating dependence on the changing policy of Downing Street seemed the only alternatives for the Cape. Out of office he jealously upheld the principle of complete liberty for internal concerns coupled with the British flag for defence, and during his five years as Prime Minister converted it into an axiom in the relations between the Colonial and Home Governments.

III

Rhodes's internal administration is hardly less memorable than his external policy. When he took office in 1890 the Colony was passing through a severe financial crisis: one of the principal banks had suspended payment, money was hard to get and even as late as 1892 a Cape loan could not be raised in London on better terms than 93 per cent. But between them Merriman, by his economies in the public service and his knowledge of finance, and Rhodes, by the confidence he inspired in the City as well as in South Africa, soon restored the credit of the colony. A Bank Act was passed imposing salutary restrictions on the issue of notes, and, owing chiefly to his predecessor Merriman's good management, Sprigg, in introducing the budget of 1894, was able to say that the Cape loan was quoted at 107 per cent, and that the credit of the colony was never so high.

Except for the Scab Act already described, Rhodes's principal measures, the Franchise and Ballot Act, the annexation of Pondoland and the Glen Grey Act, all bore more or less directly on the native question. When he introduced the last of these measures, which involved a considerable change in native administration, Merriman accused him of having hastily concocted the Bill during "a scamper through the Transkei," the chief native preserve. The charge, as Rhodes pointed out, was most unjust, for he had been dealing with natives for twenty years, and for the last ten years had more natives under his control than any other man in South Africa. Alone on the cotton plantation of the Umkomaas he had begun to study the ways of raw natives and continued doing so in the early days of Kimberley; in Basutoland and Bechuanaland he had been brought into touch with their chiefs and the domestic concerns of independent native states. In the De Beers compounds he was responsible for over 10,000 natives, and in Southern Rhodesia alone he was the virtual ruler of nearly 300,000. He had a right to speak on native questions, for he brought to these responsibilities great sympathy with the natives and a peculiar gift, also possessed by his brother Herbert, for attracting and attaching black men to himself. His own personal attendants were devoted to him, and Tony, his well-known factotum, was looked on more as a trusted companion than a menial. Wherever he went he made friends with the natives and had an uncommon gift for always recognizing those he had once spoken to. In his first journey through Mashonaland he had in his train a small native boy, " Pikenin," who very soon disappeared from the party: five years later, once more travelling through the country, he saw the same boy washing clothes in a stream. " Ah, Pikenin, is that you ? " he said at once, and offered to take him to Cape Town, where for many years he lived happily in Rhodes's household. At Kimberley he loved to saunter round the compounds, chaffing the natives, settling their little troubles and learning all about their tribal customs. But though sympathetic he never allowed a native to take a liberty with him and was very impatient of any sign of truckling to natives in others. He once related how he shocked the Imperial commissioner at the capital of Lerothodi, paramount chief of the Basutos, by his straight talk with that chief for harbouring a native malefactor: " Why do you keep that murderer in your country ? " he asked, " you ought to be ashamed of it. I am very sorry I have nothing to do with it, or I should keep you till you give the murderer up " ; and yet in telling the story he showed an unexpected touch of sympathy with the malefactor: " Who wandered about, prepared to murder everybody. I believe he leads a most unhappy life." He always felt that the treatment of the natives, watched, as he said, " not only here but at home," was as difficult as any question arising in South African politics, and accordingly laid down a rule that the Ministry of native affairs should be associated with the office of Prime Minister. He took pleasure in the title "father to the natives" which this association brought him, and rejoiced that the additional charge of one and a half million Cape natives to his responsibilities in Rhodesia and at Kimberley would enable him to "follow one train of thought" in formulating a policy. For he was convinced that no greater mistake could be made than to look at native policy from a local instead of a South African standpoint: the question of union was involved in the right solution, and even the survival of the Europeans. Appreciating the difficulties, as he did, he was modest in his appeal for confidence. "I have no native policy," he admitted at the outset, "I could not afford to say I have. I am a beginner at these things. . . Still, give me a trial, as I hope to do it well."

The Cape system, as he found it, differed from that of the other states in making no political distinction between natives and Europeans. The franchise for both, on a basis of a £25 yearly occupation, had been hardly altered since 1853, when the Colonial Secretary, Newcastle, refused to impose any restrictions, "in order that all the Queen's subjects at the Cape, without distinction of class or colour, should be united by one bond of loyalty and a common interest." At first, when the proportion of natives in the colony was little more than two to one, and the few qualified natives rarely voted, the practical objections to this provision were negligible: but it was very different in 1891 when the natives, by enlargement of territory and their greater productivity, had increased fourfold and the whites only twofold; and when the "blanket voters," as they were called, had already the deciding voice in certain constituencies. On the other hand in Natal, where the natives were as ten to one of the whites, the franchise law had been so contrived that only thirteen were on the voting roll; in the Transvaal and the Free State they had no franchise and in the Transvaal were expressly excluded from equal rights in Church or State. Though the Cape colonists in 1853 had generally opposed the equal franchise to the natives, since then a considerable body of public opinion had grown up in its favour on the ground that it was the best means of educating the natives and preserving them from oppression; and some of the most enlightened men in Cape politics, Saul Solomon and his relations, Innes, Merriman, Sauer and the Schreiners, upheld this view. Rhodes was of the contrary opinion. He was convinced that any attempt to unite South Africa would break down on the snag of the Cape native franchise, which the other states would never admit; and union was to him always a paramount consideration. "We have lived in the past," he said in his younger days, "under what might be called the mists of Table Mountain, and the policy of the House has been drifting like the clouds that sail round it. . . . We must adopt a system of Indian despotism in our relations with the barbarians of South Africa, so that by means of it there may be a possibility of creating a United South Africa stretching to the Zambesi," and it was no doubt such a sentiment that provoked Sir William Harcourt's sarcasm: "Mr. Rhodes is a very reasonable man. He only wants two things. Give him Protection and give him Slavery and he will be perfectly satisfied." He also firmly believed that in their own interests the natives should be treated like children. His own countrymen had won the franchise only after centuries of painful education in politics: it was absurd that natives, uneducated and barely emerging from a savage state, should have the same privilege. "It is just as if," he said, "the Lord Mayor and his Corporation were to suddenly proceed to Stonehenge and finding the Druids there discuss with them municipal legislation. It would be absurd. And the absurdity of our legislation has been that it is only within the last forty years that we found we could not put natives on the footing of the whites."

When, therefore, in 1891 Hofmeyr and the Bond urged upon him a measure which would increase the white and reduce the coloured vote, they were merely forcing an open door. But he had to tread warily, for three of his Ministers, Innes, Sauer and Merriman, were against the Bond on this question. However, their scruples were appeased by a vague resolution "to secure due weight in the future for the material and educational interests of the country," and in the following year the Franchise and Ballot Bill was introduced. The object of Rhodes and the Bond was indirectly attained by raising the occupiers' qualification to £75, by retaining the very low owners' qualification, almost entirely confined to Europeans, and by a more stringent education test. As a sop to the other members of the Ministry a provision for the ballot was introduced. In his opening speech Rhodes reviewed the electoral systems of most European countries and British colonies and pitched upon Jamaica as an example to his liking. Here, he asserted, the native franchise had led to the revolution of 1865, " when stringent measures were used by the governor, who was (as is the usual custom in such cases) recalled and disgraced": but it had afterwards been abolished with excellent results. And he did not conceal his hostility to the ballot clause in his own bill: " I object to the ballot *in toto*," he said, " because I like to know how a person votes—not, I hasten to say, for any ulterior purpose," but, as he explained, because the loafers and I.D.B. men in Kimberley, if not watched by the honest workmen, would vote in favour of " free liquor and robbery." But in spite of its foster-parent's opposition the ballot was carried with the rest of the bill. In the following year the registers showed a decrease of 3348 coloured voters and an increase of 4506 whites, and, as no existing voters were disfranchised, it became increasingly more effective for its objects.

The settlement of Pondoland was one of the first questions Rhodes was called upon to deal with when he took over the ministry of native affairs. This native state, bounded on the west by Cape Colony and on the north-east by Natal, had long been a source of trouble. Its only port, St. John's, had been annexed by the Cape, but the natives in the interior were given over to the barbarous practices of witchcraft and " smelling out " among themselves and made themselves a nuisance to their neighbours on each side. Rhodes's " unhappy man," Umhlonho, had murdered a border magistrate and his clerks in 1880 and was still a fugitive from justice; and cattle raids into the Cape territories were common. In 1890 Rhodes had been urged by Upington to stop the civil war provoked by Sigcau, one of their chiefs, and to put an end to the depredations of the Pondos by annexing their country: the Home Government, he said, would readily consent as Rhodes had so many friends on both sides of the House of Commons. But Rhodes was not to be hurried by the Irishman's blarney into taking over the care of 200,000 more natives without full consideration. In 1893, however, his hand was forced. Sir Henry Loch was treated with studied insolence by Sigcau during a tour in his territory and the chief's other neighbour, Natal, was showing a disposition to annex the country on her own account. Natal had only recently acquired a responsible Government and was hardly yet aware of her own limitations: at any rate Rhodes flared up at such presumption and determined to castigate it. On his return from the Matabele War he went for his "scamper through the Transkei," travelling in great state with eight cream-coloured horses and making a great impression on the population. The son of a Transkei magistrate, then a boy of five, still remembers the awe with which he beheld the big, broad man, who said to him: "My boy, I'll send you to Oxford," and the effort it cost him to retort "No, you won't." At Kokstad on the borders of Pondoland he was welcomed by the local magnates, but got rid of them and went off to lie on the hillside by himself, muttering, as he beheld the beauty of the place, "Oh how I wish they would let me alone—let me stay here." But he had to come down to the banquet at night, where he sat listless and bored till a local orator began to attack the Cape Government and expressed a wish for Natal to annex the country. At that he woke up to some purpose and launched out into a violent tirade against Natal, speaking of its parliament as a parochial assembly and sneering at its wretched financial state and its tiny white population. This savage attack on gallant little Natal illustrates Rhodes's inability sometimes to see beyond his immediate object. He defended it in the Cape House on the plea that it was necessary to make their neighbours realize the position. But he might have attained this object by less provocative language. It did him harm, for though the Natal people might have stood the reproof from Rhodes, they were maddened when Sprigg followed it up by a truculent reminder, "We are the big bear and you are the little bear"; and it antagonized Escombe, Natal's best statesman, from whom Rhodes was then hoping for support in proposals of union.

From Kokstad, though warned of the risk, he went into Pondoland. He announced to some minor chiefs that their country was to be annexed, then summoned Sigcau to attend him and kept him waiting three days, the exact period the chief had kept Sir Henry Loch waiting, before granting him an interview. He told him plainly that he and his Pondos were unfit to govern themselves, and then took him for a walk towards a mealie field, on which some machine-guns had been trained; at a given signal the guns opened fire and laid low the mealie crop; "and that is what will happen to you and your tribe," grimly remarked Rhodes, "if you give us any further trouble." But he took no risks and ensured the ready submission of the Pondos by a sufficient display of force. Never, said one of the magistrates appointed to take over the country, had he met so satisfactory a Minister: there was no red tape, and he had only to speak or write a word to Rhodes to get every reasonable request complied with at once. And though stern he was fair to the natives, and saved them from the depredations of concession hunters by refusing to recognize any grants previously made that did not appear just and equitable.

With further experience of native problems and increased opportunities for "following out one train of thought," Rhodes gradually shed his juvenile ideas of "oriental despotism" and saw that a more constructive policy was needed than a mere restriction of the franchise. He came to the conclusion that the privileges and higher civilization of the Europeans imposed upon them responsibilities to the natives, "those children, just emerging from barbarism," and an obligation to help them to a better use of their "human minds." "If you are really one who loves the natives," he said at Queenstown, "you must make them worthy of the country they live in, or else they are certain, by an inexorable law, to lose their country. You will certainly not make them worthy . . . if you allow them to sit in idleness and if you do not train them in the arts of civilization." Not that he believed in the Board school form of education too often given by well-meaning missionaries, which at best produced natives fit only to be Kaffir parsons or newspaper editors, both objects of his intense dislike, instead of helping them to use their capacities to the best advantage; but he heartily approved of the training in manual crafts provided at Lovedale, as an incentive to work instead of loafing. Speaking of the native loafer, he described his life as "very similar to that of the young man about town, who lounges about the club during the day and dresses himself for a tea-party in the afternoon, and in the evening drinks too much, and probably finishes up with immorality. . . . They are a nuisance to every district in the Transkei, to every magistrate in the Transkei, and to every location. We want to get hold of these young men and make them go out to work." To do him justice, Rhodes would have been quite as ready to force the English loafer and young man about town to work as the native loafer; and it was an absurd travesty of the truth for an English paper to describe him as "an English-speaking Dutch Boer, thirsting for slavery," because he wanted to encourage work among the natives. The natives then must be taught to work, but on lines of their own; and these lines were best found when they were not contaminated by too close contact with Europeans, but segregated in districts of their own. The natives in their undeveloped stage were readier to imitate the vices of Europeans than their virtues, and were especially subject to temptation from the liquor bars and canteens that Europeans always brought with them. But in native reserves it was possible to exclude the drink traffic altogether, as Khama, the enlightened chief of the Bamangwato, had done. For these reasons Rhodes decided to keep the natives as much apart from the whites as possible. But in their reserves they were to have every inducement to improve themselves. He had a great belief in the virtues of landed property as an aid to self-respect, so he set himself to introduce it gradually as a substitute for the communal tenure, which left the villagers too much at the mercy of their head-man and gave them little incentive to industry; and also in the educative value of self-government in local matters suited to their apprehension. "The natives know nothing of the politics of the country," he declared; "they have told me time after time that they do not understand these politics. 'Leave us alone, but let us try and deal with some of our little local questions.' That is the common statement they have made to me." So in their reserves the natives were not to have the colonial franchise, but as a set off were to elect representatives with a power of taxation for the purposes of education, road and bridge-making, plantations and other needs of the district. This policy, to which he had come after he had been Prime Minister four years, was a great advance on his previous utterances. But even here the development of his ideas did not cease. Within a few years he was proclaiming "equal rights for all civilized men, irrespective of races, south of the Zambesi," his final creed, when he had purged himself of all colour-prejudice and attached importance only to capacity and intrinsic worth.

These four principles, then: work, segregation in native reserves, individual property and local self-government, were embodied in the famous Glen Grey Bill, presented to the Cape Parliament late in the session of 1894. It was so called from the district near Queenstown, to which its provisions were in the first instance to be tentatively applied. "As a gentle stimulus to these people to make them go on working," a labour tax of 10s. was imposed on all male natives not in possession of landed property, who had not worked outside the district during the year; no Europeans were allowed to settle in the district; village management boards were to assign plots of eight or nine acres apiece to individual owners; and besides these village boards, district councils and a general native council of the Transkei were to manage local affairs and levy rates in their respective spheres. Rhodes introduced the Bill in a discursive speech, more illustrative of the workings of his own mind than of the details of the Bill, and then arbitrarily rushed it through the House with hardly any time for serious discussion. Immediately the second reading was carried the committee stage was begun; and after a debate of three and a half hours on one clause he said, "I have made up my mind for a night of it," and insisted on sitting till the Bill was through committee next morning. No essential injustice was done, for he had previously secured the assent of Hofmeyr and his followers to the Bill, and the chief advocates of native rights, Merriman, Sauer and Innes found no great objection to its principle; while the second and third readings were carried by overwhelming majorities.

The only provision which aroused much criticism from the advocates of the natives was the labour tax of 10s. It was resented as a badge of servitude, and was noted as singularly convenient to the interests of the Cape farmer or the mine manager, always at their wits' end to obtain enough native labour. Rhodes replied to his critics on this point with a humorous rejoinder to Sir William Harcourt's sarcasm about his fondness for slavery: "I was much more of a slave," he declared, "than any of those natives could easily be . . . for nine mortal years of my life; and it was compulsory slavery too. . . . Six years at school I had to work five hours during the day and prepare work for the next day for three hours in the evening, while at college I was compounded in the evenings and not allowed out after 9 o'clock." This pathetic picture of Rhodes, a slave at Oxford, was unkindly marred by Innes's quick interjection: "And you never went out, I suppose?" and was hardly a serious argument. The gravamen of the charge against the clause was not that it acted as an inducement to labour, but that it compelled the natives to work for white men, whereas the "poor whites," equally in need of a stimulus, were under no such compulsion. In practice the clause, which was objected to as much by Europeans most anxious to raise the natives' standard of work as by the natives themselves, very soon became a dead letter, and eleven years later was formally repealed. But the other, more important, provisions of the Bill were an unqualified success. New reserves were within a very short time added to the Glen Grey district for the purposes of native land tenure and local government; and the Act was twice amended and amplified. The natives entered into the spirit of ownership and took up plots eagerly: only three years after the passing of the Act 7088 of these plots had been surveyed and 6576 taken up, and £15,000 had been collected from natives in survey fees. Even without the stimulus of the labour tax the young men's inclination to work increased with the removal of temptations to liquor and improved educational facilities, and with their greater appreciation of necessities and luxuries to be obtained only by the earnings of labour. The native councils worked well. Thirteen years later the Transkei General Council was raising rates to the tune of £46,750, more than half of which was devoted to education and £12,700 to road improvement. The Superintendent-General for Education reported that "in those districts where the Glen Grey Act has been proclaimed, better teachers are got, schools are in better condition generally, and the people take a good deal more interest in education"; and a Select Committee of the Cape House stated in 1903 that "the operations of the Act have been, as they were intended to be, most beneficial to the natives concerned. Individual tenure and local self-government have done much, and will in the future do more, to lead the aboriginal natives in the path of improvement."

In a speech delivered at Queenstown soon after the passage of the Glen Grey Act Rhodes reviewed, with some natural pride, the achievements of his two Ministries. The settlement of the franchise question, long an apple of discord in Cape politics, the Scab Act, the completion of railway connections in the colony and the extension of the trunk system to the Transvaal border, the annexation of Pondoland and the Glen Grey Act: these were the measures for which he took chief credit. It was due to luck, no doubt, that the annexation passed off so well, but, as he said, recalling the story of the man who always backed Fred Archer, "It is good to have a Minister with luck." But the Glen Grey Act was his favourite child.

" We are prepared to stand or fall by it : it is worth fighting and worth falling by," and he added, " if the Glen Grey policy is a success, we shall see neighbouring states adopting it. . . . I hope we shall have one native policy in South Africa." Here was the secret of his affection for it, for during four patient years he had done all he could, except when he lost his temper at Kokstad, to improve relations with the neighbouring states and colonies, with the one cherished object of bringing them into closer federation for common purposes. With this note of union he concluded his speech : " I have a greater and bigger idea—and that is by steady work, which I take delight in, by keeping an object in view and at the same time not hurting the independence of neighbouring republics—to work with one broad and big idea, and that is the union of South Africa."

NOTE TO CHAPTER XIII

[See above, p. 187]

Correspondence between Sir Henry de Villiers and Rhodes on the formation of the Ministry in 1893.

CAPE TOWN,
5th May 1893.

MY DEAR RHODES—I am somewhat puzzled by your note of yesterday's date saying that you had found my condition impossible to carry out—for the only condition mentioned in our interviews was that you undertook to be unofficial member of any Ministry I should form. Let me very briefly recall the occurrences of the past week while they are fresh in our memories. On Friday morning you called on me at Sauer's request to consult me about some matter of professional etiquette which had arisen in his unfortunate dispute with Sivewright. After I had given my view we discussed the political situation and incidentally I let fall the remark that, after twenty years' service as Chief Justice, I had a strong inclination to re-enter political life in view of the important questions that may crop up in the near future. After a few moments' consideration you said that the best solution of the crisis would be that I should form a Ministry, you undertaking to be an unofficial member. You pointed out how undesirable it was that the Premier should be so frequently absent as you would be bound to be. This took me by surprise, but you asked me seriously to consider the matter and meet you again. That evening you called at my residence and we discussed the probable names of the Ministry I should form. On Saturday evening you again called, and we agreed upon the names of Sprigg, Schreiner and Faure in addition to yours and mine. Coming to Sauer's name we agreed that if he should not take office Laing would be suitable. The doubt in regard to Sauer arose from the fact that he had been a party to the dispute which was wrecking the Ministry. You offered to call again on the Sunday morning before riding to town to see Hofmeyr, but I said that I would meet you at your residence and ride with you some distance. When we met I handed you a letter agreeing to the Ministry as previously arranged except that Sprigg's name was doubtful instead of Sauer's. We both thought that one might not wish to sit with the other. I told you that I had worked with Sprigg in the struggle for Responsible Government and believed that I could again work with him, my only objection being that he had once landed us in the Basutoland War. As to Sauer I was in the difficulty that you had asked me not to divulge to him what had occurred, and I felt that it might savour of treachery if I took advantage of the interview suggested by him by taking office. In the course of our ride we had a long and, as I thought, satisfactory conversation about the political situation. I told you that my sole aim was to advance the good of the country and that my political sympathies were with Hofmeyr, whose object I thought to be to give his countrymen that voice in the government of the country which Responsible Government was intended to give. If I could have seen Sauer that day the whole matter would have been settled, but I was bound by my promise to you. The same evening (Sunday) you called again and shewed me a memo containing the objections against Sauer being included. Some of these objections I could not agree with—but I fully realised the force of most of them. I agreed that if I were to form a Ministry at all it would have to be without Sauer. I therefore said that my decision was not to undertake the task. You seemed disappointed and asked me not to give a final decision until the following day (Monday). I said as things stood it seemed impossible for me to carry out the plan, but on leaving, you said you would not take my decision as final unless I adhered to it on Monday, when you would meet me at the Legislative Council at 1.30. To this I consented. After you left I gave the whole matter the fullest consideration and decided that it would be impossible under the circumstances to include Sauer and that I would ask your consent to explain the position to him, feeling sure that he would fully appreciate it. I prepared my address to the electors and made every other preparation for the change. On Monday morning I thought of seeing you before going to town, but could not do so owing to the rain, but I sent a note to you asking you to request Hofmeyr (whom you were going to see) to meet me at the interview. My object was to explain to him personally the general lines of policy which I thought desirable. Immediately on my arrival in town I sent for Mr. Schreiner, as I felt it a necessity to consult some one on the situation, for I had stood perfectly alone up to that time. As he was not engaged in politics and I had perfect confidence in his discretion, I thought him the most suitable person to consult. I had only a few minutes to spare before the sitting of the Court and informed him of the whole situation. I had to be very guarded with him as I could not make a definite offer until 1.30, but I put it to him hypothetically whether, in case I should form a Ministry, he would take office under me as Attorney-General, and he said he would. He was perfectly candid with me and said that he could not have taken the office if it involved opposition to Sir Gordon Sprigg, with whom he had been in confidential relations. He gave me other information which satisfied me that I was doing the right thing in deciding to take office. While in Court that morning, I received a note from you saying that as Hofmeyr had gone to Somerset West for the day you could not see him and that you thought it best to see me after seeing him. Monday and Tuesday passed without my hearing more from you. On Tuesday evening Sauer called and, strangely enough, gave me a vague message from you that Hofmeyr had not returned and that you would see me later on. He told me that the Ministry had resigned but that he knew nothing more. As your message confirmed me in the view that you and I were still to meet for my final decision, I took the opportunity of asking Sauer what his position would be if I formed a Ministry *excluding* him. He said he well knew that I could not be guilty of treachery against him and that any Ministry I might form, even if it included Sprigg, would have his support. My mind was relieved and I felt that at our postponed interview a final arrangement could be arrived at. On the following morning (Wednesday), I saw in the papers that you were forming a Ministry, and when in Court that day I received the note to which I referred at the outset of this letter. On the following day I saw it announced that the same Ministry had been formed which we had provisionally agreed upon, except that the name of Frost was substituted for mine. I do not know nor am I entitled to know what induced you to change your mind on the Monday or Tuesday, but I regret that even if you thought there was some condition in the matter you did not allow me to meet you at the appointed time to give you my final decision as agreed. I was kept in suspense from Monday morning to Wednesday morning waiting for the interview which never came off. I do not write all this by way of reproach but merely to explain to you my own position. In the nature of things I could not take advice from any one, and my fear was that I might be acting unworthily towards Sauer at whose request you first interviewed me. On Monday morning I had a clear course of action before me, and if we had met at the appointed time (Hofmeyr's presence being of course not essential) everything would have been arranged, provided of course you had not changed your mind. The task you proposed to me was not sought for, and it was only a sense of duty which induced me to consent to undertake it in case His Excellency the Governor should have asked me to do so.—Believe me, yours sincerely, J. H. de Villiers.

Friday.

My dear Chief Justice—I have carefully read your letter. I left you on Monday with the belief that as far as you were concerned you would not form without one of the old Ministers possessed of Administrative training, and the one you desired was Sauer. I said I would come again on Monday as I was desirous to see Hofmeyr and consider if such a course was possible. I found on Monday morning that Hofmeyr was away. I had also had full time to consider the question, and I had personally come to the conclusion that it would be impossible for me to be a Minister of a new Ministry if one of the old Ministers between whom differences had occurred became a member of the new Ministry, but I thought I would see Hofmeyr and ask his advice on his return. He fully agreed with me, and I felt therefore in view of your decision on Sunday evening it was hopeless to ask you to reconsider your decision, in fact your answer had been so emphatic I did not expect you to do so. I had asked to see you again in order to consider very carefully whether your condition was possible in any way to carry out.—Yours truly, C. J. RHODES.

CHAPTER XIV

GROOTE SCHUUR AND THE BURLINGTON

AFTER he left the Hertfordshire vicarage at the age of seventeen, Rhodes never knew what it was to have a real home of his own or, except perhaps when he rode alone on the veld with the bush-boy by his side, to enjoy true privacy. Dwelling-places he had many, but each of them, to his mind,

> Was but a Tent where takes his one day's rest
> A Sultán to the realm of Death addrest.

Until he took office as Prime Minister he had never troubled himself about his personal comforts or the kind of house he dwelt in. At Kimberley he shared rooms with a friend or two, at Cape Town during the session he was content with a noisy lodging in Adderley Street, and took his meals at the club or an hotel ; his tastes were simple, and he had no time or inclination for such an establishment as his wealth could command. But when he became Prime Minister he felt it incumbent on him to live in a style more befitting the dignity of his position as head of the dominant state in South Africa. He soon found a house to his purpose.

At Rondebosch, on the outskirts of Cape Town, the Dutch East India Company had three barns or store-houses, De Groote, De Kleine and De Oude Schuur, in a hollow at the foot of the Mountain ; here they stored their tithes and the grain, wood, skins, wine and other necessaries for the Cape community and for revictualling East Indiamen that called at Table Bay on the voyage to or from Batavia. These store-houses had houses attached to them for the accommodation of the official store-keepers, persons of some importance in the Government, the chief of them being the

Opper-baas van de Schuur, who lived at Groote Schuur:[1] the last Opper-baas to live there was an ancestor of Jan Hofmeyr, who lies buried in the grounds. In the middle of the eighteenth century the Company sold the houses and grounds to private owners. The Groote Schuur house passed through several hands, suffering some disfiguring alterations in the process, and in recent years had been occasionally let to English governors as a summer residence. In 1891 it was in the possession of Mrs. van der Byl, who had re-named it The Grange. In that year Rhodes leased it, and two years later bought the freehold. He also acquired by degrees some 1500 acres of the neighbouring mountain and valley land; all, including the house and a small block of buildings in Cape Town, at a cost of over £60,000. On becoming its owner Rhodes restored to the house its old Dutch name of Groote Schuur, and also set about remodelling it on the lines of an old water-colour drawing he bought, which showed its appearance before the disfiguring alterations.

By good fortune, at a luncheon party in 1892, he chanced to meet Mr. Herbert Baker, a young architect who had recently come on a visit to South Africa. Baker had been wandering about the Cape Peninsula, rediscovering with joy the then nearly neglected beauty of the old Dutch farm-houses. Simple, solid, cool and spacious, they seemed almost fashioned by nature to tone in with the sunlight and clear air of the country, and were in striking contrast with the hideous and incongruous buildings of more modern days. Since the end of the Dutch Company's rule the art of good building had been fast disappearing from South Africa owing to the growing craze for cheapness and easy work. In place of the beautiful old thatched or tiled roofs, sheets of corrugated iron disfigured the landscape; instead of the local craftsmen's well-wrought metal fittings and carefully moulded doors and window-frames in the seventeenth- and eighteenth-century houses, cheap ready-made substitutes, turned out by the gross in European factories,

[1] Some account of the duties of the Opper-baas is given in *Life at the Cape in Mid-Eighteenth Century*, by O. F. Mentzel. Translated for the Van Riebeeck Society (Cape Town, 1919).

were imported. The fine hard native woods formerly fashioned into rafters or into the simple and beautiful furniture of the farmsteads were neglected for the shoddy chairs, tables and planks brought over in ship-loads. Houses were built and furnished hastily and without any regard to style or the needs of the climate. This decay in the building and furnishing arts was only a symptom of the attitude, deplored by Rhodes, of too many of the English colonists. The Dutch loved the country and intended to live and die there, and ordered their lives accordingly; many of the English came simply to seek their fortunes at the mines or as traders at the ports, and never looked on the country as a permanent home. Jerry-built houses, good to last their time in the country, did well enough for them; and unfortunately the fashion spread to the Dutch also. Baker felt all this and had a mind to see if the old art could be revived; but he was young and untried. Rhodes saw that his ideas were good, and decided to give him a trial. Bidding him come round and hear his "thoughts," he told him briefly to restore the front of Groote Schuur according to its original plan, and then left him to his own devices. The pitch of the roof had been altered by a former owner, and to avoid the danger of fire the thatch replaced by slates; by the time Rhodes came back from the Matabele War, Baker had entirely restored the front with its original gables and high-pitched roof of thatch. Rhodes said little, but told Baker to go on rebuilding the rest of the house in the old style.

Soon he began to take a deep interest in the work himself. "I want the big and simple, barbaric if you like," he would say. He had all the deal planks in the structure replaced by beams and ceilings of solid teak, and the rooms either panelled in teak or simply whitewashed. In the bathroom he had a great mottled-marble bath such as the Romans used; and the only modern note he allowed on the front of the house was a bronze plaque, by the sculptor Tweed, let in above the doorway, and representing Van Riebeeck's landing in 1652. The furnishing was of a piece. He was once shown a plain Dutch wardrobe of black South African wood, and was so taken with it that he allowed Baker to furnish the house throughout in the same style, either with old pieces discovered in Dutch farm-houses or with chairs and tables made of native timber by specially trained local craftsmen. He even went about making purchases for himself, and though at first he made some mistakes, never having thought much of such things in his busy life, he soon developed a very clear idea of his own taste, and, unlike many millionaires with a craving to form art collections, would never abdicate his own judgement. One unfortunate expert from Bond Street was brought out to help in finding old Dutch furniture, but he took too much upon himself and was soon bundled home. He refused to form a picture gallery: good pictures, he said, were too expensive for him when there were so many miles of railway to be built in Rhodesia, and there was only one, a fine example of the English school, in the dining-room at Groote Schuur. Nor did he care for small niggling objects, however valuable and beautiful. In his clean, bare, well-proportioned rooms he had a few pieces of solid furniture, some good specimens of old Dutch glass, Delft or Oriental china brought to the country in the Company's days, and one or two relics of the ancient arts of South Africa, the chief favourite being a very wise-looking stone bird, found in the Zimbabwe ruins.[1]

One of the principal rooms in the house was the library. Here again were signs of his individuality. His books were not a mere millionaire's collection of standard works, sumptuously bound, or rare editions collected without plan or personal taste, but the gleanings of his own eccentric choice. Though not a great reader—he led a too active life for that—he occasionally had great bouts of reading, especially on board ship. Then he read books likely to help him in his own schemes, mining regulations of all countries, as we have seen,[2] when he was immersed in his diamond mines; treatises on federal schemes in Canada and Australia, as Lord Grey once suggested to him, when he was revolving plans for South African union. One of his constant companions was a well-scored Marcus Aurelius, and he knew

[1] For the account of Rhodes's building at Groote Schuur and elsewhere and his artistic views, I am deeply indebted to notes kindly supplied me by Mr. Herbert Baker.

[2] See Chap. IX. p. 97.

his Bible well. Books of travel or descriptions of national customs and institutions always had a fascination for him, and generally brought grist to his mill: he once met Sir D. Mackenzie Wallace and told him that he had been reading his book on Russia with great pleasure, and derived from it some of the ideas of land tenure that he incorporated in his Glen Grey Act. He made a special hobby of everything known relating to the exploration and history of Africa, and eagerly sought out for his library old maps of the continent, accounts of the early discoverers and investigations into the tribal institutions of the natives. In 1892 he sent Mr. Wilmot, a member of the Cape legislature well known for his interest in African antiquities, to secure copies of documents in the Public Record Office and in the Vatican Library, and to buy for the library at Groote Schuur manuscripts and rare books about the early history of South Africa. Another feature of his library is the collection of type-written translations of Greek and Latin authors. This collection arose in this wise. One of his favourite authors was Gibbon: he loved him for the majesty of his conception, for his language, and still more for the connection he traced between Gibbon's account of the grandeur of Imperial Rome and his own idea of Great Britain's Imperial mission. Talking of Gibbon during a country-house visit in England, he expressed regret that his knowledge of Latin and Greek did not enable him to read all the authorities quoted in the *Decline and Fall*, and that there were no good translations available. On his host's advice he went to see if Mr. Humphreys of Hatchard's could help him to get the translations he needed, found he would undertake it, and left him a cheque on account with instructions to procure literal and complete translations of all Gibbon's authorities. Scholars were engaged to translate, typists to copy, and clerks to index the required versions, which in due time began to flow in to Groote Schuur. Rhodes perhaps hardly realized what he had let himself in for: with Suetonius and Tacitus and such like he was well pleased, but when it came to the apparently endless series of the complete works of the Fathers of the Church, from whom Gibbon quarried, he had to cry halt, and issued an order that the Fathers must cease.

Such as it is, the collection cost him some £8000, and is a freak hardly worthy of Rhodes; the money would have been much better spent in publishing for the benefit of the world some of the excellent versions of interesting works not hitherto rendered into English. But it is unfair, as some do, to judge the whole library from this piece of extravagance; for it was composed, as a library should be, of books that reflected the owner's tastes in history, travel and adventure, social questions and novels, not always the best, but those he fancied himself; and it was the room that he used most for his work and his play, and where his guests could come and browse to their liking.

In December 1896, when Rhodes had many other calamities to afflict him, the house, as restored by Baker, was burnt to the ground. Happily most of the books were saved and a few of the treasures, but most of the furniture perished and nearly all his private papers.[1] Baker was at once instructed to rebuild the house in the same style, which he faithfully did, only once more abolishing the thatch roof, owing to its inflammability, and substituting for it not slates, but beautiful tiles made in South Africa. Such as the house was then built and furnished for Rhodes's use, it now remains unaltered as the official residence of the Prime Minister of the Union.

Rhodes gave no less care to the grounds than to the house itself. He carefully preserved all their old beauties and associations and added new ones in keeping with the Mountain, the dominant feature from the back-stoep. He treasured a great avenue of trees as an approach from the road and the beautiful clumps of stone pines which give the foreground of the Mountain the look of a Turner landscape. The glen Wolvegat in the further distance, which still had its wolf-trap till the middle of the century, had recently been stripped of its splendid oak trees, but Rhodes saw that its wild growth of vines, maiden-hair, pelargonia and arum lilies was left undisturbed. He loved hydrangeas, so he

[1] For this reason the Rhodes Trustees unfortunately possess very few personal papers dating further back than 1896. There is a small bundle of half-charred papers of an earlier date labelled "Fire Papers," but it contains little of much importance.

completely filled a hollow within sight of the stoep with great masses of hydrangeas that in their season blaze with a riot of blue, purple and lilac. He was fond of birds and beasts, and tried to acclimatize rooks and singing birds from England; without success, however. He had better luck with African fauna. He made a huge enclosure in his park, in which buck, zebras, ostriches and other wild animals were allowed to roam as they pleased. He also kept some lions in a cage, meaning some day to build a lordly edifice with portico and marble courts to fit the dignity of the king of beasts: this he never accomplished, but he and the poet Kipling got much enjoyment from the lion-cub, Sullivan, until he became too stout to be a safe plaything for children or to be able to escape through the bars of the elder lions' house. But before all he thought of the view of his beloved Mountain. He bought up the interests of water companies in order to be able to remove their hideous reservoir from the summit of its ridge. He cut down trees here, planted new and rare ones there, always with a view to big effects and to enhance the majesty of its aspect; for in planning grounds he had what Chatham called "the prophetic eye of taste." He made roads and paths to give access to the finest views on the Mountain, and would sit by the hour on the stoep watching the mists roll over it or the changing light playing upon its peaks and kloofs. But his favourite spot for musing by himself or with a chosen friend was on a buttressed ledge, whence he could see both the Atlantic and the Indian Ocean. Here now stands Watts's Physical Energy, with the stately lion portico that commemorates the vigilant watcher.

His grounds were thus made beautiful, not for a morose and solitary pleasure, but that all his fellow-citizens might have enjoyment. Always open to the public, they were crowded on Saturday afternoons and Sundays by holiday-makers, who came from Cape Town to picnic and wander about. There were no rules or warnings against trespassers, and even when a party strayed on to the stoep where he was sitting, the only request he made of them was not to light a fire there. He refused to close the grounds when the depredations in the flower-beds became too flagrant, and when they were shut by a cautious overseer on a scare of rinderpest, he ordered them to be reopened immediately. He always treated his property on the slopes of the Mountain not as a personal possession, but as a public trust. "I love," as he said, speaking of the road he had made through his grounds and continued right round the Mountain, "I love to think that human beings will walk that road long after I am gone."

His house, too, though he could not make it quite so public as his grounds, he looked on less as a personal home than as a fitting frame for the hospitality he dispensed with regal lavishness. Toward the end of his life, when he was ailing and obsessed with the idea that his money would not go far enough for all his public objects, he was inclined to worry over the expenditure on Groote Schuur, which, without food, came to over £400 a month for upkeep and wages alone; but such considerations troubled him little before the Raid. He was still content for himself with a shanty at Kimberley or a tent on the Rhodesian plains to live in; but at all times he enjoyed a good table and good wines, which he needed to support his large frame and vast energy. He never ate or drank to excess and could, if necessary, put up with privations as well as any man; but, whenever it was possible, whether on the veld or in town, he was particular that the fare should be abundant and good, both for himself and for his guests. At Groote Schuur he kept almost open house. His colleagues in Parliament would often drop in for lunch and a talk, especially tried allies like Hofmeyr, Fuller, who wrote some charming reminiscences of him, and, during his first Ministry, Sauer and Merriman; old Kimberley and Johannesburg friends passing through Cape Town were always sure of a welcome, and so were Dutch farmers come from remote districts to have long slow talks with their friend the Prime Minister. Once a large party of country folk were coming to lunch with him and one of his servants suggested that, as they were persons of little importance, they need not be given of the best wines. "No," said Rhodes; "be sure you give them that special hock: they will like it." One old farmer, Coetzee, come with a deputation to protest against the Scab Act, was so taken with his host's welcome that he picked up a stone as a memento of his day at Groote Schuur. "Throw it away," says Rhodes, "and take this instead," presenting him with a beautiful old snuff-box: and some years afterwards old Coetzee sent a message through a friend that "if all Englishmen were like Mr. Rhodes, he would not mind being an Englishman instead of a Dutchman." He even had a tolerance for globe-trotters, and was often glad to give them something new to think about the country by a talk at Groote Schuur: to more serious visitors from the old country he always gave the warmest welcome. Young men bound for Rhodesia were generally asked to the house on their way through Cape Town; for the Founder always liked to see of what stuff his boys were made and to give special chances to the most promising. For the poet Rudyard Kipling he built a little cottage in the grounds of Groote Schuur, the Woolpack, and for several years in succession persuaded him to come and live there for some months. When a daughter of Bishop Alexander was to marry one of his pioneers, Bowen, he invited the bishop and both daughters to stay with him and had the marriage from his house.

In the bishop's *Life* there is a delightful picture of this visit. Rhodes is seen in his most charming moods: galloping in the early morning over the Cape Flats with one of his guests and perhaps Hofmeyr, silent and wrapped in his thoughts for a space, then suddenly moved to unceasing talk. One morning it was all the Sherlock Holmes game, for he had just been reading the book and was full of it, and he would give the most whimsical accounts, based on a fleeting observation, of every passer-by's past history and recent crimes. At lunch he was eagerly discussing some problem of the moment with Cape politicians or a pioneer from the north, or launching out into a dreamy monologue. The House of Assembly took him off in the afternoon; then at supper simple talk with the bishop and his daughters on the last book he had been reading, on religion or on some other general topic. He had a way of wandering in and out of the room during a conversation, sometimes disappearing before he had had the answer to his last question: and he had a childish liking for the most absurd topics and games. "Who is the cleverest man you ever met?" he once put to the company, his own answer being the Prince of Wales: another time he started a game of capping quotations, at which he proved surprisingly expert, until the bishop discovered him, like a naughty schoolboy, cribbing from a book under the table. Some of his games were of a grimmer nature. Lord Haldane recalls a particularly dreary one he once started in an English country house. It was a wet afternoon and some lady suggested a drawing-room game to relieve the boredom. Rhodes woke up with a jerk: "A game? Yes, certainly," and he made the ladies sit round him in a ring, with Lord Haldane armed with a Whitaker in the middle. The game was for Rhodes to ask such questions as "How many regiments are there in the British Army?" or "How many ships in the Navy?" and for Lord Haldane to verify the answers of the other players from Whitaker. After an hour or so of this the ladies became restive, and Rhodes dismissed them with a dry, "I think we've learned something from our game."

At the wedding of Miss Alexander, Rhodes gave away the bride, and was so much moved that he almost broke down. Indeed Miss Alexander's whole account of this visit to Groote Schuur is enough to prove how mistaken are the stories of Rhodes's hatred of women's society. He was exceedingly courteous to women, and was by no means indifferent to the company of those who would talk with him sensibly. One of his favourite guests was the great Dutch lady, Mrs. van der Byl, the former owner of Groote Schuur, to whom he showed great deference, always fetching her and taking her away from his house in his own brougham. Miss Olive Schreiner, before she quarrelled with him, found few people so sympathetic with her work as Rhodes; and when she began attacking him as a murderer and one who ought to be an outcast from society, he would never speak of her except with respect for her ability. He certainly did utter disparaging and even brutal remarks about the marriages of some of his friends;

but his objection to marriage was only in those cases where he thought the wife would interfere with her husband's work in the world, and where the husband made his wife an excuse for neglecting his duties. Once, after he had addressed at length two packed meetings of Chartered Company shareholders and was worn out, a friend brought up his bride to introduce to him. Rhodes at once took her into a little private room and spoke to her charmingly, telling her especially how much help a wife could give her husband. When he was as busy as he could be with the Matabele War and negotiations with the High Commissioner, he finds time to send two telegrams to Mrs. Colenbrander telling her that her husband at the front is well and begs her acceptance of one of his horses. He himself indeed once contemplated marriage, but later he came to the conclusion that he could never marry: his reason being that he had so much to do in the world that he could not give a wife as much of his thought and care as she was entitled to get. Possibly, had he met the right woman, he would have changed his mind. It would certainly have been happier for him to have had a good wife: she might have saved him from many mistakes of his later years and calmed the fiery outbursts that did him and his cause no good: and there is no doubt that she would have had a most considerate husband.

Though he naturally did not agree with his religious views, the bishop came to the conclusion that Rhodes's earnestness of purpose and lofty ideals were as good as the religion of many Christians; and a very different evangelist, General Booth, came to the same conclusion. His church was not a building but the veld or, at Cape Town, the Mountain. "The fact is, if I may take you into my confidence," he told some chapel-goers assembled to see him lay the foundation-stone of their place of worship, "I do not care to go to a particular church even on one day in the year, when I use my own chapel at all other times. I find that up the Mountain one gets thoughts, what you might term religious thoughts, because they are thoughts for the betterment of humanity, and I believe that is the best description of religion, to work for the betterment of the human beings who surround us." Prayer, he admitted to General Booth, was "useful, acting as a sort of time-table, bringing before the mind the duties of the day and pulling one up to face the obligations for their discharge," and when Booth suddenly knelt down in a railway carriage and began to offer up prayer for him, he knelt down devoutly also, and was pleased to have Booth's promise that he would continue praying for him. His own brave habit of "looking at the comparative" and thinking, in every trial, how much worse off he might have been, stood to him for the consolations of religion; and, however unorthodox he may have been, he was convinced that every man should have some religious creed. He realized, perhaps, with all his courage, his own loss in having no definite religious beliefs; and Bramwell Booth records the impression of gloom and melancholy his appearance gave him. "Happy? I happy?" he exclaimed in answer to Booth's question; "Good God, no!" and added, "I would give all I possess to believe what that old man [the General] believes in the next carriage." So when he was setting up schools in Rhodesia he insisted that half an hour each day should be devoted to the teaching of religion by denominational teachers; "I must say," he wrote to Milton, "that experience teaches us the world prefers *religion* in its instruction to the young." There was also to be a conscience clause, but those profiting by it, he shrewdly added, must have lessons during that half-hour, lest they should get into the habit of saying, "Thank goodness my good old Dad is an atheist and I get an extra half-hour in the playground." He was very human in his religious ideas as in everything else.

Having once made a beautiful home of his own, he turned his thoughts to creating beauty elsewhere. He had a Roman's passion for interpreting to the dwellers therein the majesty and beauty of their own country through noble monuments fitting to the natural surroundings. He sent Mr. Herbert Baker on a tour "to see Thebes, Paestum, Athens and the tomb of Lars Porsena," as he curtly expressed it, in order to get ideas for South Africa from some of the greatest monuments in Greece, Egypt and Italy.

When he discovered the grandeur of the Matoppo Hills, he found in one of the caves the remains of the old Matabele warrior Moselikatze. "He had desired to be buried seated upright on the summits of his kingdom, so that even in death he might look over the limitless expanse below him. . . . What a poet that man was!" exclaimed Rhodes, recounting the story to Watts. Here he determined should be his own burying place, here the Valhalla for Rhodesia. He made a beginning with the Wilson memorial, for which the sculptor Tweed made the bronze panels, explaining his intention to a father to whom he was showing the drawings: "Your boy died for his country, and now I want him to teach others to be ready to do the same." All his designs were on spacious lines. Buluwayo he planned as if it were a capital of a great state, and to connect it with Government House he planted an avenue a mile and a half long; to Umtali he presented a park, and urged on the administrator the planting of another mile-long avenue of stone pines and flamboyant trees, adding that if the country could not pay for them, he would. At Kimberley, his home for twenty years, he caused a great arcade of vines and rows upon rows of fruit trees to spring from a thirsty soil, and planned a huge bath or fountain in Pentelican marble to commemorate the siege. At Cape Town he erected the statue of Van Riebeeck on the quay and scrupulously preserved the few historical landmarks of the Dutch Company's time. He saved from destruction the blockhouses on the Mountain, and tried to rescue the Castle on the seashore from the neglect into which it was falling from the Imperial authorities' use of it as a barracks and office.[1] He co-operated heartily with Mrs. Koopman, a very influential lady in Bond circles, in her efforts to preserve and make accessible the interesting old archives of the Cape. In a debate on the proposal to build a modern Town Hall on the Parade adjoining the Castle ditch, he and Merriman played up to each other well in support of "the sentimental aspect." "It is true," said Rhodes, "the Parade is wind-swept and unsightly at times, but there are

[1] He failed to purchase it for the Colony from the Secretary for War owing to the prohibitive price asked.

many old associations with it, and further I would point out that it is the only open space left in the city. Even the Saturday market has been a pleasant custom for two hundred years. . . . Oh, let us," he concluded, " keep up some of those old things. There are not many in the country, and I say it is good for the people to see those old things preserved." One of the most lasting services Rhodes rendered to the people of South Africa was in helping to stimulate pride in their ancient history, and to restore the elements of beauty and fitness to their public and private architecture. Mr. Herbert Baker was the genius who created so many of the beautiful private houses that distinguish Johannesburg and Pretoria, who brought a note of distinction to the commonplace cathedral at Cape Town by the stately chapel he built for it, and gave splendour and dignity to the administrative capital of the Union by the Governor-General's house and the magnificent Government buildings on Meintjes Kop: but assuredly he would not have been so readily recognized by South Africa as the great architect he is, had it not been for the early chance given him by Rhodes and the example he was able to set by his work at Groote Schuur.

The secret of the great influence wielded by Rhodes in South Africa was that he was so transparently and wholeheartedly a South African. He always spoke of the country as his home, and never felt quite happy for long away from it. Unlike so many English South Africans, he much preferred having to do with Englishmen or Dutchmen of the country than with new arrivals from England. Thus most of his secretaries, Grimmer, Jourdan, Lange, Milton, were chosen from men with associations in South Africa who intended to spend most of their lives there. Oxford men he liked to see about him and to talk with, and he was always anxious they should settle in the country, but for his personal dealings with the people of the country he preferred those who knew the people. For, as he boasted at a time when he was accused of causing disunion, he had done the contrary in Rhodesia, " by taking up young men from the south and putting them into our administration of affairs, because our country is not one in which ' no

Afrikander need apply.' " So it was with his managers and overseers and the other men he employed in his business. Sometimes they were brought from overseas on account of their special knowledge, but they were generally men prepared to stay. One of the qualifications, for example, that he urged to Hofmeyr for using the services of Sivewright was that he intended to remain permanently in the country. His great friend Jameson was such another. At a time of life and after an experience which would have inclined most men to live comfortably at home, he did as Rhodes, and began his life anew in South Africa. This identification with the country thus accounts for the extraordinary position Rhodes enjoyed as a colonial statesman by the end of 1895. There was some opposition but no organized opinion against him at the Cape from English or Dutch, for it was recognized that he had brought appeasement and prosperity to the colony such as it had never enjoyed before. Sprigg was his henchman, Hofmeyr his good friend, and it seemed inconceivable that any one could take his place as Prime Minister.

His position in the world was only less remarkable. In Germany, France and Italy he was not yet personally known, but had become an object of awe and mystery : in Portugal he was the *homen horribel* : in Constantinople he was received with honour by the Sultan and given a jealously guarded favour. In Egypt he and Kitchener, as early as 1893, talked over their plans of connecting north and south of Africa with telegraph and railway, discussing the route and the gauge, and starting their friendly rivalry to reach the centre first. In his yearly visits to London he had become the lion of society and the hero of the financial and political worlds.

His home in London, after he became Prime Minister, was invariably the Burlington, a discreet hotel of irreproachable standing, where his wishes were known and studied and the same set of rooms always kept for him. Here he could live as he pleased ; he had no need to seek out people, for the world flocked to see him and do business with him. The diamond amalgamation, his power at the Cape, and above all the glamour from his achievements in the north, all helped to captivate the imagination of the London public. His rough uncouth figure, his carelessness in dress and manner, his massive well-cut head, recalling, as he himself was pleased to fancy, the Roman emperor Titus, all added to the mystery and attraction of his personality. And no one could mistake that here was a real person, quite independently of any passing achievement or timely good fortune; he could be ignored no more by opponents than by admirers. Great ladies sought for the honour of entertaining him; he had but to nod and great men were eager to forward his schemes or enlist his support for theirs. He frankly enjoyed all this flattery. He was especially pleased at the favour shown him by Queen Victoria, and used to tell with much complacency one of his conversations with her. "What have you been doing since I last saw you, Mr. Rhodes?" says the Queen. "I have added two provinces to Your Majesty's dominions." "Ah," rejoins his Sovereign, "I wish some of my Ministers, who take away my provinces, would do as much." In society he was moody and ill at ease when bored, and would talk of anything but South Africa to silly women who asked him silly questions. But to those who interested him he talked without reserve. "He could conquer hearts as effectually as any beauty that sets herself to subjugate mankind," said of him a great lady; for he had, according to another, "great grey eyes and a smile of singular and persuasive charm . . . like the sun on a granite hill," and more than that, a most winning and contagious enthusiasm in communicating his ideas. Years afterwards one writes to remind him of his advice to her at a dinner-party, always to speak well of the United States and make all English-speaking people understand one another, and humbly hopes that the attempts she has made to carry out his behest will meet with his approval.

He knew, too, that the deference paid to him at Londonderry House, at New Court or in Printing House Square were all useful to the great schemes he had at heart. He was very sensitive to criticism, especially in the newspapers, and took much pains to blunt its edge. Of his methods of doing this, Sir Sidney Low gives an illuminating example. He had recently attacked Chartered finance in the *St. James's Gazette*, and shortly afterwards had his first meeting with

Rhodes, who received him in a towering passion. "Look at your newspapers," exclaimed Rhodes; "see what *Truth* says about me and the *Daily Chronicle*," and that at a time when almost every other newspaper in the kingdom had been belauding him. "Jameson and I came home," he continued, "after giving a new dominion to the Empire, and we found that nobody took any notice of us, but that all your people were full of excitement because a Mrs. Somebody hadn't been elected to the School Board." After this outburst he set himself patiently to explain his views to Low, and gained one more adherent. *The Times*, which at one period had spoken somewhat sceptically and slightingly of his plans, became a whole-hearted convert. Moberly Bell, the all-powerful manager of the paper, was admitted to Rhodes's confidence, and in turn gave him his full support, and Miss Flora Shaw, one of the most brilliant and accomplished members of its staff, was allowed to share many of his secrets, and brought all her gift of enthusiastic advocacy to his cause. And there was always Stead, a very vociferous and influential prophet. In the City Rhodes had the powerful Kaffir ring at his command, and, thanks to the Rothschilds' cautious and weighty approval, was fast becoming a gilt-edged security of the Empire.

In political circles he had closer relations with Liberals than Conservatives. Though he obtained the Charter from Lord Salisbury's Government, he never seems to have quite found his footing with that reserved and fastidious statesman. It is true Lord Salisbury once spoke of Rhodes as "a very considerable man, a man of very many remarkable powers and remarkable resolution and will," but he paid very little regard to his vapourings, as he probably thought them, on the German and Portuguese treaties, and expressed a profound disbelief in the stability of Chartered Companies. In the Liberal camp he found more personal sympathy. That party was in power during most of his term of office at the Cape, and on the whole allowed him to do much as he pleased. Lord Ripon, the Colonial Secretary, though somewhat distant in his relations, generally fell in with his views, and the Under-Secretary, Mr. Sydney Buxton, and Sir Robert Herbert and Mr. Fairfield, two of the principal officials at the Colonial Office, were on most cordial terms with him. Lord Rosebery shared many of his opinions on Imperial federation, and was a powerful friend in the Cabinet. Harcourt was his chief stumbling-block. Personally, the Chancellor of the Exchequer was friendly enough to Rhodes. Though he admitted to Mr. Wilfrid Blunt that "Rhodes was an astonishing rogue and liar," his own rollicking humour had some affinity with the blunt directness of the rough South African. He invited him down to Malwood one Christmas, holding out as an inducement that he would find the Forest almost as savage as Matabeleland, and could obtain there all the poles he needed for his Trans-African telegraphs. But Rhodes never shared this friendly feeling. He looked on Harcourt as a typical little-Englander, and never forgave him for refusing to grant the concession to Cape wines and rejecting his preferential tariff clause in the Rhodesian constitution.

Once, however, partly by his own manœuvring, he had the satisfaction of seeing Harcourt's little-England policy defeated, an incident which also brought him into conflict with Gladstone himself. When the Liberal Government took office in 1892, they were called upon to decide promptly on the knotty problem of Uganda. The I.B.E.A., then responsible for its administration, had announced that they were no longer in a financial position to hold the country, so, failing Government intervention, Uganda would be lost. Rhodes, who happened to be in England at the time, was of course strongly against abandonment, both on general principles and because Uganda was an essential link in his Trans-African railway and telegraph systems. Gladstone sent for him to talk it over. "Our burden is too great," was the tenor of Gladstone's opening. "We have too much of the world, and, as it is, I cannot find the people to govern all our dependencies. We have too much to do. Not that I blame you, Mr. Rhodes," he added in his courtly manner; "you never give us any trouble." "If you will only take the country," Rhodes replied, "you will have the people capable of administration," and went on to urge his favourite doctrine that unless we annexed every suitable market we should find ourselves excluded from all markets by a hostile world. Gladstone took up the point with zest, and tried to indoctrinate Rhodes with his own free-trade opinions, but neither was shaken in his convictions. Rhodes then went off to see Harcourt armed with a large map. Harcourt's horrified account of the interview, as reported by Mr. Blunt, is as follows: "It is not Egypt only they want us to swallow, but the whole of East Africa. Rhodes was with me yesterday, and showed me this map, where you will see the territories he has grabbed. He has put up a telegraph already as far as Nyassa, and means to carry it on to Uganda and then to Cairo. He has offered to run Uganda for £25,000 a year, though he admits there is nothing to be made of it commercially." Nevertheless, Lord Rosebery backed up Rhodes's views to such effect that he persuaded the Cabinet, before irrevocably giving up Uganda, to adopt the compromise of a Government Mission to report on the outlook. Rhodes's brother Frank was a member of the Mission sent under Sir Gerald Portal; Rhodes himself advised Portal as to route and methods of transport, and, as every one expected, once hopes of annexation had been raised, the Government found it impossible to draw back. Sir William Harcourt himself introduced the Bill to guarantee a subsidy for the Uganda railway.

Besides Africa, the chief question that interested him in Imperial politics was the Home Rule Bill, with the principle of which he fully sympathized, especially now that Gladstone proposed to retain the Irish members at Westminster. He kept himself informed of the progress of the measure, and in 1893 restated his views on the importance of Irish representation by means of a letter written to *The Times* by his friend Mr. Maguire. Otherwise English politics did not interest him. They seemed to him too much an affair of "Mrs. Somebody and the School Board election," and he somewhat unreasonably expected the Imperial Parliament to be always thinking imperially, unmindful of the resentment he would have felt had it directed its Imperial thoughts too meticulously to South Africa. His real conception of the Imperial Government's proper function is brutally expressed in an election speech he made in 1898: "We are not going to be governed from home. . . . We do everything. We pass a

Bill and the Queen just puts her name to it. She never objects. . . . But what she does do for us, and without our paying for it, is this: she protects us with her fleet, and when I take a new country for you she protects me from the German and the Frenchman. . . . Whenever I took a country I simply said to the Queen: 'I have taken that: you must put your flag over it.'"

But though little attracted by English domestic politics, he was profoundly interested in fundamental social questions, and, as far as he could during his short visits, studied them at first hand for himself. From his talks with Stead and General Booth, and from visits to his own working-class property at Dalston, he was appalled by the mass of poverty, ignorance and distress he found existing in England. He paid a visit with General Booth to the farm colony at Hadleigh for the "submerged tenth," and was only confirmed thereby in his belief that the only hope for such people was the provision of "homes, more homes" in uncrowded and healthy surroundings such as he could offer them in Rhodesia. He accordingly invited the General to settle as large a colony there as he chose, and offered him assistance and full control over the experiment. In his own eyes the power to make such offers and to make the world a happier and healthier place to live in was the justification and chief advantage brought to him by his vast wealth and the great expanses of territory he had conquered.

Apart altogether from newspapers, politicians, financial houses and society dames Rhodes always had in his shareholders of the British South Africa Company, whose numbers had very soon risen to eight or nine thousand, a compact body of English public opinion behind him. The Board, as we have seen, had very soon become his dutiful agents and the willing interpreters of his actions: the annual meetings of the shareholders served, whenever he chose, as a platform from which to proclaim *urbi et orbi* not only his views on Chartered policy but his opinions on political affairs in general. These meetings were held at the Cannon Street Hotel, which had the largest hall available in the City, and whenever Rhodes was announced to speak it was always packed to overflowing. Twice in the first six years of the Company's existence he came to meetings, in November 1892 and January 1895. On the first occasion he had to meet an assemblage by no means satisfied with their own or the Company's prospects. Their shares worth £3 : 15s. in 1890 had sunk to 12s.; the expenses of administration had been enormous; the promised gold was not forthcoming, while the stories of distress and discontent among the pioneers had produced a most discouraging effect. But his massive appearance, his evident faith in himself, and the sense he conveyed of enormous strength gave even more confidence than his simple straightforward words: all doubts vanished and success seemed more than ever assured. In 1895 he came flushed with victory in the Matabele War, with his railway completed from Beira to Umtali, the main trunk line advancing and the telegraph carried forward to Blantyre, and all he had to do was to recount these triumphs. Then, having given a satisfactory account of his stewardship, he would turn to the still more congenial task of educating his audiences, and through them the English people, in the elements of his Imperial creed. In both these speeches he dwelt on the advantages of his Trans-African telegraph, not only as a dividend-earning but also as a patriotic concern. It was already earning 4 per cent as far as the Zambesi, he told them in 1892; and its very conception would make it impossible to abandon Uganda, through which it must pass, and rendered it imperative either to "deal with" the Mahdi or reconquer the Soudan. Another topic common to both speeches was the advantage to the community of his extension of territory. He took as his text in 1892 the argument brought forward by Labouchere for his policy of "scuttle," that new colonies had never done any good to his bootmaking constituents at Northampton, and retorted that without these open markets in the British Empire the Northampton bootmakers would see their foreign markets extinguished by the McKinley and other foreign tariffs. In 1895 he tried to picture what the "man in the street" gained from the Chartered Company's enterprise. He would have gained more, he said, had not the Ministry of the day been too wedded to Cobden's "beautiful theory" to agree to his preference clause for British manufactures brought into Rhodesia. They would have done much better, he added, to accept the real solution of social difficulties he offered them than to spend their time talking on platforms about "three acres and a cow," "a social programme," and "ethical discussions about the House of Lords (we all know you are not going to be guilty of the folly of making only one Chamber)"; and he ended with the injunction to his shareholders to give their votes to Jones or Brown at the forthcoming election on one condition only, "that they engage to put that clause in the constitution of Matabeleland."

The chief value of these artless talks to the shareholders was that they gave people a practical interest in Imperial questions, such as they had never felt before. It needed his magnetic personality to make men at home realize that they were personally concerned in the new countries he was developing and that success or failure depended partly on them. "More homes," preference, dividends from gold mines, railway and telegraph connections formed a mixed assortment of arguments but all of a nature to appeal to the man in the street. And from the interest aroused by Rhodesia they turned naturally to other parts of the British dominions. When therefore Chamberlain took the Colonial Office in July 1895, with long-meditated plans for a sympathetic administration of the colonies, which should lead to a more living sense of union with the Mother Country, he found that Rhodes, as much as any man, had prepared the ground before him. Rhodes, too, led the way for the later and less fortunate advance of Chamberlain to colonial preference. There had been protectionists and "fair traders" before Rhodes, but since Peel's day they had made little headway, and even Lord Randolph Churchill had found a preferential tariff an unremunerative venture. Rhodes was the first to arrest attention to the proposal and even to induce the City to consider it; for here was no mere theorist, but a hard practical man of business prepared to back his beliefs by restricting his own power of raising revenue in Rhodesia. And with Rhodes, as later with Chamberlain, the moving force for his creed of tariff reform was not self-interest, but a belief, however mistaken it may have been, that in it he had discovered a panacea for social ills and a " practical tie " with the colonies.

But when all is said the shareholders of the Chartered Company came to care far more for Rhodes himself than for his opinions or even his achievements. They cheered him to the echo when he appeared and at the end of his speeches burst into a tornado of applause. They submitted willingly to all he asked of them. They even accepted, on Hawksley's assurance that he approved, the watering down of their stock by 100 per cent in order to buy off the United Concession Company's claim to half their profits. They consented to his demand for a large issue of debentures at 6 per cent in 1893 : in January 1895 they took his advice to create no more ordinary shares, and seven months later, merely at his written request from South Africa, agreed to issue 500,000 more at a premium.[1] Chartered shares have not yet paid a dividend, but their possession, thanks largely to Rhodes's finance, was an advantage. They were generally at a premium after 1892 and so could be sold at a profit, and they also carried rights in remunerative undertakings such as the Rhodesian railways. But a large number of the shareholders held to their shares purely out of gratitude to him for allowing them thereby a part in his great enterprise. Certainly no man ever had a more loyal body of supporters than he in the shareholders of the Chartered Company : and the time was to come when he would need all the loyalty and sympathy they could give him.

[1] This transaction proved very profitable to the Company. The 500,000 new shares were issued at £3 : 10s., and with the proceeds of this premium the debenture debt of £750,000 was wiped out, while £1,000,000 new stock still remained for railway development and administration.

CHAPTER XV

THE RAID

I

THE union of South Africa had ever been the principal object of Rhodes's colonial policy. Without union he felt that all his achievements in the north, all his success in drawing Dutch and English closer together at the Cape were maimed and incomplete. He was the first to recognize that the obstacles to union were great: the antagonism between the Dutch and English races, the strong national feeling in the Transvaal and the almost equally strong particularism of Natal, the difference in native policy between the Cape and the other states, even the hostile customs tariffs and antagonistic railway policies, from which union was the only escape, all were being used as entrenchments behind which the separatist tendency in each colony or state was constantly gaining fresh strength. From the outset Rhodes had recognized that such obstacles could not be surmounted or even circumvented by any sudden stroke, but that patience, tact and faith were essential to achieve his purpose. And for many years he had displayed all three qualities to an eminent degree. The faith that union would come never forsook him; his tact in appreciating the value of the Dutch and the need of bringing about union with their co-operation and goodwill had been exceptional for an Englishman; and his patience had been learned in the hard school of Kimberley and in his early dealings with Van Niekerk and the bloodthirsty Groot Adriaan De la Rey. "It took me twenty years to amalgamate the diamond mines," he told the Bond in 1891; "that amalgamation was done by detail, step by step . . . and so your union must be done by detail, never opposing any single measure that can bring that union closer, giving up even some practical advantage for a proper union, educating your children to the fact that it is your policy and that you must and will have it, telling it them and teaching it them in your district Bestuurs and households. . . . In connection with this question I may meet with opposition; but if I do I shall not abandon it." As we have seen, he had been as good as his word and had gone some way towards mitigating the bitterness of racial feeling by his moderating influence as Prime Minister. He it was who tried to soothe the indignation of the Cape Dutch farmers at the Transvaal's outrageous tariffs; he had succeeded, where others had failed, in inducing Kruger to admit the Cape trunk lines into the Transvaal, and by his native legislation had paved the way for a better understanding on this radical cause of disagreement.

Already by 1894 he was looked up to as the one hope for a settlement of South African differences on federal lines. Albert Grey and other statesmen in England, who looked forward to this solution of the perennial race trouble, were eagerly watching his efforts in this direction; he had Hofmeyr and the Bond with him; he was always impressing on his Rhodesians that their destiny was to be merged in a united South Africa; and even in Natal, still smarting from his Kokstad speech, there was a disposition to follow him. Albert Grey, after a visit to that colony in 1894, sends Rhodes the following message from Escombe, with the full concurrence of Escombe's rival, John Robinson, and of the Governor: "'Inter-colonial and inter-state free trade in the produce of each colony and state' is Natal's policy, and they look on you as their leader, recognizing you as the only person who can bring this about. If you will make this a fundamental part of your policy," adds Grey, "he will wheel his Colony into line behind you, engaging to carry his people in spite of the opposition of those who fear a customs-union means dear bread and cheap brandy for Natal. He says, 'Let Rhodes, who has the statesmanship and imagination, strike a high note when he goes to Pretoria.'

Small men might be turned away from the high advantages of this policy by narrow sectional self-interests, and be unable to go in for the big idea because they fear the Cape may suffer from the free import of Natal sugar, or that Natal may be drowned in cheap Cape wine and brandy, but he looks to you as strong enough to emancipate your people from the tyranny of low ideals. Under your leadership Escombe feels strong enough to do the same in Natal. Now is the time: the Colonies should not go hat in hand to the Republics but *vice versa*. But this is a dogged little English colony and it won't do to threaten them as you did in your Kokstad speech. You would make it much easier for Escombe to play up to you if you could find an opportunity of saying something sympathetic to Natal which will cause them to believe that you have their interests at heart."

Sentiment, however, far more than material causes, played, as is generally the case in national differences, the greatest part in perpetuating disunion in South Africa. It was unfortunate, from Rhodes's point of view, that before he came into the field with proposals for union, he had been forestalled by the Bond's original proposals. These included a Republican form of government for South Africa, freed from all English tutelage and under its own flag. It is true the Bond had been persuaded by Hofmeyr to drop the Republican flag, but the idea was still cherished in many Dutch hearts, and was the only condition which Kruger, had he entertained union at all, would have accepted. To Rhodes such an idea was out of the question: he had no wish to cut adrift from England himself and was convinced that the English Cape colonists and Natal would never consent to it. He was once approached by Borckenhagen, the editor of a Dutch paper at Bloemfontein, with the proposal that they should both work together for an independent South Africa. His reply was short and unmistakable: "I am neither a knave nor a fool. I should be a knave to leave my own people and a fool to join yours, because I should be hated by my own people and despised by yours." At the same time he was equally convinced that the Boer states would never willingly part with their independence. The Free State had come to value an independence originally thrust upon them; the Transvaal cherished theirs the more dearly for having lost and then regained it.

To overcome this sentimental difficulty, Rhodes's proposal was to leave the Republics their own flags and their independence in certain spheres of government, but for federal purposes to create a central government under the British flag. "I have my own views as to the future of South Africa," he said as far back as 1883, "and I believe in a United States of South Africa, but as a portion of the British Empire. I believe that confederated states in a colony under responsible government would each be practically an independent Republic, but I think we should also have all the privileges of the tie with the Empire." Again, in one of his first public speeches as Prime Minister, he said: "I know myself that I am not prepared to forfeit at any time my own flag. I repeat I am not prepared at any time to forfeit my own flag. If I forfeit my flag, what have I left? If you take away my flag, you take away everything. Holding this view, I cannot but feel the same respect for the neighbouring states, where men have been born under Republican institutions and with Republican feelings." In the following year, in his speech to the Bond at Kimberley, he had deplored the mistakes of the past, which had led to the creation of independent states, and took the occasion of some criticisms elicited by this speech to restate his views on union to President Reitz:

"I hear from so many quarters that the meaning of a portion of my speech at Kimberley has been so misunderstood at Bloemfontein that I think, in justice to myself, I should state the views I expressed as to our future relations with the neighbouring Republics. I simply repeated what I have repeatedly said before, that our efforts should be to obtain with them a customs union, railway communication, and free trade in the products of the country, always respecting their independence and never in any way attempting to undermine that position, in the same way as I felt sure they would not attempt to interfere with our relations with our Mother Country. It is perfectly true that I also stated that if we were all to commence again to civilize Africa, starting from Cape Town, I think we should all agree that it would have been better for the people of South Africa to have had one system from Cape Town to the Zambesi, and I used the line of argument in reference to the North Extension being made on a friendly understanding with the system of the people of the Old Colony, so that [we] . . . should not repeat the policy of fifty years ago of practically forcing the voortrekkers . . . to form an independent system. . . . Through the errors and blunders of the then Government these people were forced to part company from [their] compatriots, to strike out for themselves and seek relief elsewhere." [1]

Kruger and the Transvaal were the greatest obstacle to the attainment of even this modified form of union. With the old President, do what he would, Rhodes seemed fated to be in almost continual conflict. First it had been Bechuanaland; then Swaziland, the Adendorff trek, railway construction and customs had followed, though both in Bechuanaland and in Rhodesia Rhodes had made it plain that he welcomed Transvaal subjects if they would acknowledge British laws. But behind all these difficulties, some of which were easily susceptible of arrangement, there loomed a vital difference of outlook best illustrated by the great Uitlander question. Kruger's predominant idea was to keep his Republic unpolluted by British interference or British ideas, and his conduct to the gold-diggers of the Transvaal was a natural outcome of this idea. There they were, 80,000 of them, chiefly of English birth and already four times the number of his burghers, and more of them flowing in: he could not drive them out, nor did he really desire to do so, for their activities had raised the Transvaal from bankruptcy to the height of affluence. The Rand taxes produced nineteen-twentieths of the state's total revenue, which, since the discovery of gold, had risen from £178,000 to nearly three millions. But without driving them out and so cutting off this bountiful source of supply, Kruger could at least make

[1] From an incomplete draft in Rhodes's handwriting. I have struck out a few words and added two, in square brackets, in the last few lines, to bring out the sense.

them feel that they were intruders of little more account politically than the natives. The franchise law of the Transvaal, most liberal before the discovery of the Rand, had been so restricted that it had become impossible for an Uitlander to obtain a vote in the country to which he contributed most of the revenue;[1] he had no control even over the affairs of the city he had founded and built up, for Johannesburg was still treated as a mining camp under a mining commissioner. The language of instruction in the State schools of Johannesburg, supported by the Uitlanders' rates, was Dutch, and Englishmen who wanted their children instructed in their mother tongue had in addition to pay heavy fees at a private school. Though denied the ordinary rights of citizenship and treated as an alien, the Uitlander was nevertheless liable to be impressed for service in native wars, as occurred in 1894. He also had more material grievances. The wealth he had brought to the Transvaal had attracted a swarm of needy adventurers, who buzzed round Kruger as if he had been a second Lo Bengula, and extracted from him all manner of concessions at the expense of the gold-mining community. A specially iniquitous concession was that for the manufacture of dynamite, which was not really made in the country, but imported by the monopolists, and then sold at such a price to the mines that it was equivalent to an extra tax on the industry of £600,000. Another set of adventurers obtained the concession for carrying coal along the Rand, which they did at almost prohibitive rates: the group owning the liquor concession succeeded in passing a liquor law, with so few restrictions that the natives on the mines were being rapidly debauched. So strong, indeed, was the influence of the monopolists that a judge who ventured to give a decision adverse to one of these concessions was promptly dismissed by Kruger. Even Van Oordt, the President's partial biographer, is driven to admit the scandal caused by the unprincipled crew who beset the old man's stoep and the lobbies of the Volksraad in search of every conceivable concession. The scandal was

[1] By a law of July 1894 it was made practically impossible for anybody not settled in the Transvaal before 1876 or the son of a burgher to obtain a vote; whereas burghers obtained the vote at the age of sixteen.

all the greater because the beneficiaries were not even his own ignorant burghers, but foreigners from Holland, Germany and any other country but England, far less likely to become loyal and permanent settlers in the Transvaal than the Uitlanders themselves.

Foolish as Kruger's treatment of the Uitlanders was, it was wisdom compared with his fiscal policy to the Cape, whereby he did all he could to alienate his best friends. He would not hear of entering the Customs Union, which even the Free State had joined, and did his utmost to exclude Cape produce from the Transvaal. Colonial pigs, brandy, cattle and coal could be imported only on payment of fantastic duties. His railway policy was equally obstructive: he finally consented to the Cape system crossing the Vaal only when his own railway was in such desperate financial straits that he was obliged to accept for it a subsidy from the Cape and in return to allow the extension to Johannesburg. Even when the extension had been made, fresh difficulties arose about the rates, which he put up so high on this section that the goods were almost forced round to the rival Delagoa Bay route. In 1894 Rhodes had a conversation with Kruger at Pretoria on this point, but without avail. "I told him," was Rhodes's version of the interview, "it was contrary to the spirit of our agreement that he should go and raise the rates, and he said he had the right to do it. I said, 'Well, this is rather breaking the spirit of the convention; it is most unfair. We lent you £700,000 to build this line when you could get it from nobody else. The result was that Rothschilds lent you one and a half millions to complete the Delagoa Bay railway, and as soon as you have got that line you have broken the spirit of the convention.' He said he did not care, he should raise the rates. I warned him, 'If you do not take care, you will have the whole of South Africa against you. You are a very strong man; but there are things you may do which will bring the whole of the Cape Colony and the north, and indeed the whole of South Africa against you, and so strongly that you will not be able to stand against it.'"

This question of railway rates was to Rhodes's mind the strongest illustration of the need for union. It was not merely a duel between the Cape and the Transvaal for cheap rates, but Natal also came in as a competitor for the Johannesburg traffic, and in the rate war of 1894 Kruger was able to play off the Natal line as well as his own against Rhodes. "I am sometimes told," said Rhodes to the Cape House, "that the question of South Africa at the present moment is the question of a united South Africa; others say it is scab or labour or stock-thefts, but I think it is the settlement of tariffs between Delagoa Bay, Durban and the ports of Cape Colony, because if we do not settle these tariffs it will be ruinous for us all." But he would not be driven hastily to acts of reprisal. "The Transvaal is foolish," he admitted, "but we should not be foolish too. Let us look at it with sorrow, and hope the Transvaal will change. . . . Our waggons, fruit, wine, butter and cattle are being taxed as in the past. But do not let us lose our tempers over it. The Transvaal and President Kruger will have to consider whether a system should continue which refuses nine-tenths of the population under it the franchise and which refuses to a friendly state, which helped it in the time of need [*i.e.* in 1881], any commercial advantages, and which says: 'We will have nothing you can produce.' Is it possible to maintain an action of that kind? If the President succeeds in doing so, he would be the most remarkable man since the commencement of the world, because such a position is impossible. Still, all we can do is to negotiate anew and maintain a statesmanlike and dignified position."

Up to the end of 1894 the struggle between Rhodes and Kruger had been straight and open. The antagonism of the two men was quite intelligible. Kruger's one aim was to keep his Transvaal a sanctuary for his chosen people; if the alien gold-seekers liked to bring wealth into the country, well and good, but there must stop their privileges. Rhodes was one of these aliens, for he had some of the largest gold-interests on the Rand. Besides, Kruger felt that he had legitimate grievances against the nation of which Rhodes was the outstanding figure in South Africa. Though he had loyally carried out his promise to Hofmeyr in 1890 to damp down the Adendorff trek as a condition for the first

Swaziland convention, he had two more conventions to sign before the matter was finally settled. And even then, though he had at first been led to expect that he might take a railway through that country to the sea, he found all his hopes dashed by England's annexation of the intervening territories, besides the ports of Kosi Bay and St. Lucia. He felt himself hemmed in by the English north, south, east and west, and he feared and hated Rhodes, because he knew that his adversary's aim was to destroy the isolation in which he gloried. Rhodes opposed Kruger not from any animosity to his race—on the contrary, no Englishman of his time appreciated and sympathized more with the Boers—but because he saw in the other's obstinate determination to keep alive the old bitter feeling, which had prompted the great Boer trek, the main obstacle to harmony between the races. He had been fighting Kruger ever since he engaged in politics, and hitherto had generally got the better of him. It was an unequal contest between the man of modern ideas, the owner of millions, backed by the greatest Empire in the world, and the solitary old man, strong only in the obstinacy with which he clung to the ideas of his childhood. But though the contest was unequal, the victory was not yet won. Rhodes had been very patient and forbearing, but his patience had limits, and already he had shown the fatal weakness of underrating his adversary. Utterances such as "I pity the man," "the President must have been a very disappointed man," are jarring notes in his otherwise skilful diplomacy, and they are the premonitory signals of that ὕβρις, as the Greeks called it, which so often attends success so overwhelming as his.

Rhodes must have exercised enormous self-control to display the patience he did in some of the most important affairs of his life, for his was a turbulent, volcanic nature, more naturally disposed to brush aside or crush opposition than to "sit down and argue with it"; and sometimes, in spite of all precautions, or perhaps because he thought a pose of brutality would serve his purpose best, the natural man had blazed out. But by 1895 a subtle change was coming over him: he was losing some of his powers of self-restraint and of waiting upon the occasion. His health was partly to blame. Although his big burly form seemed to have overcome the early disposition to consumption, he had recently had warnings of the heart trouble which in the end was to prove fatal. At the end of 1891 he broke his collar-bone and had a bad attack of influenza, which gave some anxiety to his friends—"The thought of where we should be if we were to be deprived of the help of your brain and guiding hand is an ugly sort of nightmare," wrote Grey—and he never afterwards quite recovered his elasticity. He himself had no illusions: he used often to say that he would not live beyond forty-five, and that, within his few remaining years, he must accomplish all he still had left unfinished. With this obsession upon him, he began to feel that the time for patient and laborious methods was past and to give rein to his natural impatience. Power, too, and success had begun to spoil him. He became strangely arrogant: old friends noted with pain the change from his former simple and boyish good-fellowship to the almost pompous and overweening attitude of the later Rhodes. "Newspapers," he once roared out; "do you think I care a continental fig what the newspapers may say? I am strong enough to do what I choose in spite of the whole pack of them." He was beginning to say in his heart that he was not as other men, but like a god, and that he had only to say, it shall be so, and it was so. This arrogant spirit was encouraged and pampered by his surroundings. He had turned away or lost many of his old friends, and in their place had come a horde of flatterers, secretaries and second-rate Dutchmen, who lived on him and treated him as Canute was treated by his courtiers. At the Burlington his ante-chamber was thronged, like my Lord Chesterfield's, with needy parasites in search of a favour; and the Dr. Johnsons too rarely found access. At the Cape he was jealously shielded by secretaries and cronies from the rude blasts of outside opinion, and his every word received as an oracle. His court was specially remarkable for its array of doctors. "I like doctors for my work, because their calling gives them such an insight into humanity," was his polite way of accounting for this taste: his more brutal explanation was: "because, when there is blood-letting to be done, they are less squeamish." Such brutal sayings should not be taken too literally: Rhodes always took a malicious delight in trying to *épater le bourgeois* and shock the *unco guid* by such remarks, which he did not mean very seriously. In the same way, though he enjoyed flattery, he was able to take it at its proper valuation, and turn to serious and well-tried friends, Jameson, Beit or Grey, in times of real trouble and stress. But, like all forceful men, when he had once mapped out his course, he preferred for his agents those who would not trouble him with arguments, but simply get on with the work.

His relations with the Governor illustrate well his growing impatience of contradiction. Sir Henry Loch and he had never hit it off. Rhodes suspected the High Commissioner of desiring to curtail his privileges and freedom of action in Bechuanaland and Rhodesia; nor was Loch always tactful in his dealings with his formidable Prime Minister; for he rarely forgot that he was the representative of Royalty or remembered that Rhodes was not a man to whom you could apply the ordinary rules. At any rate Rhodes was not displeased to hear in 1895 that Loch was averse to returning from his leave in England. His own choice for a successor was his old friend Sir Hercules Robinson, Loch's predecessor, with whom he had always worked well. There were objections to Sir Hercules, for he had been recalled for his remarks on the Imperial factor, he was getting old, and also he was thought to be too closely connected with De Beers and other South African companies. But Lord Ripon and Mr. Buxton were naturally much influenced by the Cape Prime Minister's opinion and accepted his view that Robinson would be the best Governor they could find to work harmoniously with Hofmeyr and the Dutch: so, in spite of some protests in the House of Commons, Robinson was chosen.[1] The new Governor was well aware that he owed his renewed term very largely to Rhodes; but his gratitude was doubtless tempered with some apprehension. "I file that letter,"

[1] It is interesting to find that in April 1895 Chamberlain, though not yet in office, was informally consulted as to Robinson's appointment to the Cape and made no objection.

was his caustic comment on Rhodes's pledge in his letter of congratulation: "If we come to disagree on anything, I promise to take that as indicating that I am wrong." On his side Rhodes was maturing plans which required the presence of a sympathetic Governor.

II

Whatever may have been the cause—flatterers, fear of death or natural impatience—a period came in Rhodes's relations with Kruger when he felt there was nothing more to be gained by open diplomacy. This conviction was borne in upon him gradually. On customs and railway rates he never had any real anxiety; the colonists held the whip-hand of Kruger in those matters when, as now, they were united. But the Uitlander question was a different matter. The indignation of the Uitlanders, mostly men of British birth, had been gradually rising at their failure to obtain any redress for their grievances. Twice the President received serious warning that they were not to be trifled with indefinitely: once at Johannesburg in 1890, when an angry mob surrounded his lodging and trampled on the Republican flag; and again at Pretoria four years later, when a rowdy crowd took out the horses and dragged the carriage, in which Sir Henry Loch and he were seated, and waved a Union Jack over his head. But the only answer he vouchsafed them was to impose further restrictions on their liberty. A law was passed forbidding meetings of more than six persons; and when in 1894 and 1895 they presented largely signed petitions to the Volksraad for the redress of grievances, they were received with jeers and told that if they wanted the franchise they must fight for it. Kruger did indeed withdraw the commandeering order in 1894 on Loch's stern representations, but immediately afterwards began casting about for means of strengthening his position.

In the first place he very largely increased his military budget, spending most of the money on supplies of guns and rifles. He also sought external alliances. Since 1872 he had been trying to enter into a defensive alliance with the Free State, without success during President Brand's lifetime; but after Brand's death he had found his successor Reitz ready to sign a treaty of mutual guarantee against aggression. He had also sought a more powerful ally. In the autumn of 1894 he had sent his State Secretary, Mr. Leyds, to sound Germany, where he had been so well received himself in 1883. Leyds seems to have met with an encouraging reception, so encouraging that at a banquet of the German Club in January 1895 Kruger proposed the Emperor's health, and said he knew he could thenceforward count on the Germans. "I feel certain," he added, "that when the time comes for the Republic to wear larger clothes [*i.e.*, presumably, to shake off all English tutelage], you Germans will have done much to bring it about. . . . The time is coming for our friendship to be more firmly established than ever."

This speech aroused once more all Rhodes's apprehensions of German interference in South Africa, and he afterwards attributed his participation in the plot against the Transvaal Government largely to this cause. Moreover, as managing director of one of the chief companies on the Rand, he was naturally concerned at the unrest in Johannesburg, and during his visit to Kruger in 1894 on the railway question had discovered from conversation with Leonard, Hays Hammond and other friends that there was every chance of a spontaneous rising against the Government. Sir Henry Loch, too, after his recent experience at Pretoria, had been convinced of the danger, and had actually had a force of police ready on the Bechuanaland border to act in case of emergency. Early in 1895 both he and Rhodes had warned the Colonial Office. But as yet there was no organized plot. The leaders of the gold industry did not, as one of them said, care a fig for the vote: they were only troubled at the hindrance and loss to their business caused by the dynamite and other concessions, and pinned their faith chiefly on what was euphemistically called an "election fund" for securing a more friendly Volksraad. Such men feared Rhodes's impulsive nature and were obviously much relieved when Beit advised them in 1894 not to consult him on their difficulties. The chief agitators for more drastic action were some of the working men and the business people who intended to make their homes in Johannesburg; but both Rhodes and Loch saw that they were as sheep without a shepherd and had neither arms nor plans for a successful revolt. The conviction was gradually forced upon Rhodes that if the rising was not to be a fiasco he must himself take a hand in it. He had a third motive for action: a fear that unless the movement were directed on the right lines it might impede rather than advance his own plans for union, by simply replacing a Boer by a British Republic. "You might be sure, sir," was his comment on this idea, "that I was not going to risk my position to change President Kruger for President J. B. Robinson."

Early in 1895, therefore, Rhodes decided to organize the rising in Johannesburg and ensure its success. At first he took only a few people into his confidence. With Beit he arranged to share the expenses; Hawkesley, the Chartered Company's solicitor, Mr. Maguire and a few others in London were let into the secret; there were one or two chosen confidants in Johannesburg; Jameson, the administrator of Southern Rhodesia, and Dr. Rutherfoord Harris, the Cape Town secretary of the Chartered Company, were to take an active part in the conspiracy. In taking this decision judgement and the sense of honour had alike deserted Rhodes; for as Prime Minister of the Cape and managing director of the Chartered Company he had no business to interfere with the internal affairs of a friendly state except on behalf of his Colony or of Rhodesia. As it was, from the outset he placed himself in a false position. To ensure the success of a revolt two factors had to be considered: a supply of arms for Johannesburg and the provision of a force on the border ready to enter the Transvaal and support the rebels at the first signal of a rising. Rhodes proposed as a private individual to buy and smuggle into the Transvaal arms which it was his duty as Prime Minister to stop, and by the use of his authority as managing director of the Chartered Company secretly to place a force on the border for a purpose entirely alien to the trust imposed on him by the Crown.

The Chartered Company was at that time so uncontrolled in its actions that no difficulty was anticipated in secretly concentrating a force of police ready to enter the Transvaal at the right moment; but they had no good "jumping-off ground." The most suitable trysting-place was in the neighbourhood of Mafeking; but that region was still directly under the Crown. Already, however, before he had embarked on his plans for a Johannesburg rising, Rhodes had been trying to obtain the transfer of the whole of Bechuanaland from Imperial control. With respect to the Crown Colony of British Bechuanaland, memorable to him for his early associations with Stellaland and Goshen, he had no difficulty. The British Government had always been ready to hand it over to the Cape, when that Government was prepared to undertake the administration. Accordingly, when Rhodes proffered the request, Lord Ripon raised no objection; and the terms of transfer were finally settled by his successor, Mr. Chamberlain. In August 1895, therefore, ten years after his lament over the Cape's lost opportunity through Warren's policy, Rhodes had the satisfaction of passing in the Cape House an Act for the annexation of British Bechuanaland. Although Rhodes came in for some friendly criticism on the provisions required by Chamberlain, limiting the Cape's right of interfering with the natives, and was told that he had been worsted in his first encounter with the new Secretary of State, the Colony made a very good bargain; for it took over this new province without being asked to repay to the Imperial Government any part of the large sum spent on its development. But this addition to the Colony still gave Rhodes no satisfactory jumping-off ground, for he had no right to post his Rhodesian force in Cape territory: for this he required a footing for the Chartered Company in the Protectorate.

The Bechuanaland Protectorate was in fact within the Company's sphere of operations, which in the Charter was defined as all the region to the north of Mafeking: but, although they already possessed nearly all the concessions there, they had not hitherto been granted powers of administration. In a letter to the Duke of Abercorn Loch had thus explained the position: "An enormous area was included in the Charter and if all had to be taken up and worked at once, the Company would have required a capital of nearer £5,000,000 than one, but the position, as I understand it, is this. The B.S.A. Company were to establish themselves first in Mashonaland and develop the wealth of that country before embarking in further liabilities; the Imperial Government in the meanwhile administering the remainder of the country under the High Commissioner with as much economy as the necessities of the position permitted, so that the Company might have breathing time to gradually feel their way and establish themselves in Lo Bengula's country before undertaking further responsibilities." But apart from any ulterior designs, this arrangement did not suit Rhodes at all. He suspected Loch and the Imperial Government of an attempt to cozen him out of his rights, and, in his letter of November 1894 to Lord Ripon asking when the engagement to the Company was going to be fulfilled, remarked with some asperity that he would never have undertaken the railway northwards had he thought he was not to control the Protectorate. Lord Rosebery's Government had no objection to giving Rhodes what he asked, but they were already tottering to their fall and were afraid of taking a decision that might arouse opposition. For Rhodes and the Company still had enemies: their financial operations were sharply criticized, and the Exeter Hall party distrusted their native policy none the less for the Matabele campaign. Accordingly Ripon put off a decision until the Government's defeat on cordite in June 1895 left the matter over for his successor.

In the new Secretary of State, Joseph Chamberlain, Rhodes met a man no less masterful and with even greater means of exercising authority than himself. Unlike Lord Ripon, whose official existence depended on a precarious majority of some thirty votes, Chamberlain had at his back an overwhelming majority in the country. He had come to the Colonial Office, not as most previous Secretaries, because their services to the party did not entitle them to a more important department, but of his own deliberate choice and with a settled purpose of making its true importance appear. He was not one to fall under the influence even of a Rhodes, as his two predecessors had unconsciously done: he had formerly distrusted him;[1] and though he had come to sympathize with many of his aspirations, he had no idea, even in carrying out any objects they might have in common, of allowing Joseph Chamberlain to play second fiddle to Cecil Rhodes. Politely but firmly he indicated this in his answer to Rhodes's letter of congratulation on his appointment; and he very soon made it evident that, though willing to honour his predecessor's promise to transfer the Crown Colony to the Cape, he had no immediate intention of handing over the Bechuanaland Protectorate to the Company. So Rhodes had to try another tack, and commissioned Dr. Rutherfoord Harris, then acting as his agent in London, to secure a strip on the Protectorate border for the purposes of railway construction.

Before the negotiations for this strip, however, were concluded, Chamberlain gave a foretaste of his decisive methods and of the control he intended to exercise in South Africa, when Imperial interests were concerned. The rates war with Kruger was still dragging on without much prospect of settlement. When the Transvaal railway manager had proposed to put up the rate from the Vaal above 6d. a ton, in order to kill the Cape traffic, Kruger had light-heartedly urged him to make it 1s. Thereupon the traders in desperation forsook the railway at the Free State border and carried their goods over the short stretch to Johannesburg in bullock-waggons. Not to be outdone, Kruger proclaimed that the Vaal drifts, by which they had to cross, would be closed. This last stroke united all parties at the Cape against the obstinate old President, and Rhodes carried even the Bond members of his Ministry with him in appealing to Chamberlain to take action against what his Attorney-General, Schreiner, declared to be a breach of the London Convention. Chamberlain took the same view and described the President's act as "almost . . . one of hostility"; he also declared his willingness to back up a protest by a display of force, on condition the Cape Government undertook to pay half the cost; for "Her Majesty's Government," he stated in the despatch, "do not intend that such an expedition

[1] See Chap. X. p. 136.

should, like most previous colonial wars, be conducted solely at the Mother Country's expense." Rhodes did not quite relish the condition, but recognized that Chamberlain was not to be trifled with, and secured the consent of his Cabinet. No force was needed, for Kruger saw he had gone too far and climbed down.

The negotiations between Chamberlain and the Colonial Office on the one hand, and Dr. Harris and the other Chartered Company's agents on the other, have been a subject of such acute controversy that it is essential to bring out as clearly as possible the conditions under which they were conducted. When Chamberlain entered upon them, he had held the seals of office only a few weeks and was barely posted in the outlines of the case he had to deal with. He found that his predecessors Knutsford and Ripon had pledged themselves more than once that the Protectorate should ultimately revert to the Company. But the date of cession had been left open, and Chamberlain himself was anxious to postpone it, for he had a firm belief that, where natives were concerned, the Imperial Government's rule was the fairest, and he himself, unlike some of his predecessors, had no fear of shouldering responsibility. In this view he was confirmed by the extreme unwillingness he found in the principal Bechuana chiefs, Khama, Sebele and Bathoen, to exchange Imperial protection for that of the Company, and by the enlightened government of Khama himself. He also felt that the Company already had quite as much territory to administer as they could manage for the time being, and that any sudden increase " would," as he drily remarked, " be deemed by any person of administrative experience to contain in itself the elements of failure." On the other hand, he had great ideas of developing the empire by railways and other means, and kept pressing Rhodes to fulfil his engagement to continue the extension of the railway northwards. To this demand Harris's answer, on behalf of Rhodes, was that for a railway he must have at least a strip of territory along the Protectorate border under the Company's complete control; and to this, in principle, Chamberlain at once agreed. The other outstanding question in South Africa to Chamberlain's mind was the trouble in Johannesburg. The Colonial

Office had long been aware that a rising might at any moment occur, and that the Imperial Government might be called upon to interfere in the interests of peace in South Africa. Loch's action in having a body of police on the border in 1894 was fully approved, and next year Lord Ripon and Mr. Buxton had discussed with Sir Hercules what steps he should take. It had been arranged by them that, if Johannesburg revolted, he should at once go to the Transvaal and have a sufficient force at hand to ensure respect for the advice he might proffer. On assuming office, Chamberlain had confirmed these instructions and arranged that troops should be available, if required.[1] By his prompt and decisive attitude on the Drifts question he showed that, if necessary, he was prepared to strike hard.

Dr. Harris, Mr. Maguire, Hawkesley and Albert Grey carried on the negotiations with the Colonial Office on behalf of the Chartered Company. The first three certainly, probably the last, knew what was foremost in Rhodes's mind in his anxiety to obtain the border-strip, though the ostensible reason was simply to facilitate the railway construction. Of these agents Dr. Harris took the leading part. By his own account, he was the repository of nearly all Rhodes's secrets. "I do not think," he told the South Africa Committee, "anybody was more intimately associated with all Mr. Rhodes's affairs, private, political and public, than I was. I did everything for him." If that was so, it does not indicate much discrimination on Rhodes's part. Dr. Harris was an extremely able and energetic secretary to the Company, a very successful man of business, and a good whip to Rhodes's party in the Cape Parliament; and Rhodes was no doubt grateful to him for his readiness to take trouble off his shoulders. But he had little acquaintance with large political questions, and was certainly not of the calibre to deal on equal terms with a leading English statesman. He came to the business so full of Rhodes's plan of putting an emergency force on the border that he seems to have worked himself quite sincerely into the belief

[1] For several months the troopships conveying drafts to or from India were ordered, instead of going through the Suez Canal, to take the longer course round Africa and call for orders at the Cape.

that any one with whom he discussed the possibility of a revolution or the railway strip was as much aware of the secret scheme as he was himself. He and some of the others in the secret certainly confided it to Miss Flora Shaw of *The Times*, with the expectation that she would prepare the way discreetly; and she even went so far as to draw up a memorandum for *The Times* correspondents abroad that they might know the line to take when the rising occurred. A few privileged individuals in society were also admitted into the secret, and a favourable atmosphere of vague expectation was created. Frequent visits were paid to the Colonial Office and long conversations were held with Fairfield, the head of the South African section, on Chartered Company business. In these conversations the state of Johannesburg, the possibility of a rising and even the attitude to be adopted in face of such a rising were not unnaturally touched upon; and Dr. Harris certainly received the impression that Fairfield was more aware of Rhodes's particular plan than he actually was.

Chamberlain himself met Harris only twice. The first time was in August, when the question of the strip was first discussed, and Chamberlain agreed that if Rhodes could come to terms with the various chiefs concerned he might have his railway-strip, leaving large reserves for the natives. At this interview Harris tried the effect on Chamberlain of what he called a "guarded allusion." According to his own account, he hinted "in confidence" that troops placed at a certain point on the border might be useful in case of a rising in Johannesburg. But Chamberlain cut him off very short, telling him coldly that he wanted no confidences from him, as the High Commissioner could be trusted to give him all necessary information; he did not catch his allusion to troops, and had obviously no inkling of Harris's real meaning. The second interview in November was at a purely formal meeting attended also by the Bechuana chiefs, when there was no opportunity for "guarded allusions." At this meeting Chamberlain, with the consent of the chiefs, handed over the border strip to the Company on terms which he justifiably regarded as very advantageous to the country. In return for the six-mile strip along the Livingstone road, the Company agreed to the creation of large reserves for the natives under the High Commissioner, to abandon their claim to a subsidy of £10,000 a year for the railway, promised them by Ripon, and even to save the Imperial Government the large expenditure on the Bechuanaland police by undertaking responsibility for the security of the strip and the border. On Rhodes's representation that it was essential to secure immediate protection for the construction parties, Chamberlain allowed him to recruit for the Company's police from the disbanded Imperial police, and to collect an adequate force at Pitsani, a few miles north of Mafeking.

Rhodes had thus obtained the "jumping-off ground" he needed; not a day too soon, for the Johannesburg rising had been timed for December;—though at a price of which he complained in no measured terms to Dr. Harris. But he was also brought to believe that he had the indirect approval of Chamberlain for his scheme. The hints and innuendoes made to Chamberlain and Fairfield were reported for all they were worth to South Africa, as well as Dr. Harris's optimistic impressions of the sense in which they were accepted. There is no doubt that Dr. Harris, and, chiefly through his reports, Rhodes and several of the other conspirators, were fully persuaded that their course of action was countenanced by Chamberlain. Rhodes himself was not one to insist on an explicit sanction from those in authority in a case of difficulty. As he himself said to a young English officer whom he blamed for not exceeding instructions in Uganda: "You cannot expect a Prime Minister to write down that you are to seize ports, etc. But when he gives you orders to the contrary, *disobey* them." But there is not a tittle of evidence that either Chamberlain or the Colonial Office officials really understood, still less approved of, Rhodes's scheme. What Chamberlain certainly knew was that a rising in Johannesburg was probable, and he had provided for the intervention of the High Commissioner in that case, and for a military force to support him, if necessary. It may even have occurred to him that the police on the border might possibly be called upon for assistance, though a man of Chamberlain's masterful nature, had he contemplated such a case, is much more likely to have retained the police in his own hands. But that Chamberlain had any inkling that Rhodes himself was actively plotting for the revolution, and that part of his plan was to send in a Rhodesian force as soon as the rising occurred is neither proved nor credible; for the reports by Dr. Harris of his impressions are not evidence.[1]

III

While the discussions about the strip were going on, the rising in Johannesburg was being organized. Jameson paid several visits to the Rand to feel the ground before he finally broached the subject of Rhodes's plans to the leading members of the National Union, an organization started to secure rights for the Uitlanders. The arrangements then proposed and accepted were that 5000 rifles and a million rounds of ammunition should be smuggled in from Kimberley, that on the eve of the rising the arsenal at Pretoria should be surprised, and that at a given signal Jameson should cross the border at the head of 1500 men with guns and Maxims. The date tentatively fixed for the rising was December 28. The only doubt still left in the minds of the leaders was as to the flag under which the revolution should be carried out: the Republican Vierkleur or the Union Jack. In other words, was the Transvaal to remain independent or be annexed to England? Rhodes and Jameson were suspected of designing annexation; the Johannesburg leaders were convinced that such a design spelt failure, for though the majority of the Uitlanders were English, many even of these, besides the Germans and Americans among them, had no wish to upset the Republican institutions, if their just grievances were removed. To clear up the point, a deputation went to see Rhodes in October. His answer was quite satisfactory: he had, he said, two objects in embarking on the revolution—first, to get rid of abuses which affected him as one of the largest mine-proprietors, and secondly, to obtain free trade with the other South African states. "That is what I want," he said, laying his finger on the word "free trade" in the Uitlanders' declaration of

[1] For a further discussion of this point see Chap. XVI. pp. 282-283.

rights, "from that will flow a customs union, railway amalgamation and ultimately federation." He assured them further that he had no intention of changing the flag by violence, and that if a plebiscite after the revolution decided on a Republic he would not oppose it, provided the Republic came into close fiscal union with the rest of South Africa. It was, in fact, his old idea of independence for local affairs with the British flag for union.

From this date preparations both in Johannesburg and on the border began in earnest. Rhodes himself, beyond providing the funds with Beit, took little active part, trusting to subordinates not always well chosen. His brother Frank, a cavalry colonel of exquisite charm but no business capacity, was sent in a nominal capacity on the Gold Fields, to take charge of the plot in Johannesburg. The Chartered Company's office at Cape Town was used as a clearing-house for messages to Rhodes and between Johannesburg and Jameson on the border; officials of De Beers at Kimberley took an active part in smuggling arms over the border, concealed in oil-drums or under truck loads of coal, and in enrolling men, such as the "eleven fine diamonds" sent to Johannesburg in December, to stiffen the conspirators. A Dr. Wolff, another of Rhodes's Kimberley doctors, was sent to the Transvaal to buy up stores and horses and place them at suitable points on the road between the border and Johannesburg, for the relief of Jameson's column. Touches of melodrama were introduced by mysterious agents, ostentatiously engaged on secret intrigues. A certain Captain Holden dropped one fine day from the clouds on a wretched forwarding agent at Port Elizabeth, who was so cowed by the other's formidable gift of silence that he at once complied with his demand on him to forward some oil-drums full of arms surreptitiously to Johannesburg. "He was most extraordinary. He asked me to ask him as few questions as possible. I have never found a man so silent before. He was like an oyster," said the forwarding agent; and he had never seen him before or since. The plot was referred to as the "flotation of the new company," or the "polo tournament," the conspirators as "subscribers" or "shareholders," or what not, in the telegrams these agents showered on one another. How little Rhodes himself controlled the details of the plot is evident from his friends' testimony. "Mr. Rhodes was always trying to remember details, but he never could," said one of them. He did not even trouble to sign his own cheques, and contented himself with giving the vaguest instructions. "That is not the way Mr. Rhodes does things," Dr. Harris told Sir William Harcourt. "If Mr. Rhodes has an agent he trusts him and gives him *carte blanche* in that way. He does not say, 'If you think fit to do so and so, do it.' He says, 'You know the whole thing; do the best you can, when the circumstances arise.'"

The trouble about this method of conspiring is that the chief conspirator should have a very clear idea himself of his object and agents thoroughly to be trusted to carry out that idea. Unfortunately Rhodes was rather vague on the crucial question of the flag; though he had not insisted on the revolt being under the Union Jack, he certainly had every hope, nay intention, that the Transvaal should vote itself British. In that sense he may have spoken to his intimates. But Dr. Harris seems to have gone further and wanted the revolt itself to be a British affair, and, after his return from England in the middle of December, the Johannesburg leaders were becoming disquieted at rumours emanating from Cape Town of Rhodes's intention to insist from the outset on the British flag. Jameson, the appointed leader of the border force, was another who was inclined to interpret very largely any licence to "do the best he could when the circumstances arose."

Gallant and devoted to Rhodes as Jameson was, he was naturally impetuous and self-confident, and none the less so for his recent success in Matabeleland; and he was soon so much taken up with his own side of the plot that he began to forget the subsidiary rôle originally assigned to his force. The enrolment of its members had been proceeding apace since October, when a detachment of 250 Mashonaland mounted police was brought down to a camp at Pitsani, in the six-mile strip, north of Mafeking.[1] Recruits were

[1] This was possible at that date, as Rhodes had purchased from Montsioa a tract of land at Pitsani with Chamberlain's approval.

obtained from Cape Colony, and by the end of December, when many of the disbanded Imperial police had joined him, Jameson had 600 men at Pitsani; a well-equipped force, yet less than half the 1500 promised to the Johannesburg leaders. As military advisers he had Major Sir John Willoughby of the Horse Guards and some other British officers seconded for police work, who in April had conducted a secret reconnaissance of the country round Pretoria. If Jameson himself was rash, these regular officers gave him very little ballast; all seem to have regarded the success of the expedition as a foregone conclusion and to have undertaken it with the light-hearted carelessness of cheery schoolboys. One curious precaution Jameson did take. He obtained from the Johannesburg leaders a letter of invitation to himself, which described the disturbed and discontented state of the city, the likelihood of a conflict with the Government and the consequent danger to "thousands of unarmed men, women and children . . . at the mercy of well-armed Boers," and concluded with a request that he should come to their help if a disturbance took place. The date of the letter was purposely left blank; Jameson was to fill it in when he started and use its appeal for the helpless women and children as a justification for invading the Boers' territory. As a further safeguard to his officers Jameson felt justified in assuring Willoughby in general terms of the Imperial authorities' goodwill to the scheme; and Willoughby passed on these assurances to the others. Jameson based his belief partly, no doubt, on the optimistic reports sent from London about Chamberlain's attitude, partly also on recent conversations with Sir Hercules Robinson. Naturally neither Rhodes nor he informed Robinson of their scheme—Rhodes, indeed, as will appear, carefully concealed it from him—but they had discussed with him the action to be taken in case of a rising in Johannesburg. Robinson had told them confidentially of his instructions to mediate, and possibly Jameson suggested to him that, if he wanted armed support, the police on the border might prove useful. But this is a very different thing from Robinson approving of the unauthorized invasion of the Transvaal that Rhodes and Jameson contemplated. But, like Dr. Harris, Jameson seems to have believed that others understood his hints in the same sense that he gave them.

Meanwhile there was more misunderstanding in Johannesburg. Arms had been smuggled in, but not in sufficient quantities, and the tale of 5000 rifles promised had not been nearly completed by the end of December. The leaders also required a definite assurance that the High Commissioner would come up to protect them, as soon as the revolt broke out. Rhodes gave the necessary assurance, quite unjustifiably, for his knowledge of Robinson's intention came to him only in confidence as a Minister of the Crown, and was never meant to be used as a stimulus to the revolt. Finally, the question of the flag came up again in an acute form. The Reform Committee, organizing the revolt, discovered that many of the rank and file were very lukewarm about rising at all and were certainly not prepared to risk their lives for the Union Jack. Accordingly *The Times* correspondent, Colonel Younghusband, who was in the Committee's confidence, volunteered to see Rhodes in Cape Town. On arriving at Groote Schuur on December 22, 1895, he found Rhodes with a large party on his stoep. "Have you seen my hydrangeas?" said Rhodes, catching hold of his arm, "come and see them"; and, as soon as they were out of earshot: "Now tell me quick what it is, as we can't stay here long; we are being watched." On hearing Younghusband's message: "All right, if they won't go into it, they won't; and I shall wire to Jameson to keep quiet." As, however, he was strolling off to the station for his three days' journey back, Younghusband was overtaken by Dr. Harris, who said, "Oh, Rhodes says that when any rising takes place it must be under the British flag." When this message was reported, the Reform leaders were in dismay: they sent telegrams and messengers to Jameson to delay his departure, and two more delegates to have it out with Rhodes. The delegates saw him on December 28, and were reassured by his statement that there would be no question of the Union Jack—Dr. Harris's message had probably been another case of "doing the best he could"; and in the evening it was agreed to postpone all action for another ten days, when it was hoped more arms would have arrived. Rhodes himself thought the revolution had "fizzled out like a damp squib."

Even before this Rhodes had quite decided that all action must be postponed till the Johannesburg people were readier. Throughout the 26th, 27th and 28th telegrams of increasing urgency were being sent to Jameson from the Chartered Company's office, bidding him stand fast. Dr. Harris was evidently moved almost to tears by the hesitation of Johannesburg, and concludes one of his telegrams "Ichabod"; but he makes it quite plain to Jameson that he must not move: "All our foreign friends are dead against flotation and say public will not subscribe one penny towards it even with you as director. . . . We cannot have fiasco."

But Jameson was tired of delays and of all the excuses of Johannesburg for postponement—the flag, the High Commissioner, a race meeting or what not—which he began to suspect were simply signs of oozing courage; and he came to the conclusion that if left to itself Johannesburg would never rise at all. Well, if they hesitated to take the plunge, he would drive them in. Moreover, there were signs that the secret was leaking out: everybody in Mafeking knew that some plot was afoot; there were rumours in the Free State and in Cape Town, and even the old President in a speech at Middelburg had hinted that he might be more wide awake than was suspected. For all these reasons he decided he must act at once if at all: "You may say what you like," he is reported to have exclaimed, as he rose from reading Macaulay's essay, "but Clive would have done it!" So, in spite of Rhodes's direct and reiterated orders, he prepared to "do the best he could as circumstances arise." One of the Johannesburg messengers, the silent gentleman of the oil-drums, sent to stop him, finding, when he arrived at Pitsani on December 28, that his message was spoken to deaf ears, decided to cast in his lot with the column and go in with it. The other messenger startled the inhabitants of Mafeking by thundering at the door of a Jewish storekeeper in the early hours of the following morning, and after getting a pair of top-boots from the store rode on post-haste to Pitsani on the same fruitless mission. On this day, Sunday, December 29, Jameson and his officers harangued the men, read out snatches of the "letter of invitation," which he dated December 20, and exhorted them to ride in with every prospect of an easy success. Parting healths were drunk, in one case too freely, for the trooper sent to cut the wires to Pretoria was so befuddled that he carefully cut and buried long strands from a farmer's fence in mistake for the telegraph wire. The careless young officers had no doubts or fears; they had been told that "it would be all right" with the Imperial authorities, and so easy were they as to the event that one of them carried in his kit a complete collection of incriminating documents, code-telegrams, a code to interpret them, and a diary recording his talks with Rhodes and Jameson. At 9.30 P.M. the magistrate of Mafeking was sitting peacefully on his stoep after evening service with his wife and mother, when the quiet was suddenly broken by loud cheering from the police camp hard by. It came from the Imperial police, transferred to the Chartered Company's service, starting out to join the Rhodesians at Pitsani. So sallied forth Jameson's troop of 600 across the border into the Transvaal.

On the morning of that Sunday Rhodes received a telegram from Jameson saying that he was starting that night. Rhodes at once drafted a telegram ordering him on no account to move. But the telegraph offices were shut for the rest of the day, and by the evening the line to Cape Town had been cut by troopers unfortunately more sober than their comrade; so this telegram was never sent off. Hitherto Rhodes had confided his plan to only two men in the Imperial service. One of these was his Oxford friend, F. J. Newton, formerly on the Governor's staff, but now Commissioner of the Protectorate, where his acquiescence was almost essential to Rhodes's plans. Newton had felt some qualms at this knowledge and thought he ought either to resign or inform his chief, but Rhodes had quieted his scruples, saying it was unnecessary and absurd for him to resign and that it might do harm to speak to Robinson prematurely. The other was the Imperial Secretary himself, the High Commissioner's right-hand man, Sir Graham Bower. In October Rhodes, on obtaining his word of honour that he would keep it secret, told him of the force he was collecting at Pitsani for action in the Transvaal, adding, "If trouble comes, I am not going to sit still. You fellows are infernally slow: you can act if you like, but, if you do not act, I will." Later he told Bower of the money he was spending on the Johannesburg rising, but at the end of December informed him that the plot had miscarried. Great then was his astonishment and distress, when he was summoned to Rhodes's house at eleven o'clock that Sunday night, and Rhodes showed him Jameson's telegram. Rhodes still professed to have a faint hope that Jameson might be recalled by his own message; but he was evidently crushed by the news and kept saying, "I know I must go; I will resign to-morrow."

Naturally Rhodes had said nothing of his designs against the Transvaal Government to his ally Hofmeyr, though he seems to have thought of giving him a hint when all the preparations were completed; nor did he tell his colleagues in the Ministry. He appears to have thought that success would justify him in their eyes. Two of his Ministers, however, had been disturbed by persistent rumours connecting his name with the rising in Johannesburg. One of them, Schreiner, had gone to see him at Groote Schuur on the memorable Sunday and warned him against having anything to do with the Johannesburg movement, as people would be watching him. "Oh, that's all right," said Rhodes, shrugging his shoulders: he then still hoped his telegram would recall Jameson. On Monday 30th Schreiner had telegrams from the magistrate and police inspector at Mafeking, sent by despatch rider to the nearest station below the interrupted wires, announcing Jameson's departure into the Transvaal. Schreiner did not believe it and told the magistrate not to get unduly agitated; but he went to consult Rhodes. He was out riding with a friend, so Schreiner left a message and went home to dinner. Hardly had he finished when Rhodes's boy came with a lantern to guide him through the woods to Groote Schuur. Schreiner came into Rhodes's study with the telegrams in his hand:

"The moment I saw him," is Schreiner's own account, "I saw a man I had never seen before. His appearance was utterly dejected and different. Before I could say a word, he said, 'Yes, yes, it is true. Old Jameson has upset my apple-cart. It is all true.' I said I had some telegrams. He said, 'Never mind, it is all true. Old Jameson has upset my apple-cart.' . . . I was staggered," continues Schreiner; "I said, 'What do you mean, what can you mean? . . . Why did you not say anything to me yesterday when I was here?' and he said then at once, 'I thought I had stopped him. I sent messages to stop him and did not want to say anything about it if I stopped him.' . . . 'Why do you not stop him [now]? Although he has ridden in you can still stop him.' He said, 'Poor old Jameson. Twenty years we have been friends, and now he goes in and ruins me. I cannot hinder him. I cannot go in and destroy him.'" Then for three hours the two friends talked about this tragic ending to their partnership, for both at once saw that Rhodes's Ministry was doomed. "During the entire interview," says Schreiner, "Mr. Rhodes was really broken down. He was broken down. He was not the man who could be playing that part. Whatever the reason may have been, when I spoke to him he was broken down. . . . He was absolutely broken down in spirit, ruined. . . . I left in very great distress." That one may well believe; for Schreiner was one of Rhodes's most faithful followers. His mother, tied as she was to her up-country home, never saw Rhodes, but had long watched his career with passionate devotion, used to write him letters full of the pride she felt in him, and had brought up her son William almost to worship him. In parting from this friend on that Monday night Rhodes had a foretaste of what the Raid might mean to him. The agony had begun, but the worst was yet to come: for he still believed that Jameson might perhaps by a miracle win through to Johannesburg, and, though he could have felt little hope, he yet went on fighting fiercely for his friend.

Early next morning Sir Graham Bower told the High Commissioner of Jameson's intention to enter the Transvaal;

and on the same day a cable message came from Chamberlain saying that rumours of such an intention were current in London, and that any such violation of a friendly territory must be repudiated forthwith. Rhodes's secret designs, confided to *The Times* and to too many other people in London, had evidently leaked out. At any rate, this message effectually disposes of the suggestion, afterwards put about, that Chamberlain was privy to Rhodes's plot, for it was sent before Chamberlain could possibly have known whether Jameson had been called in by the Johannesburg people or not, and whether he was likely to succeed or fail. Rhodes was at once called upon by Robinson to disown Jameson's action, but would not do so, and even avoided meeting the High Commissioner until he thought that he could do some good to Jameson by seeing him. But he sent in his resignation as Prime Minister, which Robinson did not accept for a few days, as he was just starting for Pretoria to interview the President on the crisis. On the 31st all Cape Town knew of the Raid, among others Hofmeyr. "If Rhodes is behind this, he is no more a friend of mine," he said, and straightway telegraphed to Kruger, wishing his burghers success against "Jameson's filibusters"; he also called on the High Commissioner to issue a proclamation against the raiders, as Kruger had done against the Adendorff trek. Robinson not only agreed, but accepted Hofmeyr's draft. Then Rhodes was roused to come and plead with Robinson for delay, at least until Jameson's fate was known. In Sir Graham Bower's room he met Hofmeyr face to face. He told him that he had offered to resign and of the reason: "I have been so intimately connected with Jameson people will not relieve me of responsibility." "Mere resignation is not enough," was Hofmeyr's retort; "you must issue a manifesto repudiating Jameson, suspending him as Administrator of Rhodesia, and declaring that the law will be set in force against him." "Well, you see," answered Rhodes, "Jameson has been such an old friend, of course I cannot do it." "I quite understand," said Hofmeyr, "that is quite enough, you need say no more." With that he turned away, and told a friend a day or two later that he felt about Rhodes's conduct as if he had been deceived by the wife of his bosom.

To Rhodes this loss of a fifteen-year-old friendship was a bitter blow : hearing of his deep distress, Hofmeyr consented to visit him once more at Groote Schuur. But the breach was only widened by this, their last, interview. Rhodes went away convinced that Hofmeyr meant to attack his Charter, and would make no admission of guilt ; Hofmeyr came away saying Rhodes had been spoilt : " He imagines himself a young king, the equal of the Almighty," or, as another version has it, " a Clive and a Warren Hastings rolled into one." Rhodes afterwards would veil his feelings by brutal and cynical allusions to Hofmeyr and their previous relationship, but he felt the loss none the less deeply.

While any hope remained that Jameson might win through, Rhodes and his associates did their best to promote his success. They could not stop the proclamation outlawing him, but hoped through their influence on *The Times* to win the sympathy of England. The " letter of invitation," with its date now altered to December 28 by Dr. Harris, was cabled over to Printing House Square and, by its appeal for helpless women and children, stirred up a wave of popular enthusiasm for the Doctor and his troopers, and inspired one of the worst sonnets ever indited even by a poet-laureate. Dr. Harris kept up the appearance of success as long as he could, and a report was circulated that a victory had been won and Johannesburg nearly reached. But on January 2 the stunning news came through that on that morning Jameson and his whole party had surrendered to the Boers at Doornkop, near Krugersdorp, twenty miles short of their goal : he had not been assisted by the Johannesburgers, and it began to look as if he was not even wanted by them. However, this was the very moment obligingly chosen by the German Emperor to divert attention from Rhodes's and Jameson's misdeeds by an uncalled-for telegram of congratulation to Kruger. The British nation were not going to stand any German interference in South Africa, and promptly ordered out their fleet as a warning. In South Africa even Hofmeyr was stirred to anger at the Kaiser's " blundering utterance " : " Nobody," he suggested caustically, " knows better than his Imperial Majesty that the first German shot against England would be followed by . . . the acquisition by England of all German colonies —Damaraland included—which would not be an unmixed evil for the Cape." Rhodes himself, when he met the Kaiser three years later, bluntly described what a good turn he had done him: "You see, I was a naughty boy, and you tried to whip me. Now my people were quite ready to whip me for being a naughty boy, but directly *you* did it, they said, 'No, if this is anybody's business, it is *ours*.' The result was that Your Majesty got yourself very much disliked by the English people, and I never got whipped at all."

However, the Kaiser's bluster could not veil the fact that Jameson and his men were at the mercy of the Boers, and had made themselves ridiculous by their easy self-confidence; that the Johannesburg rising, partly through the blundering impatience of Rhodes's own trusted agent, had collapsed ignominiously, and that the leaders, among whom was Rhodes's own brother, were to be put on trial for their lives as traitors to the Republic. The Transvaal was put on its guard, and redoubled precautions against a menace to its independence. Rhodes had implicated the British South Africa Company's officials in his plot and had brought its Charter into jeopardy; he had perverted the De Beers Company and the Gold Fields from their legitimate objects, and had destroyed a Cabinet which seemed to have no possible rivals. Above all, by this attempted short-cut to success, he had undone his patient labour of years to unite English and Dutch and to promote the union of South Africa. Before the world, and especially before his enemies, he kept a proud, almost arrogant, demeanour, barely admitting his error, or admitting it only so far as to claim credit for the admission. But in his own house, during the week succeeding the Raid, he unbared to a few intimates the agony of his soul, an agony like that of Saul—

> drear and stark, blind and dumb.

He had failed not merely in his plot—that touched him least —but failed for the time being in the object of union closest to his heart, and failed through his most trusted friend; and he had lost the confidence of those through whom he had the fondest hopes of achieving his aim. Never afterwards was he the leader of the community, but only of a party based chiefly on the racial lines which he detested : a few good friends still remained to him among the Dutch, but the Dutch as a whole had been carried off by Hofmeyr from him for ever. Many of the English too. For Mr. Merriman represented the feelings of many of his English fellow-colonials, as well as of the Dutch at the Cape, who objected as strongly as Rhodes himself to Kruger's treatment of the Uitlanders. "I was heartily in favour of the Reform movement," he said, "and it was the Raid that stopped the movement. The Raid was not only wrong in its inception, but it is the deceit and treachery which accompanied it that I object to; and the Raid has put Mr. Kruger back into his old position and rehabilitated him in the civilized world. That is the pity of it, and for that we have to thank Mr. Rhodes. . . . I do say, Mr. Rhodes is unworthy the trust of the country."

Lastly, he had, by this unworthiness, lowered the tone of South African politics. In his solitude and sad repining he may well have felt what Schreiner, revealing the depth of his own loss, expressed in this bitter cry: "You cannot trust a man altogether and be absolutely mistaken in your trust and remain with regard to the rest of the world just as full of trust and confidence as ever: and that is what hundreds of people are feeling in South Africa to-day; they have lost their leader. Yes, they have lost him absolutely, a leader who cemented around him such loyalty and devotion as I do not suppose in the colony any man ever had, or is likely soon to have again. . . . [The result is that] people do not confide as they did; they do not take a statement that a thing is so as necessarily proving that it is so; it may be so, or it may not be so."

CHAPTER XVI

THE NEW BEGINNING

RHODES had no David to harp to him during that week of agony, to tell him :

> Each deed thou hast done
> Dies, revives, goes to work in the world ; . . .
> . . . each ray of thy will,
> Every flash of thy passion and prowess, long over, shall thrill
> Thy whole people, the countless, with ardour, till they too give forth
> A like cheer to their sons, who in turn fill the South and the North
> With the radiance thy deed was the germ of. . . .

He had no David to

> . . . Snatch *him* the mistake,
> *Him* the failure, the ruin he seems now,—and bid him awake
> From the dream, the probation, the prelude, to find himself set
> Clear and safe in new light and new life,—a new harmony yet
> To be run and continued and ended—who knows ?—or endure !

He had no David ; but during those sleepless nights and days he found a voice in his own heart to tell it him : and he came forth to face the world with the words on his lips :

"I am just beginning my career."

I

For the time being he had ceased to count at the Cape, except as a suspect, but there was yet much for him to do elsewhere. "What does it matter what the people say about us, so long as our work goes on ? Hey ? I am sure you realize that," he once told a friend : and it was a principle he always followed out himself. There was the fate of Jameson and the Reform prisoners to be thought of. Jameson and his officers were handed over by Kruger to the British authorities and, after a trial at bar, were sentenced to terms of imprisonment. Rhodes made it his business to provide for their legal expenses, and to ensure them every comfort it was within his power to give, and he wrote saying that he was prepared to stand his trial also, if the Government wished to prosecute. The Reform prisoners were put on trial in the Transvaal, and Frank Rhodes and the other leaders were sentenced to death. Rhodes encouraged his sister to go up and do all she could for Frank while he was in prison; and when the death sentences on Frank and the other three were commuted for fines of £25,000 apiece, Rhodes cheerfully paid them as part of the expenses of the Raid. These expenses, which included the cost of all the agents employed in the plot, a press fund to secure a favourable public opinion, compensation to sufferers, arms smuggled into Johannesburg, and pay and equipment for the raiders, amounted to considerably over a quarter of a million sterling, a debt which was promptly settled by Rhodes and Beit between them. He also had it at heart to make a clean breast of his own share in the Raid. There was no definite charge on which he could be brought to trial, as Jameson had been; but two Committees inquired into the plot against the Transvaal. The first, a Committee of the Cape House of Assembly, sat in 1896, and, after hearing all the evidence available in South Africa, reported that, though Rhodes did not direct or approve Jameson's entering the territory of the South African Republic, yet he could not be relieved of responsibility for the unfortunate occurrences that had taken place, as he had concurred in the previous arrangements. Rhodes himself was not present at this inquiry, as he was then engaged in suppressing the rebellion in Matabeleland, but he concurred in the verdict.

The second inquiry was in 1897, before the British South Africa Committee of the House of Commons. When he started from South Africa to "face the music"—so he called it—a considerable revulsion of feeling had already set in. Kruger, not for the first time, had had all the cards in his hand after the Raid, and by a display of generosity might have brought nearly all South Africa to his feet. But he had shown clemency to the Reform prisoners only grudgingly, and under pressure of an almost general expression of opinion from every other colony and state: and he had not made any concessions to the Uitlanders' real grievances. This obstinacy, for one thing, had helped to rehabilitate his great rival. Rhodes himself also, by his masterly settlement of the Matabele trouble, had recalled to men's minds the great qualities of their lost leader: absence and his silence to the world, while he was "doing his duty," as he said, in Rhodesia, did the rest. So, when he came round from Beira on his way home to England, his journey was more like a triumphal progress than the penitential pilgrimage of a culprit going to meet his judges. Invitations to public receptions showered upon him from town after town on his way, but he refused them all except those from Port Elizabeth and Cape Town. At Port Elizabeth he began his speech nobly: "If I may put to you a thought, it is that the man who is continuously prosperous does not know himself, his own mind or character. It is a good thing to have a period of adversity. You then find out who are your real friends. . . . I am confident enough to say that I do not feel that my public career has closed. . . . I am determined still to strive for the closer union of South Africa. . . ." On his railway journey to Kimberley and thence to Cape Town crowds thronged to the stations to welcome him, and among them he was rejoiced to recognize the faces of many of his old friends among the Dutch farmers. He was deeply touched: "It is very moving to see one's fellow-beings feel so kindly to one. Such appreciation as this generally comes after a man is dead," he said to Fuller, and at a private dinner with some former parliamentary colleagues was moved to the frankest expression of his contrition. "I do not so much regret," he admitted, "joining in an attempt to force President Kruger into a juster and more reasonable policy. . . . But what has been a burden to me is that I was Prime Minister at the time, and that I had given a promise that I would not do anything incompatible with the joint position I held as director of the Chartered Company and Premier of the Cape Colony. On every ground I was bound to resign if I took such a course as assisting in a revolution against an officially friendly state; and I did not. I can only say that I will do my best to make atonement for my error by untiring devotion to the best interests of South Africa." Unhappily he never went so far in public. He had promised to make this apology at the public reception in Cape Town, but as he was beginning it the apology was drowned in a hurricane of applause, and he did not continue. It was indeed not a humble Rhodes, and many doubted if his repentance was sincere when, in that first public speech at Port Elizabeth, he had blurted out his contempt for the "unctuous rectitude" of his countrymen in England, before whom he was about to appear.[1]

No such scene greeted him at the inquiry in London as that immortalized by Macaulay in his description of the trial of Warren Hastings. It is true some of the greatest in English politics were to sit in judgement upon him: Chamberlain himself and Hicks-Beach, the jealous watch-dog of the Exchequer, whose rough tongue had no respect of persons; Harcourt, Campbell-Bannerman, and Buxton; Blake, the Irish-Canadian orator; Labouchere, who from the outset had pursued an untiring vendetta against Rhodes, his Company and all their proceedings; the Attorney-General, Cripps and Bigham, all three learned in the law and adroit in cross-examination; and there, too, primed with Rhodes's case by a recent sojourn with him in Rhodesia, "the delight and ornament of the House, and the charm of every private society he honoured with his presence," that modern Charles Townshend, George Wyndham; the poet, had he not dallied with politics, the great statesman, had he not trifled with literature.[2] To assist the Committee in coming to a just decision were assembled many of the great leaders of the Bar: Cohen, mellifluous

[1] An ingenious and cautious friend suggested to him that the words he meant to use and which should be inserted in the official report were "*anxious* rectitude." But Rhodes, as might be expected, replied, "No, I said it and I stick to it."

[2] Charles Boyd relates that Rhodes, when he had known him only a year, said of him, "Thought he was a spring poet: instead of that he is all chapter and verse."

and most deadly when with exquisite courtesy he seemed to be yielding every point; Pember, harsh and domineering, whose rough decision overbore all argument; and silver-tongued Pope, the unquestioned monarch of the Parliamentary Bar, who in his weighty and measured utterances seemed always, with consummate art, to be pleading not for a mere client's interests but for truth and public policy. All these were there; yet it was but a drab spectacle. The setting was not Rufus's Hall, but a dull committee-room adjoining. No beauty, rank or eminence graced the proceedings, for all but those connected in some way with the case were rigidly excluded. Dramatic moments, indeed, there were: Sir Graham Bower's startling revelation of his own privity to the plot and his concealment of it from the High Commissioner, some passages in Dr. Harris's evidence, where his word and Chamberlain's seemed almost irreconcilable, and Hawkesley's refusal to produce telegrams in his possession; but there was no eager crowd, swayed by divergent feelings, to share in and murmur at the exciting moments.

The two chief points of interest at the Committee were Rhodes himself and the question of Chamberlain's foreknowledge of the plot. Rhodes took the inquiry very seriously, and on his voyage to England spent two hours every day on ship-board rehearsing his evidence with a friend: the friend had to ask the sort of questions he imagined Labouchere or Harcourt would put. "Yes, that is a very fair question," Rhodes would say, and carefully consider how he would answer it. In spite of all this preparation he was evidently nervous when he really found himself walking up to the little table placed in the centre of the horse-shoe round which the Committee were sitting. He came in looking, as to features, very much like a Roman Emperor—massive head, masterful nose, and sleepy eyes, yet with a veiled fire in them—but in gait and gesture very unlike any Roman Emperor: ill-fitting clothes huddled on to an awkward body, a rather shambling walk and a half-dazed appearance. The first unfavourable impression was confirmed when he began to speak. His voice was squeaky and staccato, he sat humped up in his chair and was obviously ill at ease before his inquisitors. The answers he gave seemed involved and sometimes off the point. One began to wonder if this were really the great Colossus who bestrode half a continent. He seemed heavy, even stupid. Then came the hour for luncheon, which, with characteristic disregard of ceremony, the Committee and witnesses ate off little trays brought in by a waiter, so that the proceedings were not interrupted. Rhodes murmured his order to the waiter and then went on as before. The luncheons were brought in; and before Rhodes was set a solitary sandwich and a large tankard of stout. One bite of the sandwich, one long draught from the tankard; and then, as if suddenly aroused by this diversion, he shook himself together, like a lion just awaking, pulled straight his coat, sat up square to his tormentors, sent forth a gleam from that hitherto sleepy eye, and then—he just took that Committee in hand. Hitherto they had seemed to play with him, henceforward the *rôles* were reversed. There was no longer any question of examining Rhodes on his misdeeds; Rhodes himself took the floor and began examining the Committee on their knowledge of South Africa and lecturing them on things he thought it good for their souls to know. He enjoyed himself vastly. He dragged them away from the Raid, not because he wished to conceal his own part in the business—he stated quite frankly at the outset that he accepted full responsibility for it—but he brushed it aside as irrelevant, because he wanted to make that Committee, and through them the British public, understand their own mistakes and responsibility in South Africa and the policy for which he stood. Germany's part in Transvaal affairs? Oh, Germany's susceptibilities must be considered, and we must observe the correct diplomatic reticence, was the attitude of most of the Committee. Diplomacy go hang, said Rhodes in effect; you've got to know what I believe to be the facts: and these facts he proceeded to tell them. He had five days in that witness chair; but once he was on his mettle he never let that Committee go. Unmoved alike by Sir William Harcourt's grand manner and by Labouchere's insidious thrusts, he answered their questions indeed, but often told them more than they bargained for. He was accused of having made money by selling shares at the time of the Raid, so Wyndham asked him a friendly question about his transactions. Yes, I've sold plenty of shares, cheerfully responded the culprit; when the work on the telegraph or railway lines was hung up for lack of funds, I would sell large blocks of shares to enable me to pay for them out of my own pocket; I did likewise at the time of the Matabele War, "when I was afraid the Doctor might have bad times." But nobody had the courage to ask him the specific question about the Raid time: it would have been too absurd, for any one who had seen and heard him, to suspect him of having tried to make money out of that adventure. After his five days under examination the Committee seemed only too glad to let him go. Would you like to have me up again? blandly inquired Rhodes; I shall be happy to come, but you must remember that my work in Rhodesia keeps me very busy. Later, perhaps, said the Committee; but "later" never came.

As to Chamberlain's supposed privity with the plot against the Transvaal, nothing came out that has not been recounted in the previous chapter. The only unsatisfactory incident of the inquiry was that Hawkesley, on Rhodes's orders, refused to produce some documents, presumably telegrams and letters sent by Rhodes's agents to South Africa, which he had shown privately to Chamberlain the previous year; nor did the Committee insist on their production. This was unfortunate, because there was a suspicion abroad, partly fostered by Rhodes's friends, that Chamberlain was, in the current phrase, "in it up to the neck"; and the belief is even yet not quite dead that, after secretly countenancing the conspirators' plans, he threw them over when the fiasco came. Complete mathematical proof of Chamberlain's innocence is, of course, not possible, since these communications have never been revealed; and by this time probably all copies have been destroyed. Rhodes himself certainly believed that he was serving his country's interest in forbidding their production; but it is significant that all the cables in code which passed between agents in London and Rhodes himself or the Company's officials at the Cape were duly produced, and that the utmost they go to prove is that some of these agents believed that Chamberlain had an inkling of Rhodes's plans.[1] If the banned documents went any further, the most probable solution of the mystery is that Chamberlain may, in some utterance to Rhodes or his friends, have expressed a hope that the expected rising in Johannesburg would succeed, or have alluded to the instructions given to Robinson as to his course of action in the event of a rising. If that was so, Rhodes may have thought it prudent to avoid the disclosure of such utterances at a time when the rising had failed and the best hope of securing appeasement in South Africa was by concealing from Kruger what might have happened in other circumstances: and Chamberlain, though he said he had no objection to their disclosure, may for the same reason not have regretted Rhodes's decision. But though mathematical proof is impossible, it may confidently be asserted that, whatever sympathy Chamberlain may have had with the rising, he was not privy to, still less approved of, Rhodes's machinations in connection with it.[2]

The verdict of this Committee was very much the same as that of the Cape inquiry. The Raid was condemned, and Rhodes was severely censured for the misuse of his office as Prime Minister of the Cape and managing director of the Chartered Company; that was the least which the national honour demanded, especially in view of assertions, such as Jameson's, "I know, if I had succeeded, I should have been forgiven," and Rhodes's "unctuous rectitude." It must be admitted, however, that the sting of the rebuke to Rhodes was very much taken out by the subsequent debate in the House of Commons. Courtney, that jealous keeper of the nation's conscience, and other

[1] Some documents purporting to be the suppressed communications were published subsequently in the *Indépendance Belge* and are quoted in Jeyes's *Life of Chamberlain*. But they carry us no further.

[2] The view expressed in the foregoing paragraph is borne out by a statement attributed to George Wyndham by Mr. Blunt (*My Diaries*, i. p. 346). Wyndham, who was in all the secrets of the Rhodes group, told Blunt that Chamberlain was not involved in the Raid but was concerned in political intrigue against the Transvaal, which would obviously refer to the instructions to Robinson to use an armed force, if necessary, in case of a rising in Johannesburg.

speakers made a strong plea for removing his name from the list of Privy Councillors, as a mark of the nation's disapprobation of his action; but the House would not listen to the suggestion. They were not perhaps much moved by Chamberlain's paradoxical assertion that Rhodes had done nothing inconsistent with his personal honour; an assertion which went far beyond what Rhodes himself admitted to his friends at Cape Town. But it was felt that he had been punished enough in losing his great position at the Cape as well as his seat on the Board of the Company he had himself created. They were also impressed by a generous tribute to him from his successor and former rival, Sprigg, who testified to the love and admiration in which he was still held at the Cape and to the strong feeling there that any further punishment meted out to him would appear merely vindictive.

Rhodes himself was undoubtedly enough punished, not merely in loss of position and power, but still more in the disappointment of hopes. Nevertheless the Committee, and still more the debate in the House, were, from a national point of view, deplorable. A treacherous and, in method, unjustifiable attack had been made on the Transvaal Republic, and, whatever the provocation, admittedly great, in the treatment of the Uitlanders, it would have been more in keeping with our honour frankly to have admitted the wrong done by our fellow-citizens and leave the excuses aside. The Committee, however, allowed itself to be diverted by long discussions as to the Uitlanders' grievances, the Transvaal's intrigues with Germany and such really irrelevant matters. For, however just ours and the Uitlanders' case may have been against Kruger's régime, our countrymen had put themselves irretrievably in the wrong by the Raid, as well as by the plottings and smuggling of arms which preceded it. The Committee's inability to obtain documents known to be in the possession of one of the witnesses was another unfortunate incident; and Rhodes rendered a poor service to his country by forbidding their production. For whatever they may have contained, nothing could have been more mischievous than the atmosphere of suspicion created by their non-production. And the subsequent debate in the House was worst of all, with Chamberlain's almost implicit disassociation from the condemnation of Rhodes by the Committee. The fact is that in many quarters in England there was little condemnation of the Raid. Rhodes was aware of this when he said, "I found all the busmen smiling at me when I came to London; so I knew it was all right."

II

Even before this final examination by his countrymen Rhodes had found work of the utmost importance to his hand. His first great fear, after the catastrophe, had been that his beloved Company might be deprived of its Charter, and that he himself would be allowed to have no further part in Rhodesia. Hardly had he come out of his retirement at Groote Schuur in January 1896 than he took ship to England for a week's visit to see his Board and Chamberlain. He found out from the latter that there was no immediate design of cancelling the Charter; and satisfied with this assurance, when he saw that his own continued presence on the Board might injure the Company, he made no difficulty about resigning his directorship.[1] But, director or no director, he was determined now to devote his energies chiefly to his own country. Returning by the East coast route, he called on Kitchener in Egypt on the way and obtained through him a cargo of Soudanese donkeys for use in Rhodesia, because of their immunity from horse-sickness.[2] He landed at Beira on March 20, 1896, and a few days later heard news so serious that he thought no more for some time of donkeys or horse-sickness. On March 24 the first murders of isolated settlers near Buluwayo were perpetrated by the Matabeles, the signal for the serious

[1] This resignation did not take effect till June, when Chamberlain had pointed out its necessity.

[2] Mr. Blunt in his *Diaries* reports a cock-and-bull story to the effect that Rhodes and Kitchener between them plotted that Rhodes should be allowed to kidnap 200 Soudanese men to work in the Rhodesian mines. Rhodes at the time heard of the story, and in a speech at Buluwayo promptly contradicted it: "I had hardly arranged for these donkeys to arrive here when I received a peremptory telegram asking if it was correct that I was arranging for the importation of Soudanese. I replied promptly, gentlemen, that it was totally incorrect, and that the only animals I was receiving or arranging for were donkeys."

rising, which for a time jeopardized the lives of the whole white community in Matabeleland. The Matabeles had many grievances real and imaginary against the English. Since Jameson's arrival in 1893 there had been a drought of unexampled severity; the native police enrolled by the Company, taken chiefly from the races formerly subject to the Matabeles, had shown a tactless and tyrannical disposition, much resented by their former masters, and had even sometimes been employed in securing forced labour for the mines; the reserves set aside for the natives after the Matabele War had been most unsatisfactory; "not homes, but cemeteries," they were described by a distinguished Englishman. To crown all, one of the most fatal attacks of rinderpest ever known in South Africa spread havoc and destruction among the magnificent herds which had been the glory and chief source of livelihood to Lo Bengula and his people. To Lo Bengula's old warriors the opportunity seemed good for revenging themselves on the invaders: some of their best regiments had taken no part in the fighting of 1893 and felt themselves a match for the English, whose prestige had suffered by Jameson's defeat at Doornkop; moreover, the country had been largely denuded of police by their diversion to the Raid. The revolt spread like wildfire, and very soon the 4000 inhabitants of Buluwayo found themselves a beleaguered garrison surrounded by 15,000 savages and in danger of starvation, if not worse.

Fortunately help was at hand. Earl Grey had gallantly undertaken the thankless task of succeeding Jameson as Administrator. Arriving at Mafeking within a month of the outbreak of revolt, he hurried stores up to Buluwayo. Already Colonel Plumer, now for the first time enabled to give proof of his great military capacity, had organized a relief column, which on May 24 inflicted the first defeat on the rebel forces and removed all danger from Buluwayo. Relief had also been coming from another quarter. Rhodes had arrived at Salisbury at the end of March and had at once, though ill of malaria, begun organizing a column under Colonel Beal, and in spite of his condition insisted on accompanying it. During the march to Buluwayo

Beal defeated the rebels near Gwelo, and Rhodes took his full share of all risks in this engagement and in the still more dangerous reconnoitring expeditions. He seemed to bear a charmed life, never carrying any weapon except a hunting-crop and always riding ahead with fearless courage. He was apparently not a man of much physical courage naturally, but he had the greater moral courage of being able to force himself to incur necessary dangers at a crisis; and he now probably felt that his own skin was of little worth compared with the example he felt bound to give. When his column arrived at Buluwayo in the beginning of June the Matabele impis had all dispersed into the Matoppo Hills, a large tract of tumbled country to the south-east of Buluwayo. Sir Frederick Carrington had arrived to take command of the operations and ordered a sweep round of this country by three columns. Plumer won a considerable success at Thabas Imamba, north of the Matoppos, at the end of the month, but another attack in July showed that the rebels would never be defeated by this sort of warfare. When pressed they could always take refuge in the almost inaccessible hills at their back, and from their posts of vantage could sally forth and inflict serious losses on the attackers. They could indeed be starved out; but Rhodes wanted peace not extermination. The only other course was negotiation, and this Rhodes resolved to undertake.

Negotiation was not an easy task. Carrington insisted on keeping a large force on the edge of the Matoppos, which naturally aroused the suspicions of the Matabeles that a trap was being laid for them; and Rhodes's first difficulty was to get into communication with them at all. However, an opportunity was found by the capture in August of an old old crone, a widow of Lo Bengula's father, Moselikatze, who was released with a message to the rebels. Four days later a small party rode out of Plumer's camp, Rhodes himself, Hans Sauer, Colenbrander, a man well versed in the natives' ways, who had quarrelled with the Chartered Company but came in response to Rhodes's special request, one or two other Europeans and the native scouts John Grootboom and Makunga. The party were unarmed and they rode out to the trysting-place, where a red flag was to be flying if the Matabele indunas were prepared to parley. The red flag was flying right enough, and to show that it was understood Rhodes hung beneath it his own white handkerchief. Further messages were sent in to the chiefs to induce them to come to an indaba with Rhodes to discuss grievances and consider terms of peace; but they were still very wary of approaching close to the English camp. So, to give them confidence, Rhodes with his little party moved right away from the troops and pitched a camp far in the heart of the Matoppos; there he remained, forbidding any armed force from Plumer's camp to come near him, defenceless, had the Matabeles any sinister intentions. All the time he was being watched by the Matabeles in the hills above him; and at last, seeing that he had no aggressive intentions, they gradually gained confidence enough to consent to a meeting, on the understanding that neither side should bring rifles or assegais. This first indaba on August 21 was the crucial one. Rhodes and his party were first at the meeting-place, a large smooth rock; they carried among them only four revolvers and their horses were tethered some way behind them, so that there was no means of escape in case of treachery. Soon at least 100 natives were seen approaching, all fully armed with assegais and rifles, and flanking parties thrown out to cut off any retreat. In spite of the previous arrangement and several messages the natives kept advancing with threatening mien. These were anxious moments for Rhodes and his friends. A sign of fear or hesitation would certainly have brought the whole crowd upon them. Not before they were forty yards from the rock did the natives lay down their arms. Then the talk went on between them and Rhodes for two livelong hours, Colenbrander acting as interpreter. At first the young men were inclined to be unruly and interrupt their elders, who were doing most of the talking, but were soon brought to order by the wise old induna Babyan. The following fragment of conversation shows the nature of the discussions that went on during those two hours: "Rhodes, we know," said a chief, "he is not in fault." Then a Majaka said insolently, "How do we know that Mr. Rhodes is doing his best for us? Perhaps when he goes away he tells his people to rob us." To this the chiefs answered that they trusted Colenbrander and Rhodes; whereupon, "Tell them, Colenbrander, that I am going to stay in the country," said Rhodes. After this he scattered bagfuls of tobacco to be scrambled for by the natives, and the indaba broke up. On returning to camp Rhodes remarked that the interview had just enough spice of danger to make it interesting.

After this, for nearly two months, Rhodes stayed on at his camp, holding frequent indabas with the natives, urging them to come in before it was too late to sow their crops and avert starvation, and allowing them to go freely in and out of the camp as they pleased; so gradually they came to look upon him as their Father and Protector. Such implicit faith, too, had his friend Lord Grey, the Administrator, in Rhodes and his trustful methods that he allowed Lady Grey and his daughter to stay a fortnight in the camp with no more protection from the natives surrounding them than Rhodes had himself.

The last solemn conference, held on October 13, was attended by Lord Grey, Rhodes, with Colenbrander to interpret, and nineteen of the chiefs. Grey opened the proceedings by telling them the Queen wished for peace before they were starved. It would be useless for them to resist the English, who were very strong with their railway, then being brought up to Buluwayo by Sir Charles Metcalfe, their forts and their guns. "I hear," he added, "that you chiefs are sore because you have lost authority and the young men laugh at you. Well, I will give authority to good indunas, and first to Faku and Umjeen, to whom I will give a horse and in due time a salary." Then the following dialogue took place:

Gambo. We have no leader and it is impossible for a nation to live without a ruler.

Rhodes. The chiefs will be at the head of their followers, but the Administrator will be over them.

Somabulana. We want some one to whom we can go before we go to Mr. Rhodes, to whom we can report our troubles. We want one not half a dozen heads.

Rhodes. Each chief will have his own district and the people will go with their grievances to the chiefs. The chief will go to the native commissioners, who will in turn communicate with the Administrator.

Faku. That is what we want. Give us a head and we are satisfied.

. . . . . .

Rhodes. The trouble is that the chiefs and indunas have nothing, and they will be compelled to beg food from the common people. It is not right that chiefs should do this, but if they draw salaries from the Government this will be avoided. They can then stay in their districts and thus look after their people. The chiefs must show by their conduct that they are loyal. Look at Dhlio, he is not here to-day, because he is in the hills collecting guns.

And then, after further talk from Grey, Rhodes thus concluded: "Before this meeting breaks up I wish to inform you that I am leaving the Matoppos to-day, but before you go away to your homes I should be pleased to give you some presents. I hope you will behave well to the Administrator and show your loyalty."

The chiefs then thanked Rhodes and said they would lick the ground he was treading on.

Having made peace with the indunas, Rhodes gave them a prompt illustration of the spirit in which he meant to deal with them hereafter. Up in the Matoppos the Matabeles had been almost starving, and even now were faced with many months of famine, since they had not been able to sow their lands. To relieve their immediate distress, therefore, he ordered a million bags of mealies at once, telling Grey that if the Company objected to the expense he would pay the whole cost out of his own pocket. He also promised the settlers compensation for their losses: and the Company cheerfully accepted both charges.

The settlement thus achieved by Rhodes after these long weeks of suspense and danger was never broken. He had succeeded by his confidence and courage, by his sympathetic understanding of the workings of the native mind, and above all by his ability to recapture that lost quality of patience which had characterized the old Rhodes of the breakfast with Groot Adriaan De la Rey, of the night-long vigil with Barney Barnato at Kimberley, or of the happy relations with the Dutch, when he could "sit down and argue with a man." It was one of the great incidents of his life, the most complete single achievement, and the one which gave him, perhaps, the most unalloyed satisfaction.

Unfortunately the trouble in Rhodesia did not come to an end with this settlement. Hardly had Rhodes, with most of the available fighting men in Mashonaland, arrived to relieve Buluwayo than another serious revolt broke out in the country they had just left. The Mashonas had always been regarded as an unwarlike people little likely to take up arms, but they were stimulated to revolt by the prophecies of a venerated seer, who lived in a cave, as well as by the example of their former masters, the Matabeles. Their revolt was much more troublesome to quell than the other, as they had no such corporate existence, each of the many chieftains with his kraal being a law unto himself: so each had to be defeated separately. The revolt accordingly dragged on from June 1896 to October 1897, the natives taking refuge in the innumerable caves of the country, whence they made raids on the English: and the method sometimes adopted of dealing with them was to blow up their fastnesses with dynamite. During part of this guerilla warfare Rhodes had to be away giving evidence before the Committee in London, but as soon as he was released he hurried back to his country. It must be remembered that all this time Rhodes had no official position of any kind there: for he was no longer a director and had no more status than any other settler. But Rhodes was Rhodes, and, wherever he was, could no more be ignored than the sun or the weather. He once made himself colonel of a column to bring to an end the disputes between two officers of equal rank; he told generals and others in the Imperial service when he thought their work was done, and saw that they took the hint for their departure; and everybody, high or low, looked to him for help and counsel. While the guerilla war was still going on he did not neglect the material development of the country. He set himself the task of importing cattle from the Cape, from the Argentine and from Australia, to make good the terrible ravages of the rinderpest ; finding that the Beira–Salisbury railway could not be laid to the existing site of Umtali except at a prohibitive cost, he boldly moved the whole township ten miles farther east with full compensation to the standholders ; the insurgent Mashonas had destroyed a large section of his Trans-African telegraph line, but undismayed he started laying it again at once. Where this pet project was concerned he was ruthless in hustling on his agents to almost superhuman exertions. When one of them grumbles at difficulties, he replies, "I cannot understand people undertaking a job and then not finishing it. . . . I am determined to finish the telegraph this year to Blantyre" ; and though, owing to the destruction of the line, this was not accomplished till April in the following year, 1898, he was justifiably proud of the speed with which the line had been laid through some hundreds of miles of almost unexplored territory.

All this work he loved. He felt he was doing something definitely useful for his fellows : he was, as he called it, "creating." Speaking to his Rhodesians almost for the last time, he expressed some of his joy in this "creating." "To be in this country," he said, "is surely a happier thing than the deadly monotony of an English country town or the still deadlier monotony of a Karroo village. Here at any rate you have your share in the creation of a new country. . . . You have the proud satisfaction of knowing that you are civilizing a new part of the world. Those who fall in that creation fall sooner than they would in ordinary life, but their lives are better and grander." He loved, too, the roaming life on the open veld, which this work of supervising the development of his country entailed. There he was most at home, there most himself. He was fortunate in having with him then in Rhodesia the friend most suited to his mood, Lord Grey, gallant and courageous as himself and of a sunnier nature. Grey had many stories of his talks with his friend as they rode together over the plains or sat beside the camp-fire, stories which reveal softer sides of the man's nature rarely shown to others. "Why," asked Grey of him one day, "do you always give away cheques of £20, £30, £50 or more to every ne'er-do-weel who whines to you for help?" "Well," said Rhodes, "a man once came to me in Cape Town and said he was on his beam-ends, could I lend him something? I didn't like the fellow's face and refused, and that same night he committed suicide. That was a lesson to me; and since then I have never dared to refuse money to folks who are hard up." One night Grey was sleeping soundly in his tent after a hard day's ride when suddenly he awoke with a start to find Rhodes, clad only in a flannel shirt, leaning over him and shaking him: "Wake up, Grey, wake up!" "Eh, what's the matter? Is the tent on fire?" sleepily murmured Grey. "No, no, but I just wanted to ask you, have you ever thought how lucky you are to have been born an Englishman when there are so many millions who were not born Englishmen? And that's not all: there you are, over forty, with a clean and healthy body and a sound mind when you might have been riddled with disease. That's all: that's all I wanted to say." "The dear old fellow," said Grey to himself, "he had been thinking of the Raid and was trying to do a bit of his 'looking at the comparative.'" Then there is the well-known story of Grey breaking to him the news of the burning of Groote Schuur. "I've bad news for you," said Grey, with a telegram in his hand. "Tell it me quick, then," said Rhodes, "so that I may know the worst"; and when he had heard, "Nothing worse than that? That's all right. Why, I thought you were going to say it was the Doctor."

III

At first he took little part in Cape politics. In 1896 he did not appear at all in the House, in spite of an urgent appeal from some of his truest friends to make at least one speech in extenuation of his fault, by reminding the House of all he had done for the colony as Prime Minister. But in refusing he was probably wiser than they, for his work in Rhodesia was the best acknowledgement of repentance he could offer. But on his return from England next year he was in his place for a few weeks and made a couple of speeches on indifferent matters. The House maintained its reputation for courtesy, for nobody attacked him or made any allusion to the past; while some of his old Dutch friends, who used to call him affectionately "De Oud Kerel," said after hearing him: "There spoke our old Rhodes. It is the first time we have heard him since the Raid." At the end of that year he began to take a more active interest again in Cape politics. He was stung by the suggestions made by some of his old friends that his best retreat was "a hermit's cell somewhere on the Zambesi"; "but," he added, "I have not the slightest intention of being driven out." He was especially taken up then and during the succeeding year in the elections, in which the Progressives, the party newly formed to resist the Bond, made their first appearance. In consequence of the Raid the Bond had gained a great many new adherents, such as Sauer, Merriman and Schreiner, who was appointed by Hofmeyr its leader in the House. The old race-antagonism was reviving, and the coolness towards Kruger had quite disappeared. The principal tenets of the Progressives were anti-Krugerism, redistribution, to remove the unfair advantage of the country districts over the towns, and the union of South Africa: a programme inspired by Rhodes.

On both sides great activity was displayed at these elections of 1898 and much money spent. The Bond were accused of drawing funds from the secret service chest of the Transvaal, and Rhodes himself spent lavishly on the election, an expenditure which he frankly admitted and defended when charged with it. He stood himself for two constituencies: Namaqualand, a safe seat for his party, and his old seat, Barkly West, where the large Dutch element made it rather doubtful if he would succeed. But he himself was determined to get elected at Barkly West for that very reason. "It may be asked," he told his electors there, "why do I worry or bother with this constituency? My answer is that I wish to show that, whatever may have been my mistakes, I still keep the strong support of a large section of the Dutch people, that I have a broad idea as to the union of Africa, and that I have not altered my ideas in the least about the equality of the races, and that I am prepared to meet Dutch audiences equally with English. . . . I want to show that I still have a large section of the Dutch electors in my favour." He travelled all over the constituency, meeting the Dutch farmers, regretting that he had not been born in the country, so that he could talk to them in Dutch, and expounding his views in every village. He also made speeches for the party at Cape Town and Port Elizabeth, and was consulted on every electoral difficulty that arose. A suggestion was made that the Doctor should stand; and Rhodes, whose tender devotion to him after he had "upset his apple-cart" is one of the finest traits in his character, was all for it. But most of his friends wisely decided that the time had not yet come; and Jameson postponed to a later date the rehabilitation he so splendidly achieved. Had not Rhodes felt, as he surely did now, that his own days were numbered, it would in some ways have been better for his fair fame could he also have waited. For in the heat of the election he said many hard and bitter things of old allies and friends, parted from him solely on account of his own misdeeds, things that one would willingly forget. But Rhodes's theory was, "What is the good of friends to me when I am right? I want them when I am wrong"; and to those who had left him at such a time he was brutal and unforgiving. However, he achieved two objects by his campaign. Though his party were defeated in the country, his own triumphant return for his old constituency, Barkly West, proved that he was right in believing that many of his former friends among the Dutch still remained faithful to him personally. He also made men talk and think of his dream, a united South Africa.

Speaking of union Rhodes would always adopt a severely practical line of argument. He would begin by pointing out to his audiences, mostly composed of farmers, the intolerable burdens they suffered from excise laws, from customs barriers at every state frontier, from the irritating tariffs of rival state railways, matters they could all understand. Then he would lead them on, with some such remark as, "After all, the general questions of South Africa and the parish pump are wonderfully intermingled," to consider that a federal union under which all these material squabbles would disappear would also be the best means of abolishing the perennial sore of racial strife. One of the suggestions he made was that, if the Republics hung back at first, Rhodesia and the two colonies should form a federation into which the others would soon be bound to come. To this he was reduced largely owing to his own plottings and the Raid; for Kruger had hardened his heart the more in consequence, and the Cape Dutch, who alone could have brought in the Transvaal, were estranged. Perhaps the most important disciples he made were in Natal, a colony hitherto inclined to stand aloof from the rest of South Africa. Escombe, it will be remembered, was already a convert to his views on union, and with time he became more enthusiastic. He writes to Rhodes in 1898 that he has sent a letter to Laurier in Canada asking for suggestions and is digesting other federal constitutions: he even proposes a motion in the Natal Parliament in favour of union. In the following year he had actually made a draft constitution for the "South African Commonwealth" based on Australian Acts, on the lines Rhodes had always laid down: the Governor-General to fly the flag of the United Kingdom, and each colony, state or province to maintain its own flag and, subject to the constitution, its own laws. But the most remarkable symptom of the growing feeling for South African solidarity in Natal was the invitation given to Rhodes in the last year of his life to sit for Newcastle as their representative on the Legislative Council.

All these signs may well have cheered Rhodes, but he was not destined to enter into the promised land. Plans and hopes of union were all brought to naught by the outbreak of the South African War. The antagonisms of race he had laboured so long to allay were started into fresh malevolent growth. Escombe, too, his strongest supporter, died prematurely. But even at this dark time, burdened himself and fevered with impatience by his own failing vigour, Rhodes never despaired. And, indeed, his ideas did not die. When he himself was dead and men had forgotten his faults, remembering only what South

Africa owed him, their thoughts turned more and more to the solution of their chief difficulties that he had preached to them in and out of season. When the Union Convention met, many of its members said to themselves, as Jameson did and as his master Rhodes would have said: "We must give up many small things if we are to attain the bigger thing, Union; for that cannot be attained without sacrificing many of our personal predilections." So when the first great difficulty appeared, the language question, it was Jameson who proposed that the English and Dutch languages should be on an absolutely equal footing: while his great fight was on equal voting powers for all: in both respects following out Rhodes's maxim, "Race feeling will go on until equal rights are given." So on the native question, which Rhodes had foreseen would be one of the great stumbling-blocks, the Cape consented, without giving up her own liberal franchise, to the compromise by which the other provinces retained their more stringent law. And so was fulfilled the aspiration in one of Rhodes's most combative election speeches. "We must forget the past," he said, addressing the Afrikanders, "we must forget the past, and work with you again in the future, for we are convinced that our main objects—the gradual acquisition of Africa and the union of South Africa—are one and the same."

CHAPTER XVII

THE ST. MARTIN'S SUMMER

THE four years in Rhodes's life succeeding the Raid are, as an example of his grit and dogged determination in overcoming difficulties, the most marvellous even in his meteoric career. He knew himself to be under sentence of death, he was still reeling from a blow which would have crushed many of the strongest, and he had every inducement that wealth and friendship could give to pass the remainder of his days in peace and comfort. But peace and comfort did not enter into his scheme of life, and never less so than when he felt that his days were numbered and that he had a fault to retrieve. He dropped none of his old interests, but took up new ones with zest and seemed to bring to them all the old energy and directing capacity. Certainly his fellow-shareholders in his great commercial concerns, De Beers and the Gold Fields, could not complain of any neglect on his part. In the midst of the excitement caused by his journey to London to "face the music," he found time to preside at the De Beers General Meeting at Kimberley and give the shareholders a lucid and most encouraging account of their concerns. For this Company he was always thinking out fresh plans of economizing in the workings and increasing its usefulness to the community. He took very seriously his trust to dispose of the surplus profits for public objects, such as grants for educational purposes, a sanatorium for Kimberley, which, he said, "I have always thought would be an admirable place for people with chest complaints from home," volunteer corps and a local exhibition. He also took the chief part in establishing a dynamite factory for the benefit of both companies, to save them the extortionate charges made by the importing firms; and induced De Beers to devote large amounts of its earnings to experiments valuable to the colony, such as horse-breeding and farming.

One subject, however, though it still interested him deeply, he never touched: the internal affairs of the Transvaal. He had burnt his fingers there once, and, as he said to a German interviewer, "a burnt child dreads the fire. I keep aloof from the whole Transvaal crisis, so that no one may be able to say if things go wrong that Rhodes is in it again." This self-imposed restraint was much eased by his complete confidence in the new Governor, who came out in May 1897. Sir Alfred Milner was a man after Rhodes's own heart. A pupil and follower of his friend Stead in the new conception of the British Empire as a power to be strengthened for good in the world by the closest union of its parts, he had come to South Africa far otherwise equipped for his task than the ordinary colonial governor, both in mental attainments and by his long training, first in social work and the best kind of journalism and then in high Government posts at home and abroad. The two men met on the veld in Rhodesia and conceived a liking and admiration for each other. Rhodes naturally did not attempt to obtrude his advice about Cape politics or Transvaal affairs on Milner, nor would Milner have allowed it; for he was determined to take his own line in dealing with the problems which had been agitating South Africa so long and to rely on his own judgement. But they had occasionally to confer on Rhodesian affairs, especially when Milner came on a visit of inspection to that country at the end of 1897, and discovered that each was big enough to do his own work without interfering with the other. Indeed the relations between the two men redound to the credit of both; for they were not easy relations. Rhodes was not wont to make it easy for any one who came in his way, governor or no governor; and there was Milner, practically sent to take out of his hands affairs he had mismanaged. In respect to that particular business Rhodes used to say, "Oh, it's all right in Milner's hands," and left it there quite contentedly. Later, when the war had fixed policy irretrievably, the two men saw one another and corresponded rather more freely. Rhodes sends Milner long letters about his proposed scheme for the settlement of English colonists in the country districts to the end that they might mix more with the Dutch and help to break down the bitterness of racial feeling, largely due to want of acquaintance with one another. Milner helps Rhodes with suggestions for getting over difficulties in Rhodesia, encourages him in his trans-continental railway and telegraph plans, and gives him a friendly hint as to the best moment for approaching Chamberlain on a guarantee scheme for the Rhodesian railways. "The objection you may take to all this is," he writes, "that you are going over now and not in the autumn, and I quite agree that, as your personal advocacy of the scheme in London is essential to its success, it would be a bore for you not to be able to settle it now, as this might involve another journey at an early date. I admit this, but I fancy that, if my arguments are good, and the chances of your succeeding six months or a year hence are far greater than now, you would make very little of the personal inconvenience."

But the letter which best shows the relations between the two men is one written by Lord Milner when some busybodies were trying to stir up strife between them. Rhodes had apparently once done the same thing on his side, "a confidence," says Milner, "which you once showed me, and for which I have always felt grateful." As to the present attempt, he continues, "it is a crazy scheme, and it is not from any fear of your lending an ear to it, especially after the generous and consistent support you have shown me through all this trying crisis—and that at a time when my position was much weaker than it is to-day—that I am writing these lines; . . . [but] in view of the future and of the infinite importance, for public reasons, of a continued good personal understanding and absolute frankness between you and me about the lies, innuendoes and suggestions which may be poured into your ear in the course of it. Therefore I say to you precisely as you once said to me—if you are told anything about myself, which implies either that I distrust your co-operation with me, or that I wish to hamper your own big work or detract from the influence which you exercise and always must exercise in the development of S. Africa—please, do *me the justice and the kindness absolutely to disbelieve it.* I don't for the life of me see why we should ever clash, for there is work enough for both of us in all conscience, in the next year or two, in working out the future of the great British country here, which is going, I trust, not only to federate itself, as a free nation like Canada and Australia, but to be one of the means of federating the Empire.

"Of course, we may differ, here and there, as to policy. If so, I am sure we can in the future, as in the past, discuss all differences frankly and with mutual trust, brushing aside the suspicions and the *arrière-pensées* which certain reptiles are never tired of trying to implant in the minds of both of us."

Among the schemes Rhodes took up with special zest after his fall was model farming on a great scale. He had been ruminating such a project when he was Prime Minister, "as an example which will be a large benefit throughout the colony," but he does not seem to have taken it up seriously till he was released from the trammels of office. His original idea was that it should be an enterprise financed with De Beers money, and so he proposed to the shareholders in his speech at Kimberley in 1896. But, as was often his way, he began the work as a private experiment of his own in partnership with Beit. His own modest account of the experiment is given in a letter he wrote to Lord Milner: "In a small way I have tried to encourage fruit cultivation in the Cape Colony and possess some twenty or thirty farms in the Paarl and Stellenbosch districts. Owing to their special knowledge the men in charge of these farms are almost entirely English, who have studied fruit-cultivation in California; and for the first time we have a number of English on the land in these districts. At first they were looked upon with suspicion and distrust by their neighbours.[1] This feeling has now totally altered.

[1] When Rhodes first began to purchase farms, there was a hubbub in *Ons Land*, the Dutch paper, Rhodes being accused of sinister designs on the Dutch. So great secrecy had to be maintained at first about the sales.

They mix socially with the neighbouring farmers; they are intermarrying with the Dutch and the whole tone of these two districts is changing." The experiment was begun about 1897 with the engagement of Mr. Pickstone, a man of great experience in the methods of Californian fruit growing and packing, who had hitherto failed in his South African ventures, but whom Rhodes unhesitatingly picked out as the very man for the job. Rhodes's confidence was fully justified, for no man could have been more whole-hearted in his devotion to his employer's interests or to his idea in starting the scheme. Under his careful management the farms were rapidly developed and made examples to the whole of South Africa in scientific fruit culture. Within four years some 150,000 fruit trees—pears, apples, prunes, apricots, peaches and Japanese plums — were planted on the quincunx system; and it was calculated that in the fourth year from planting the orchards should pay their expenses. Vines also were planted on some of the farms, and plans were made for artificial irrigation, for a cannery and for a light railway to take the produce to market or on shipboard for export. Special attention was paid to this export trade, to develop which Rhodes spared no expense in bringing over expert sorters and packers from America. This proved so successful that the first sample cases sent to Covent Garden and to America were a revelation to the dealers and gave the start to a new South African industry, an industry which has now attained such large proportions that Cape plums, once a rarity for the millionaire's table, are now seen everywhere, even on the humble coster's barrow. Both Rhodes and his manager were determined that the experiment should not be a mere luxury, but put on a paying basis as soon as possible, for, as the latter said, "A scheme founded on philanthropic lines is of no benefit to the community, but a business scheme, which can pay a dividend, is of undoubted assistance to any country."

But the farm experiment did not end there. Mr. Baker discovered that one of the farms had excellent clay for tile- and brick-making; just the thing needed for the introduction of a South African tile industry, which he and

Rhodes were anxious to create; so the latest brick-kilns and tile works were established and a new manufacture started. Rhodes also built a model village on another of the farms for the coloured labourers on the estate. The village was designed by Mr. Baker, and had a church and a parsonage for the Dutch parson engaged to look after the spiritual wants of the inhabitants. One of the coloured women was once describing to a visitor how she came there. "Let me tell you," said she, "that I was living with all my family in a little one-roomed *pondokice* [*i.e.* mud hut], as most of us coloured labourers are obliged to live, and the 'Big Master' came to see me and he looked at me and my hovel and said, 'Now if I give you a nice cottage, all beautifully clean and pretty for the same rent you pay for this hovel, viz. 10s. a month, will you promise me to ever keep it as you find it, clean and bright?' 'Yes,' I replied, and the 'Big Master' smiled and did as he said, and now I and all who live here keep our cottages as you see them to-day, always *skoon en blink* [*i.e.* clean and shining], for you see at any moment the 'Big Master' may come and we must keep our promises. Don't come and tell us any lies about him, for we know what he has done and we love him." Rhodes, indeed, was a model employer. Whereas most farmers tried to influence their boys entirely through the wine bottle, the rule on Rhodes's Farms was that no wine was given; and it was found that the boys were best influenced by the managers being able themselves to do the work.

Finally, after Rhodes had proved the success of the experiment, the estate and business of "Rhodes's Fruit Farms" was turned into a limited liability company, in which nearly all the shares were held by Rhodes himself, Beit and De Beers, each of these having provided over £60,000 of the initial capital required, and Rhodes having made all the first advances out of his own pocket.

He also had two farms of his own, which he dearly loved, in Rhodesia. He loved them perhaps for the reason he gave in one of his speeches: "Because life on a South African farm gives a good deal of time for thinking." One was a vast estate of 100,000 acres at Inyanga, in

Eastern Mashonaland, which he bought in 1897 for over £50,000. This was given over to the management of his friend Grimmer, and was especially valuable as grazing ground. Here Rhodes made trials of various kinds of stock, Angora goats, sheep and cattle of different breeds, to see if they were suited to the climate of Rhodesia. He also tried cereals, vegetables and fruit trees, but without great success. "Do you not think Inyanga the best place in Africa for farming?" he asked one of his farmers; "I should like to see it next year about February or March, as I am very fond of the place." The difference between this and the other farm, Westacre in the Matoppos, was thus expressed by one who knew them both: "Inyanga is a country like Scotland, which to enjoy one must walk over: Matoppos one rides through."

During his long sojourn in those Matoppo Hills in 1896 he had discovered two spots which made a lasting impression upon him. One was the hill with the wonderful view which he came upon in the course of a long ride with George Wyndham and Grey, and promptly christened the "View of the World." Near by was Moselikatze's grave, which had made so strong an appeal to his sense of fitness and grandeur.[1] Some Philistine had rifled the remains, and Rhodes had immediately recovered them, summoned all the chief Matabeles, and re-interred them with fitting barbaric pomp. He had also determined to make the "View of the World" the Westminster Abbey of Rhodesia, —"My church is the Mountain," he used to say at Cape Town,—there to put up the Wilson Memorial and the monuments of any who should hereafter deserve well of Rhodesia. Here, too, was to be his own last resting-place, his bit of 6 feet by 4 feet, that he was wont to speak of as his last possession.

The other discovery was a tract of singularly rich soil by a gap in the hills. "Providence," he said, "left this gap in the hills for a purpose, and we must respond. Get a good engineer and arrange for him to prepare surveys for a dam and furnish us with an estimate of the cost." Hardly sooner said than done. Mr. M'Donald, the factor to whom

[1] See Chap. XIV. p. 231.

charge was given of the estate Rhodes had promptly bought near the gap, was told to get the work going. The plans for the undertaking, which was to cost some £30,000, took a year to prepare, hardly quick enough for Rhodes's impatience; but then he himself was largely to blame, for during the preparation of the plans and also during the whole course of the work he was always making fresh suggestions. He made friends with Aird, the contractor for the great Nile dam, and was always taking hints from him and others about the best models of valve or other new devices in dam-construction. "Mr. Rhodes," says M'Donald wearily, "keeps making alterations, which I admit have so far been good. He talks dams with everybody that has one, and gets new ideas which his secretary writes me at his request." The construction, which was pressed on with the utmost goodwill by factor, engineer and workmen, took nearly four years. As always happens in such enterprises, faults in the rock and other unexpected troubles occurred; but when at last completed it was a triumphant success. The scale of the undertaking may be gauged from the measurements of the embankment, which was 1200 feet long, 75 feet high, 15 feet wide at the top, and 390 feet at the bottom; the reservoir stretched back from this embankment a quarter of a mile and held 50 million gallons of water, and it was calculated to irrigate 2000 acres in the valley below.

The Matoppos farm, like Inyanga, was principally used as an experimental station for the benefit of the settlers, a purpose that was perpetuated by the clause in the will directing the trustees to cultivate both farms "for the instruction of the people of Rhodesia." Oats, maize, mangels, potatoes and lucerne do best on the Matabeleland farm, which also makes a good show of pigs, poultry, cattle, ostriches and fruit trees. Rhodes here, as at Groote Schuur, wanted others to share what gave him so much delight. At the opening of the railway to Buluwayo in 1897 he invited all the assembled guests to a huge picnic he gave there, and he always encouraged chance visitors or holiday-makers from Buluwayo to come out and see the View of the World. Later he had an hotel built in the neighbourhood and a light railway made from Buluwayo; none too soon, for his sorely tried factor complains that he had had to entertain about 150 visitors within two and a half months. But, with Henry V., Rhodes could exclaim, "I care not who doth feed upon my cost." Rhodes was particularly fond of sending out thither tired secretaries or friends, believing that quiet meditation in that glorious scenery was the best cure for jangled nerves. For the same reason he kept on one of his quite impracticable farmers, a regular Diogenes he is described, because, in spite of his vile farming, "his philosophical meditations" were suited to the place.

In April 1898 Rhodes was restored to the board of the British South Africa Company: not that it made any real difference to his power, for during the two years he had been off the board he had taken a greater part in the affairs of the country than at any previous period; and the chairman said he had always been consulted on every important decision: but it pleased and touched him. The meeting at which he was re-elected was packed. His name was proposed by one of his old Rhodesians, Weston-Jarvis, who gave as his best qualification that he was accessible to all men, and seconded by the Duke of Abercorn. By the cheers from the whole hall that greeted this nomination and that were redoubled when Rhodes appeared and stood forward to address them, the shareholders showed that they had lost nothing of their old enthusiasm and affection for him. He had already been negotiating with the Colonial Office about the new constitution for Rhodesia, rendered necessary by the Jameson Raid. The chief points of interest in the new Order in Council, issued in November 1898, were three. First, the Imperial Government took definite powers of exercising control over the administration of the country by providing for a resident commissioner to act as the High Commissioner's eyes and ears, and an Imperial Commandant-General over the Company's police and volunteers. Secondly, Rhodes secured his long-cherished object of a clause to prevent the raising of the Rhodesian customs duties on British imports above the existing Cape tariff, a first step, he hoped, to a general system of preference for the Empire, and, by its insertion in the constitution, as difficult to alter, he argued, as a clause in the United States constitution. Thirdly, a move was made in the direction of self-government by the establishment of a legislative council, of which the settlers were entitled to elect a minority of the members. In his speech at Buluwayo in June 1896 Rhodes had indicated that he was in favour of this, and at Salisbury in the following November had dwelt more explicitly on the near approach of a representative system, with the sole reservation that, as long as the shareholders paid for the country, the Company must have the deciding voice. Since the directors endorsed his views Chamberlain was only too willing to give effect to the proposal.

No trouble seemed too great for him and no detail too trivial when it was a question of Rhodesia. He looked forward to the day when Southern Rhodesia, as a self-governing community, would take a decisive part in South African politics, and he was convinced that the best means of hastening the day was by developing the country's resources and making the settlers self-supporting. Sir Arthur Lawley and Sir William Milton, the joint-administrators who succeeded Grey, were helped by him in every effort to improve conditions and remove grievances. He founded settlements of Fingoes and Bechuanas to increase the labour supply and give an example of good native methods of agriculture to the Matabeles and Mashonas; he sanctioned a Salvation Army colony under General Booth, and, as always, welcomed new Dutch and English settlers. He sent Mr. E. B. Sargent, an authority on questions of education, to plan a good system of national schools. He encouraged by judicious concessions all efforts by genuine workers to develop the gold mines, in which he had the greatest confidence as the chief resource of the country. Northern Rhodesia also, though he never visited it, was not forgotten. He sent two men, Codrington and Coryndon, in whom he had confidence, to govern it, and kept a sharp look-out on their proceedings. There the conditions of climate were so different and the white settlers so few that he insisted on native police instead of an expensive and useless European force, of whom he caustically observed: "They would do nothing excepting get fever. Their day's work would be eating three meat-meals, lying on their backs on stretchers: for the balance, reading *Tit-Bits* and devoting their conversation to cursing the country and the Chartered Company. I don't blame them." He did all he could to help prospecting companies, such as Mr. R. Williams's Tanganyika Concessions Syndicate, to discover new openings for mining or agricultural enterprise. And everywhere peace and good order were gradually established. Lord Selborne, who visited Northern Rhodesia in 1907, only seven years after the Chartered Company took over full responsibility for it, thus testifies to the value of the work inaugurated there by Rhodes: "I travelled through the country with the same safety and in the same atmosphere of the existence of a civilizing influence that I should find in the native territories of Cape Colony or in Basutoland. . . . And yet it is not more than fifteen years ago since the Matabele perpetrated their last wholesale massacre on the Batoka plateau, or since the Barotse themselves raided one of their subject tribes. . . . It is less than that since masters killed their slaves at will, and since people were constantly being executed for witchcraft."

He was not so successful in his dealings with the Government about railway extension. The Matabele rebellion had brought home to him the need of a more rapid construction of the railways to connect the isolated parts of Rhodesia with sources of supply and reinforcements. Thanks chiefly to the exertions of Sir Charles Metcalfe and the contractors the railway was brought into Buluwayo by 1897: in the same year Beira was connected with Umtali and two years later with Salisbury. But Rhodes had another railway, not so obviously necessary for the defence of Rhodesia, almost equally at heart: the Cape to Cairo railway. The first section he proposed to lay was from Salisbury across the Zambesi through N.E. Rhodesia to the southern end of Lake Tanganyika: the Imperial Government had already agreed to a railway in Uganda, and he had arranged with his friend Kitchener [1] to bring the Egyptian and Soudan system to the northern border of Uganda; arrangements were even made for securing that the gauges of the Egyptian and South African systems should be identical: the only portion left over, therefore, was from Tanganyika to the south of Uganda, which he hoped could be settled with the German or Congolese Governments. The demand he made on the British Government was for a guarantee on the section from Salisbury northward to Tanganyika. Chamberlain was at first not averse to the proposal; but Hicks-Beach, the Chancellor of the Exchequer, would agree only upon such impossible conditions that Rhodes gave up the idea of a Government guarantee in disgust. Though he contained himself enough in his public statement to the shareholders to earn Chamberlain's thanks, in private he remarked of Sir Michael that "he reminds me of the young man in the Bible with our Saviour when asked to part with his wealth." But he was not beaten, and set himself doggedly to collect the capital from shareholders of the Chartered Company, friends in the City and other companies interested in Rhodesian development. The route was changed from a north-easterly to a north-westerly direction chiefly in order to tap the recently discovered Wankie coalfields: this route had the additional advantage to Rhodes's eyes of crossing the Zambesi just below the Victoria Falls; "I should like the spray from them to dash against the railway carriages," he said, and added pathetically, "I want to get there at once, as there is little satisfaction in knowing the railway will reach there after one's death." But he never saw the Falls.

As his Trans-African telegraph approached Tanganyika, he began to be anxious about the strip between that point and Uganda. It is true that by the Rosebery treaty of 1894 provision had been made to connect the line through

[1] Kitchener and he had long had an understanding about a junction between their respective spheres of work. Chaffing telegrams were interchanged between them when Kitchener got to Sobat and later to Khartoum in his Soudan expedition, Kitchener telling Rhodes he was likely to be behindhand at the trysting-place, and Rhodes answering that that was the only fly in his ointment. Kitchener also took special care to tell Rhodes of his brother Frank's wound in the campaign and of his reinstatement in the army.

Congo territory, but unfortunately King Leopold had not received the stipulated payment of the Lado enclave;[1] and Rhodes's opinion of that monarch was "that it will be very difficult ever to get him to any practical conclusion unless he has by far the best of the bargain." The alternative route to Uganda was through German East Africa. So in March 1899, on his way back to England from Egypt, where he had been making arrangements with Kitchener and Cromer for linking up his line with theirs, he paid visits to Leopold II. and the Kaiser, to find out from which of the two monarchs he could get the better terms. Little is known of what actually passed in his private interviews with them,[2] but the results are clear. He always afterwards spoke of Leopold with the utmost loathing, and as he came out of his room caught hold of our military attaché, who happened to be passing, and hissed in his ear: "Satan, I tell you that man is Satan." At any rate he got nothing out of him.

With the Kaiser he found himself at once on the best footing. The interview seems to have started happily with the genial interchange of chaff about the Kaiser's telegram of January 1896;[3] and when it was over Rhodes came out with a promise that he should have every facility for taking his telegraphs through German East Africa. At an Embassy dinner where the two met again they had another long talk together, at the end of which the Emperor called up one of his Ministers and said, "Make a note of this, that when Mr. Rhodes gets into our territory he does not require a military escort for his workers, as that would put him to unnecessary expense." Some of the details had to be worked out between Rhodes and Von Bülow and other German Ministers, and the final agreement was not signed till the end of the year, after the despatch of a cable signed "C. J. Rhodes": "What about my telegraph? I am close to the German border and should not like to enter German territory without authority. The only alternative dismissing whole staff"; the cable happily arrived when the Kaiser was

[1] See Chap. XII. p. 181.

[2] Rhodes sent a long letter describing the interviews to the Prince of Wales (afterwards Edward VII.); but the letter does not seem to have been preserved.

[3] See Chap. XV. p. 274.

about to visit England and wanted to improve English feeling by publishing the fact of the agreement. In a letter to the Foreign Office Rhodes explained that the Germans naturally required a *quid pro quo* for their concession, in the shape of permission to land their trans-Atlantic cable at Waterville or Valentia, on the west coast of Ireland. Rhodes urges the Foreign Office to agree to these terms on the grounds that we ought not to foster the monopoly of the existing American Company and that we should have more control over the German cable if it landed in our territory than if it were laid under the sea all the way to America. Finally, the only condition for permission to carry the telegraph line through German East Africa was that the Chartered Company should not make a railway line to connect with the west coast except through German S.W. Africa; while a promise was given that if the Germans themselves could not find the capital for a railway line through German East Africa Rhodes should be allowed to construct it.

Within less than a year of this agreement the telegraph line had been laid over fifty miles in German territory; and Rhodes had calculated to a nicety the cost of construction from Cape Town to Port Said, the staff required for maintenance, the charge to be made for messages and the dividend that would be payable on capital.[1] He humorously defended to the shareholders of the Chartered Company his tariff arrangements with the Egyptian Government before he was on their borders and at their mercy on the ground that, "I will not say for a moment that they would blackmail us, but I have always found my own countrymen are particularly good at a bargain, especially if you find they are the sole people to be dealt with." Another result of his interview with the Kaiser was that he lost all his apprehensions of German designs against England in Africa, and carried away a vivid appreciation of the Kaiser's quick and business-like methods. In subsequent speeches he described him as "a big man," "a broad-minded man";

[1] It illustrates Rhodes's thorough methods that to ensure exactitude in his calculations he obtained from Australia all relative statistics about their trans-continental line.

and to a German shortly afterwards he wrote: "Your Emperor was very good to me. As far as myself is concerned, I shall not alter my determination to work with the German colonies in Africa," and in answer to a telegram of congratulation from the Kaiser after the relief of Kimberley expressed great delight at "the good feeling your Emperor showed to us." But the most remarkable testimony of his personal gratitude was the provision in a codicil to his will that the German Emperor should choose a certain number of Rhodes scholars annually from his people.

During this eventful year, 1899, Rhodes may well have felt that the seal was set to his rehabilitation by two great testimonies to the honour in which he was held. The first was at the last meeting he ever addressed of the British South Africa Company, when the vast hall at the Cannon Street Hotel could not contain the crowd of shareholders that pressed to see and hear him, and after the principal meeting he had to address an overflow meeting on the stairs and corridors, being piloted through the throng by two or three big, burly, smiling policemen. His opening words indicated unwonted shyness at this great demonstration: "I suppose that the most unhappy thing in the world is for a public man to make a speech, especially the night and day beforehand. The only simile I can think of would be, perhaps, the night and morning of one of our forefathers, just before he went to a State execution." But he soon took heart and made one of his usual rattling, practical speeches.

The other and still more welcome testimony was the degree of D.C.L., *honoris causa,* conferred on him at Encaenia by his old and much-loved university. He had the added gratification of receiving the honour at the same time as Kitchener, the friend who was working in co-operation with him from the other end of Africa, the recent victor of Omdurman. There had been some opposition to the degree in Oxford, but this was more than counterbalanced by the extra warmth of the reception accorded him. He was ingenuously pleased and said so, as soon as he got back to Cape Town. After describing his interview with the

Kaiser, he went on: " And then, sir, I had the good luck to meet Lord Kitchener in London. We met very frequently, and we rode in the park together. I think horse exercise increases the activity of the brain. And we came to a distinct understanding, and I think you will hear before very long that funds have been provided for Lord Kitchener to proceed from Khartoum to Uganda. I had the opportunity of meeting him on several occasions. We met at Oxford. Talking of Oxford, really one sometimes feels fortunate in having done very wrong, because it brings out the affection and support of one's people. Some possessed of the most complete rectitude at Oxford thought I was unworthy of receiving the degree that had been awarded to me. Perhaps it was the most fortunate thing that ever happened to me—I mean their opposition. I went to Oxford with the great general, on whom the eyes of the world were fixed. I think, sir, I should have been almost nobody if it had not been for this opposition to me. But I can assure you, gentlemen, they gave me a greater reception than Lord Kitchener, and you must remember that they were not mere undergraduates of eighteen, but Masters of Arts, gentlemen with grey beards, because after the day's proceedings, the undergraduates numbered 400 and the others numbered 5000. Gentlemen, I mention this because one's troubles have brought out one's friends."

In more serious vein was the speech he made at the luncheon given in his honour by his old college, Oriel. " Sometimes," he began, " in pursuing my object, the enlargement of the British Empire, and with it the cause of peace, industry and freedom, I have adopted means in removing opposition which were the rough-and-ready way and not the highest way to attain that object. But you must remember that in South Africa, where my work has lain, the laws of right and equity are not so fixed and established as in this country; and if I have once or twice done things which savoured rather of violence than of protest or peaceful striving, yet you must look back to far-off times in English history for a parallel to the state of things in South Africa. I believe my neighbour, the Regius Professor of History, could tell you that in those past times there have been not a few men who have done good service to the State, but some of whose actions have partaken of the violence of their age, which are hard to justify in a more peaceful and law-abiding age. It is among those men that my own life and actions must be weighed and measured; and I trust to the justice of my countrymen, of which I thought I read some forecast in the kind reception and appreciation awarded to me here in my old college."

CHAPTER XVIII

LAST DAYS

WHEN the South African War broke out in October 1899, Rhodes was a tired man. The control over himself, which the catastrophe of the Raid had for a time restored, was gradually slipping away. His temper, hot and fiery at the best of times, began to regain the mastery; and he observed no measure with those who had for any cause displeased him. He had long and heated controversies with co-directors in several of his companies, rating them for not having in all respects followed his advice and speaking with a rather sad arrogance of all his own previous services to their shareholders. He often spoke harshly and inconsiderately to subordinates for faults which in better days he would have treated with good-humoured indulgence. To an unfortunate railway manager, for example, who was slower than he liked in sending in some accounts, he telegraphs in clear, so that all might read: "I order you again to send the accounts . . to Cape Town. . . . Absolute nonsense your suggesting settlement of accounts should wait. . . . Be good enough to do as you are told"; and to the unfortunate man's protests against his "insulting telegrams" and a "fearful letter" he vouchsafes no reply. In fact it gets to such a pitch that he can barely brook a word of contradiction except from the faithful friend of happier times, the beloved Doctor, who exercises over him almost the only soothing influence. The excuse, and it is some excuse, for this loss of control is that no man's mental and physical strength could stand the tremendous strain Rhodes had been putting on his throughout his life, and especially during the last four years.

Rhodes had taken no part in the negotiations preceding the war. In accordance with his settled policy he had scrupulously left all such matters entirely in Sir Alfred Milner's hands. But he had expressed a very decided belief that it would not come to hostilities. In September he had, perhaps rather inadvisedly, presented Kruger with a lion for his Zoo, and was highly indignant when it was returned to him with scant ceremony. "I see no connection," he wrote to the director of the Pretoria Zoo, "between a Zoological Gardens and your Government's present differences with H.M.'s Government. It is the first time that *lions and politics* have been mixed up. I suppose some one must have chaffed them about the British lion." Both publicly and privately he committed himself to the forecast that "Kruger will at the final push give anything . . . nothing will make Kruger fire a shot"; for he judged from the ease with which the President had been made to climb down about the Drifts affair. The fact was that Rhodes had never fully realized the difference wrought by the Raid in South African politics. Kruger himself would probably not have yielded about the treatment of the Uitlanders, Raid or no Raid; but before that incident Kruger's own position was being so rapidly sapped by the growing alienation of the Cape Dutch and by the opposition to his policy in his own country that, had there been no Raid, the obstinate old man would ere this almost certainly have fallen. The Raid had restored his prestige and given a new lease of life to his obstinacy. Moreover, Rhodes forgot that though his dealings with the Kaiser may have convinced him that his own apprehensions of German intrigue were ill-founded, Kruger had not forgotten the telegram and assuredly counted on help from Germany.

On the eve of the ultimatum Rhodes insisted on taking his place among the defenders of his diamond mines at Kimberley. It was a great risk, because the Boers were known to be anxious to capture him, and the story went that they had planned to exhibit him in a cage as a prisoner throughout the Transvaal. He did extraordinarily good work during the long siege in practical measures for the security and support of the inhabitants. He opened a soup-kitchen to feed the poor, constantly supplied the hospital with grapes from the De Beers vines and other luxuries, arranged for the underground workings of the mines to be used as shell-proof shelters for the women and children, raised bands of natives to act as runners, provided horses and equipment for the volunteer corps, and even succeeded in getting a 28-pounder rifled gun designed and turned out from the De Beers workshops, a gun appropriately christened "Long Cecil." But when all this is said, it must be admitted that Rhodes did not do himself credit at the Kimberley siege. He could not understand that in a beleaguered town the military officers must necessarily be supreme. He was accustomed to give orders and not to receive them, and he expected the same rule to be observed on this occasion. Naturally Colonel Kekewich did not take the same view of his duties, with the result that long before the end of the siege the two men were not on speaking terms. This was bad enough, for when the principal civilian in the town was notoriously insubordinate, Kekewich's task in maintaining discipline among the inhabitants was made exceedingly difficult. But this was not the worst; for Rhodes from the outset conceived the idea that all other operations in the war should be brought to a standstill until Kimberley was relieved. Almost before the siege had begun he had started bombarding the Governor, Lord Methuen, and other military authorities with demands for a relieving force to be sent forthwith. He wrote to Colonel Baden-Powell at Mafeking urging him to take the same line, he summoned a special meeting of the De Beers directors to make similar representations, and when Roberts and Kitchener came out he was equally vociferous to them. It is, of course, absurd to imagine that he was anxious about his own skin, but he was suffering, in an intensified form, from the same malady which had characterized some of his dealings with Lord Salisbury and other Ministers, a complete inability to see the importance of anything which interfered with his own immediate object. Knowing nothing of the relative value of objectives in a campaign and having always a profound contempt for soldiers as such, he decided that the failure to relieve Kimberley at once was simply another instance of military incapacity. It is perfectly true that it would have been a serious blow to the British cause had Kimberley fallen, but not so serious, in spite of all the diamond mines, as to make it worth while to divert the whole course of the campaign to save it.

Throughout the campaign there was the same inability in Rhodes to conceive that any military object ought to stand in the way of his own plans. When it was not Kimberley it was something else. Immediately after the siege he offered to forward supplies to Roberts and Kitchener, provided "I have full power and no one to interfere with me. . . . Reply sharp as otherwise I am going to Cape Town." The Field-Marshal and his Chief of the Staff must have felt embarrassed at this peremptory offer of their would-be Moses, the more so as he showed a disposition to dictate to them what their base of supply should be and how many waggon-loads they ought to require: and the arrangement did not last long. In the later stages of the war he again came into conflict with Kitchener. Kitchener wanted to finish off the guerilla war as soon as possible and ordered that all available railway rolling-stock should be employed for military purposes: Rhodes was tired of the war and thought it more important that his rolling-stock should be employed in developing Rhodesia. It had so happened that when Kitchener was pressing forward his desert railway for the Soudan campaign, Rhodes had generously come to his help by allowing him to have some of his new engines destined for Rhodesia; and now he takes care to remind him of his debt. "Tell K.," he wires to the staff officer, "I lost a lot of time by giving up my engines for his Khartoum trip. I really think this time he should leave my rolling-stock alone." But even this personal appeal *ad hominem* seems to have met with no response.

Yet there were still flashes of the great man. One such flash came in October 1900, when Lord Roberts, having reached Pretoria and dispersed the Boer forces, declared that the war was practically at an end; and this dictum was for a short time accepted by the English, among others by Rhodes. To celebrate the victory of our arms he was invited and consented to address a meeting of the South

African League at Cape Town, a body of loyal propagandists, of which he was president. The meeting was held on a fine sunny morning of a South African spring day. The Mountain above was clear and sharp, the air fresh: a sense of joy and hope was about. In contrast to the glory outside the meeting gave a dreary impression. It was a mean hall and the audience looked dull: the time being morning, few men were present, and most of the seats were filled with fanatical-looking ladies, who seemed to regard the event they were celebrating as a national triumph of English over Dutch, and by look and tone showed that they at any rate would have scant mercy on the vanquished. Then Rhodes strode in, marched straight to his seat, looking neither to right nor left, and almost at once plunged into his discourse. He was an altered man since that other entry into the committee room at Westminster four years ago. He still had a shy manner, but not the same dazed and nervous look; physically, though, he was much changed for the worse, with the puffy face and bloated appearance that often comes with an affection of the heart. As he spoke his audience hardly seemed to exist for him. He never glanced at them or at the sordid surroundings, but kept his gaze fixed above their heads at the window in front of him, with that strange dreamer's look in his eyes, as if he were straining for a sight of his Mountain and beyond to the clean sun-washed uplands of the country he had made his own. His first words were like a trumpet-call; but it was a call little in tune with the mood of such an audience: "You think you have beaten the Dutch! But it is not so. The Dutch are not beaten; what is beaten is Krugerism, a corrupt and evil government, no more Dutch in essence than English. No! The Dutch are as vigorous and unconquered to-day as they have ever been; the country is still as much theirs as it is yours, and you will have to live and work with them hereafter as in the past. Remember *that* when you go back to your homes in the towns or in the up-country farms and villages: let there be no vaunting words, no vulgar triumph over your Dutch neighbours; make them feel that the bitterness is past and that the need of co-operation is greater than ever; teach your children to remember when they go to their village school that the little Dutch boys and girls they find sitting on the same benches with them are as much part of the South African nation as they are themselves, and that as they learn the same lessons together now, so hereafter they must work together as comrades for a common object—the good of South Africa." So spake he, and gave them a "thought."[1]

"What a hypocrite the man must be!" said an English friend to whom this scene was described, a friend still hot with wrath at the shame of the Raid, and convinced that the war was almost entirely due to Rhodes. But he was not a hypocrite: for in this speech you get the whole essence of Rhodes's life-work for union. He bungled it for his own time, by his impatience and his folly, but he never once swerved from his aim.

The speech made a great sensation, especially among his friends in England. General Brocklehurst[2] wrote: "I have been rubbing it into every one since I got back that you are the only man who can save South Africa (beginning with the Queen), and I am surprised to find how many of your enemies agree. I told the Queen you and Gordon were the same man, only with different methods—this fairly made her jump, but she 'saw my point,' as you would say. The Government, I am sure, would be only too thankful for you to come out of your tent and give them a lead. I have said you and Milner are on most cordial terms, so that he would approve. My line has been—you propose a Federal Parliament right away (no Crown Colonies), yourself at the head of it, compensation for both sides for all damage done during the war, and general amnesty. I've got rather hung up in trying to work this out in detail, but that is where Cecil Rhodes comes in, and it would mean peace, or at least an alternative to the present policy of trying to sit on bayonets, which would probably be accepted by the Boer leaders and would bring peace."

And Lord Grey, ever faithful and enthusiastic, wrote: "The full report of your speech which arrived by last mail

[1] Rhodes's exact words are not quoted in the above account, but the gist of this speech, spoken twenty years ago, and the whole scene are indelibly impressed on my memory.

[2] Now Lord Ranksborough.

has more than confirmed the good impression created by the cabled summary, and has further justified the contention of your Friends that you are the *one* man who has the qualities of Heart, Head, and Experience required for the task of fusing Boer and Briton.

"Your speech, in my opinion the best you ever made, cannot fail to make this view popular even in quarters where recently, and perhaps not unnaturally, considering all things, there has been a strong prejudice against you. I am in hopes that you may be able to find some further opportunity of impressing in your own characteristic and effective fashion, the necessity of every man doing everything in his power not only to conquer the resistance but to win the affection and confidence of the Boers."

Some of his old friends in South Africa also urged him to come forward again after the fall of the Schreiner Ministry in 1900, and Sir Alfred Milner would have welcomed him in office. But his heart was chiefly in Rhodesia, and he did not feel he had the strength to undertake what at best would have proved a thankless task. He was conscious indeed that the centre of interest in South African politics had shifted from his old "dominant state" to the north, the Transvaal or even the Chartered Territory; so much so that he signed the unfortunate petition for the suspension of the Cape Constitution, a petition which Chamberlain, to his credit, emphatically rejected.

During these last years he put the finishing touches to the Will. He made the first will, it will be remembered,[1] when he was an almost unknown boy of twenty-four, and with all the changes of detail introduced later, never altered its main purpose of making his wealth a means of advancing the highest interests, as he conceived them, of the British Empire. His first idea was to leave the Trustees wellnigh unfettered in their discretion as to the best means of carrying out his intentions. In the final will of 1899, however, he laid down explicitly his central notion of a great educational scheme to apply to all the English-speaking portions of the globe. The plan he adopted, after long consultations with his friends Stead and Hawkesley, was to provide

[1] See Chap. VI. pp. 51-52.

scholarships for young students from all the self-governing colonies and from the States of America of sufficient value to enable them to have courses at his own university of Oxford, because "I consider that the education of young colonists at one of the universities in the United Kingdom is of great advantage to them for giving breadth to their views, for their instruction in life and manners, and for instilling into their minds the advantage to the colonies as well as to the United Kingdom of the retention of the unity of the Empire. . . . And [because] I also desire to encourage and foster an appreciation of the advantages which I implicitly believe will result from the union of the English-speaking people throughout the world."

In a pencil note to Hawkesley, undated but addressed from "Near Aden," he gives his first sketch of the terms on which the "Rhodes Scholarships" are to be granted and held: ". . . The conditions for election should not only be for literary attainments, but also due weight should be given to the character and social qualities of the candidates, especially to their being moderately fond of field sports, say cricket and football, I do not want simply 'bookworms'; you might copy the idea of the All Souls condition, 'bene natus bene vestitus et moderate doctus.' Of course I object to the snobbishness of the *bene natus bene vestitus*, but I quote this to give you my idea: to sum up, I mean 'for good literary attainments and a taste for outdoor sports.' I have made the amount £250 per annum, as I think a young fellow should live for that sum at Oxford and not require to pinch himself, but my opinion is he cannot do it for less. You will note that you will really have to provide for nine [*i.e.* from South Africa], as there will be three each year for three years continuously. You might point out in the Will that I consider such a course of great advantage to young colonists '*for giving breadth to their views, for giving instruction in life and manners, and for instilling into their minds the advantage to the Colonies as well as to England of the retention of the Unity of the Empire.*' You might also add a suggestion to the authorities at Oxford to try and extend their scope and add if possible to their sphere of instruction a medical school, aiming at equalling the high standard reached at Edinburgh; there are now over fifty South African students there. I should have given some of the Scholarships to Edinburgh, but they have no residential system and I think it most disastrous that young fellows should at the most critical period of their lives be left without supervision; it leads to the ruin of many, especially of young Colonists from abroad who have no family circles close at hand to act as a check if they have a tendency to waste their time and energies in free living and dissipation.

. . . .

The successful candidates should choose whatever College they like at Oxford, it is a mistake for them to crowd together at one College, they would get too local, they should be spread through the University; they might have a yearly dinner to compare and celebrate their successes in the Schools and in the field sports.'

These provisions for the "Rhodes Scholarships" are those that attracted most attention in Rhodes's will: with these he was himself most happy. Lord Rosebery relates his saying to him: "When I find myself in uncongenial company, or when people are playing their games, or when I am alone in a railway carriage, I shut my eyes and think of my great idea. I turn it over in my mind and try to get new light on it. It is the pleasantest companion I have." The scheme has now been working for nearly twenty years, and it has proved at least as great a success as the founder hoped. At Oxford, chosen for his experiment *quia multum dilexit,* young men, from every corner of the British Empire and from every State of the great Republic our fathers founded, come yearly to be taught and to teach the common interests of good government, and to put into practice the Aristotelian theory of virtue, which Rhodes looked on as one of the great precepts of life, *ψυχῆς ἐνεργεία κατ' ἀρετὴν . . . τὴν ἀρίστην καὶ τελειοτάτην . . . ἐν βίῳ τελείῳ,* "the exercise of the human faculties in such way as to develop the highest excellence in the best circumstances." At Oxford, it is said, the Rhodes scholars from the Eastern, Middle, and Western States of America gain a better knowledge of one another's characteristics and of the wider problems of their own commonwealth than they could ever have done had they never left America; the Dutch and English students from South Africa, the French and English from Canada, the New Zealander and the Australian meet on common ground to discuss problems which for the first time they perceive they have in common; while the whole university in turn gets a closer acquaintance with the idiosyncrasies of its own citizens from overseas and of the common problems of the English-speaking races. The Germans, too, who came thither before the war, had learnt to value the peculiarly English life and teaching of Oxford: and it is one of the finest indications of the Oxford spirit conquering the passions of war that one of the colleges commemorated on the same list with the Englishmen their German Rhodes scholar, who had fallen *pro patria*.

Various provisions of the will illustrate other beliefs and aims of Rhodes. He gave munificent endowment to his old college, Oriel, with a sly indication that the *βίος τέλειος* does not consist exclusively of an undue asceticism; in his dispositions for his own family he took precautions that his wealth should never be used to encourage the abhorred breed of "loafers," but that it should help to foster the old "country gentleman" spirit, to which he attributed a large measure of England's greatness. He left Groote Schuur to the Prime Minister of the Union of South Africa, with ample provision for his comfort and dignity: an act of faith in the final realization of the policy for which he had made a lifelong struggle.

His trustees were friends who shared his views, men on whom he could rely to carry out his further unwritten desires for advancing the interests of the British Empire: Lord Rosebery, Grey, Beit, Sir Lewis Michell, his trusted banker, Hawkesley, Lord Milner, and, a death-bed choice, the Doctor. Stead had been one of the original trustees, but, though never ceasing to be personal friends, they had parted on the South African War, and Rhodes had expunged his name "on account of his extraordinary eccentricity."

. . . .

The last months of his life were tragic. He was in constant pain from his fatal heart-illness, and vainly sought relief by travel in Italy, in Egypt, or on a moor in Scotland. From this last sojourning-place he dragged himself back, almost dying, to South Africa, to deal with a sordid case, in which his name was involved. A woman in whom he had been interested had forged his name to a number of bills of exchange, and the affair was becoming a scandal in Cape Town. He had to give his evidence on his death-bed, to which he took as soon as he landed. The last home chosen for him by the Doctor, who brought him back and tended him with a love passing the love of woman, was a tiny cottage at Muizenberg, close to the seashore, where he could get all the cooling breezes to help him in the prolonged agony for breath. All old passions were hushed during this long struggle of the brave fighter, and friends rallied round him. Hofmeyr, his old ally, sent him a message of reconciliation, and those since parted, who remembered pleasant communings with him in the past, brought their sympathy. Daily a cable message would be sent to his friends in London, with Jameson's hopes or fears of his progress, and daily a message of encouragement would come back.

Rhodes himself, dying, had all the humility of the great man who has aimed high, and, as with all those who aim highest, has failed in reaching the utmost height At one time, in his pride, he had felt that at least he had achieved success which would ensure undying glory for his name: but latterly he had come to see the vanity of all human striving and the many points in which he, the strong, the powerful, had failed. "Everything in the world is too short. Life and fame and achievement, everything is too short," he had once said in these latter days to Lord Rosebery: so now, one of his latest utterances, before he breathed his last on March 26, 1902, less than fifty years of age, was "So little done, so much to do."

He was buried in his chosen resting-place, the View of the World in the Matoppos. A huge concourse greeted him for the last time from all parts of South Africa. Besides his own most faithful friends those who mourned him most deeply were the people of his own chosen land, among whom he had come to rest: the settlers and the natives, to both of whom he had always stood as the great protector. For the settlers Milton, once his secretary, now the administrator he had picked out, thus spoke of the "profound gloom and sorrow throughout Rhodesia caused by the passing of the great figure to whom all the inhabitants have from its earliest days been wont to turn in their difficulties and doubts for guidance and help. It may be hoped that during the trials of his later days our founder and friend may have been cheered and sustained by the thought that the fabric he had reared rested on no unsure foundation." For the natives he had conquered and then succoured Faku, one of the chiefs of the 1896 indabas, thus spoke: "I am an old man and am on the brink of the grave. I was content to die knowing that my children and my people would be safe in the hands of Mr. Rhodes; who was at once my father and my mother. That hope has been taken from me and I feel that the sun has indeed set for me." As the coffin was lowered into the rock-hewn grave Faku's tribesmen gave him the royal salute, only given to their kings.

A simple slab with his name carved on it marks the spot—

> Is Saul dead? In the depth of the vale make his tomb—bid arise
> A grey mountain of marble heaped four-square, till, built to the skies,
> Let it mark where the great First King slumbers: whose fame would ye know?
> Up above see the rock's naked face, where the record shall go
> In great characters cut by the scribe,—Such was Saul, so he did.

. . . .

This book will have been written in vain, if it has failed to give some impression of what manner of man Rhodes was, what his faults and what his fine points, his aims and his performance: still more will it have failed, has it not made plain that he was one of the great men of the world, great not mainly for any definite achievement—though in achievement he was also great—but for a personality of resistless energy and dominating force. He was one of those rare beings of whom one can say that, whatever he turned his hand to, he would have been a master; and, like all such beings, he seemed to have his star, his *aura* of success, which fascinated the world and made it yield him even more success than he had asked for. Yet, as with Caesar on the Ides of March, or with Napoleon at Waterloo, the star suddenly failed him at a crucial moment, because in his pride he presumed on success and forgot that the strongest may become intolerable. It is this gift of dominating personality which is most elusive to describe and yet which most interests the world, regardless of whether its owner succeeds or fails; the gift which makes all eyes turn to the man who has it, wherever he appears, though there may be others present who have achieved more or been greater benefactors to humanity. Who would turn to look at Brutus, who overcame Caesar, could he behold Caesar himself, or even Wellington, were Napoleon with him? A Gibbon, maybe, raised a monument to the Roman Empire and to himself greater than any single achievement of a Chatham: yet still Gibbon remains merely a man who wrote a great book, while Chatham, apart from any action, is a supreme personality. And so it was with Rhodes: you might hate him, you might loathe all he did, you might even think meanly of his actual achievement, but you could not ignore him any more than you could ignore a flash of lightning that suddenly blazes forth across a murky night.

His achievement also, partly for good, partly for ill, was great. For the worst of a man of such dominating personality is that his evil example is as potent as the good. He was no cynic for himself, nor, doubtless, was he a cynic in his outlook on humanity: he cared too much for his "fellow-beings" for that. But his Kimberley training led him deliberately to adopt a pose of cynicism, which had effects almost as baleful as if he had himself been a cynic to the core. He himself used his wealth for public objects and inspired others to do likewise. Yet by the chances of winning an easy fortune on the share market, which he offered to those whom he wanted to gain for his great designs, he tempted smaller men to think more of the bribe than of the design. Rhodes himself, like Walpole, was not accessible to motives of self-interest, but nevertheless, like Walpole, presuming too much on the temptation to others of self-interest, he lowered the standard of public life at the Cape and even at home in England. The good side of his "sitting down and arguing with a man" had thus its sinister reverse.

Grey, in one of his letters, describes a visit to Watts, then at work on his "Physical Energy": "He took me to the statue and said, 'Well, that is Rhodes!'"; and Grey adds, "I hope he may decide to give the head of the Rider some resemblance to your features, so that it may go out to the world as his conception of your character." Rhodes's physical and mental energy was indeed abounding; but this very strength sometimes proved a weakness, when he had passed away. As long as he lived Rhodesia was bound to thrive under his watchful eye. We have seen what Faku thought of Rhodes as a father and mother to the natives: and it was so with the white settlers. Had they a difficulty in farming?—go to Rhodes, and it was all right: was a railway needed?—go to Rhodes, and it was put in hand forthwith: was the gold law irksome in a particular case?—go to Rhodes and he would make the proper allowance for the circumstances. He corresponded personally with viceroys and colonial governments, he dealt with the British or any foreign government as an equal when he wanted any concession for Rhodesia. But when he was gone, there was no Rhodes to take his place, nor even a system as a substitute. Like so many strong men he found he could get what he wanted so much more easily by personal intervention and by a *sic volo, sic jubeo* system, that he set up no other for the time when he should not be there. Five years after his death the settlers were complaining that no director of the Chartered Company came near them, and they had no one to whom they could turn as in the old days of Rhodes's lifetime. The natives, too, suffered when he had gone. There was then no one to soften their hardships if they had a year of famine or were harried. When he was alive he used to send up cattle to distribute to the natives who did not "loaf" and to keep their hearts "white"; when it came to the bare rights allowed them in their comparatively small and even curtailed reserves they had good cause to echo Faku's lament.

Fortunately the evil effect of the Raid, Rhodes's worst definite fault, passed away, and the policy, of which it was a distorted symptom, the union of South Africa, remained and gained ever fresh strength after his death. His influence on the members of the Convention itself has already been alluded to;[1] on events which led to the Convention it was still greater. Before he came on the scene, the Dutch had been striving for a Dutch union under a Dutch flag, and the English toyed with such fantastic schemes as Froude's and Carnarvon's to make federation an excuse for finally crushing Dutch aspirations: it is due to him more than to any man that English and Dutch in South Africa came to see that a joint action for union would alone gain the end desired by both. Indirectly, too, he made the English and Dutch sides more equal in the bargainings for union by his services to the whole of South Africa as well as to the British Empire in the acquisition of Rhodesia. The Dutch never forgot that, had it not been for him, Rhodesia, like South-West Africa, might have passed to Germany, a power even more distasteful to them than undiluted England: and for the first time they had cause to see that English and not Dutch enterprise had brought a great new tract of South Africa under the civilizing influences of Dutch and English combined.

Rhodes was indeed a faulty hero: what hero is not? But he had great aims, some of which he attained, and he had the priceless faculty of inspiring others with the same aspirations. Perhaps the purest devotion to those aims he ever inspired was found in one of his own Rhodesians. Young Hubert Hervey in his lifetime echoed Rhodes's words, when he said, "Only believe in your idea and it will carry you through every difficulty. If you live you will do great things; if you die—well! how can you die better? And your idea will not die." For those aims later he was

[1] See Chap. I. p. 2, and Chap. XVII. p. 297.

ready to lay down his life. As he lay dying of his wounds in the Matabele rebellion, he asked for Rhodes and begged him to see that his sister was cared for after his death. Rhodes was touched. He spoke thus of him afterwards: "He never thought of himself, he was without self. . . . He was without fear—he did not know fear—and without self. . . . That feeling about the Empire was the ideal of his life. There is a great deal of talk about the Imperial idea, but unhappily self is so often beneath it. That is where it is; people say all this, but self is so often at the bottom of it. With him it was *absolutely pure*; . . . There may be cynical people who will say about the Imperial part, 'Oh yes, we know it is generally a cover for self.' But when they see that half an hour before death he still had not thought about himself, that all his thoughts were for others, they will feel there was no self in him. Half an hour before death! I had gone to him wondering what he wished—other men might have had other thoughts—but his were still, even then, only for others." Rhodes, we may believe, was so deeply stirred, not merely by his love for the young man, but yet more because he felt the nobility of that short life consecrated his own aims in the face of his fellow-men.

Such was Rhodes's influence on one among many: of this influence generally no one could speak better than that disciple of his whom he inspired with a life-long devotion to the same ideals. Earl Grey, at the Chartered Company's general meeting held in the year succeeding Rhodes's death, said of him: "He was in truth the most strenuous lover of his country, the most single-minded and the greatest-hearted man I ever met. During his life he gave all his energies and all his wealth to the service of the Empire, and in his will he has bequeathed to the entire Anglo-Saxon world the priceless legacy of an inspiring ideal. . . . I have come across, and sometimes in the most unexpected quarters, men whose characters have been entirely changed by the example of Cecil Rhodes, and whose ambition it is now to administer as a public trust considerable proportions of those fortunes, which but for him they would probably have spent upon themselves."

BIBLIOGRAPHY

I. Oral

For a Life of Rhodes there are still available the personal recollections of many who spoke with him and knew him well. I have had the privilege of talking with many such during the last six years or more that this book has been incubating. Some, alas! of these have now passed away; for it is wellnigh twenty years since Rhodes himself died. Among those to whom I am deeply grateful for information about Rhodes's career, and still more for many of those intimate touches that make the savour of a biography, I should like to mention:

The late Sir Starr Jameson.
The late Earl Grey.
The late Sir Frank Lascelles.
The late Mr. Robert Yerburgh, M.P.
The late Mr. F. C. Selous.
The late Mr. C. D. Rudd.
Col. Sir F. Younghusband.
Mr. and Mrs. Rochfort Maguire.
Mr. H. Wilson Fox, M.P.
Sir Ralph Williams.
Sir Graham Bower.
Sir Chas. Metcalfe.
Miss Louisa Rhodes.
Mr. Herbert Baker.
Rt. Hon. J. X. Merriman.
Sir Francis Newton.
Mr. F. J. Dormer.
Mr. Robert Williams.
Miss Alexander.
Sir William and Lady Solomon.
Sir Lionel Phillips.

II. MS. Authorities

The *Rhodes Trustees* possess a large quantity of letters, etc. addressed to Rhodes, his letter-books, copies of his telegrams, and various other papers relating to him. Unfortunately most of his early papers were destroyed in the fire at Groote Schuur in 1896. Some of his most characteristic utterances are contained in the telegrams, by means of which he conducted a large part of his business. Towards the end of his life he had a great distaste for writing letters himself, but in many of those dictated to his secretaries his actual words are given in inverted commas.

The *Rhodes Trustees* generously gave me unrestricted permission to see and make copies of all the papers in their possession. For their generosity I owe them deep gratitude.

The late *Mr. C. D. Rudd* allowed me to see and copy a number of letters addressed to him by Rhodes, ranging in date from 1874 to within two years of his death. These are especially useful for the Kimberley days.

To *Miss Rhodes* I owe the very interesting letter quoted in Chapter IV., and the sight of some other early letters, etc.

III. Published Books on Rhodes

MICHELL, Sir LEWIS. *Life of Rt. Hon. C. J. Rhodes.* 2 vols. 1910. (Indispensable for facts.)

JOURDAN, PHILIP. *Cecil Rhodes, His Private Life.* 1911.

LE SUEUR, GORDON. *Cecil Rhodes.* 1913.

(The last two give personal touches by former private secretaries.)

RADZIWILL, CATHERINE, Princess. *Cecil Rhodes, Man and Empire-Maker.* 1918. (Not of much account.)

COLVIN, IAN. *C. J. Rhodes.* 1912. (A slight but good sketch.)

FROST, A. S. *C. J. Rhodes.* 1902. (Slight.)

DE WAAL, D. C. *With Rhodes in Mashonaland.* 1896. (Most useful.)

"IMPERIALIST." *Cecil Rhodes.* 1897. (Chiefly interesting for two chapters of reminiscences by Jameson.)

HENSMAN, H. *Cecil Rhodes.* 1901. (Many useful facts.)

DORMER, F. J. *Vengeance as a Policy in Afrikanderland.* 1901. (Gives interesting, if unfavourable, view of the later Rhodes.)

FULLER, Sir THOMAS. *Rt. Hon. C. J. Rhodes.* 1910. (A most valuable Memoir.)

"VINDEX." *Cecil Rhodes, His Political Life and Speeches.* 1900. (Indispensable for the speeches.)

STEAD, W. T. *The Last Will and Testament of Cecil J. Rhodes.* 1902. (Valuable as an exposition of Rhodes's aims.)

Useful sketches of Rhodes are also to be found in:

WILSON, Lady SARAH. *S. African Memories.* 1909.

MENPES, MORTIMER. *War Impressions.* 1901.

LEONARD, A. G. *How We Made Rhodesia.* 1896.

ALEXANDER, E. *Primate Alexander, A Memoir.* 1913.

BERDROW, W. *Buch berühmter Kaufleute.* Leipzig, 1905.

FORT, G. SEYMOUR. *Dr. Jameson.* 1908.

ROBINSON, Sir JOHN. *Notes on Natal.* Durban, 1872.

WILLIAMS, Sir RALPH. *How I Became a Governor.* 1913.

PALADINI, CARLO. *Interviste (Rhodes, etc.).* Firenze, 1902.

VAN GOCH, H. A. *Weerstaat den Rhodesgeest.* Dordrecht, 1900.

LAURENCE, P. M. *On Circuit in Kaffirland.* 1903.

SCULLY, W. C. *Reminiscences of a South African Pioneer.* 1913.

Proceedings at Unveiling of Rhodes Memorial Tablet. Oxford, 1907.

HUTCHINSON, G. T. *Frank Rhodes, A Memoir.* (Privately printed.) 1908.

PARKIN, G. R. *The Rhodes Scholarships.* 1912.
COOK, E. T. *Edmund Garrett.* 1909.
Hansard and *The Times* are essential; and for Rhodes's speeches during his term of office as Prime Minister the *Cape Hansard* is necessary.

At least two novels have been based on Rhodes's story:

HOPE (HAWKINS), ANTHONY. *The God in the Car.* 2 vols. 1894.
ROBERTS, MORLEY. *The Colossus.* 1899.
OLIVE SCHREINER'S *Trooper Peter Halket*, 1897, is a bitter attack on Rhodes's native policy.

Innumerable Magazine articles have been published about Rhodes. Among these may be singled out articles by:

CUST, H. *N. American Rev.* July, 1902.
VARIOUS AUTHORS. *Diamond Fields Advertizer*, Christmas Nos. 1906 and 1907.
WARREN, SIR C. *Contemporary.* May, 1902.
LOW, SIR SIDNEY. *Nineteenth Century and After.* May, 1902.
WITT, R. C. *Nineteenth Century and After.* May, 1902.
THOMAS, E. N. *Empire Review.* Aug. and Sept., 1902.
SAUER, Dr. H. *Empire Review.* May, 1902.
BAKER, H. *Nineteenth Century and After.* January, 1920.

The articles on Rhodes in the *D.N.B.* by Charles Boyd and in the *Ency. Brit.* by Lady Lugard should also be consulted.

IV. SOUTH AFRICAN HISTORY

A most valuable book for the student of S. African history and literature is S. Mendelssohn's *S. African Bibliography* (2 vols., 1910). During his lifetime Mr. Mendelssohn allowed me to read many otherwise inaccessible books in his library, on which his bibliography is chiefly based; since then the library has been bequeathed to the Union of S. Africa.

Among general histories are:

THEAL, G. M. *History of S. Africa*, 1486–1872. 5 vols. 1888–93.
History of S. Africa, 1795–1894. 5 vols. 1908.
S. Africa. 1894.
LUCAS, C. P. *Historical Geography of S. Africa.* 1897, 1904.
WORSFOLD, B. *S. Africa.* 1895.
Lord Milner's Work in S. Africa. 1906.
Reconstruction of New Colonies under Lord Milner. 1913.
WILMOT, A. *History of Our Own Times in S. Africa.* 3 vols. 1897–99.
CORY, G. E. *The Rise of S. Africa* (*to* 1857). 3 vols. 1919.
LEYDS, W. J. *First Annexation of the Transvaal.* 1906.
The Transvaal Surrounded. 1919.

TILBY, A. WYATT. *S. Africa,* 1486–1913. 1914.
BRYDEN, H. A. *A History of S. Africa.* 1904.
The Natives of S. Africa. 1901.
The S. African Natives. 1909.
AMERY, L. S. (general editor). *"The Times" History of the War in S. Africa.* 7 vols. 1900–1909.

Political Biographies.

MARTINEAU, J. *Life of Sir Bartle Frere.* 2 vols. 1895.
MOLTENO, P. A. *Life and Times of Sir J. C. Molteno.* 2 vols. 1900.
WILMOT, A. *Life and Times of Sir R. Southey.* 1904.
KRUGER, S. J. PAUL. *Memoirs.* 2 vols. 1902.
VAN OORDT, J. F. *P. Kruger en de Opkomst der Z.A.R.* Amsterdam. 1898.
HOFMEYR, J. H., and REITZ, F. W. *Life of J. H. Hofmeyr (Onze Jan).* Cape Town, 1913.
MACKENZIE, W. D. *John Mackenzie.* 1902.
O'BRIEN, R. BARRY. *Life of C. S. Parnell.* 1910.

V., SPECIAL PERIODS

(1) *The Diamond Fields.*

Diamond Fields Advertizer. Christmas Number, 1901.
ANCIAUX, GABRIEL. *Puppets on Show.* (? 1896.)
MURRAY, R. W. *Diamond Fields Keepsake.* 1873.
Knights of Labour of S. Africa, *Manifesto of.* 1892.
RAYMOND, H. *B. I. Barnato, A Memoir.* 1897.
COHEN, L. *Reminiscences of Kimberley.* 1911.
MATTHEWS, J. W. *Incwadi Jami, Twenty Years' Personal Experience of S.A.* 1887.
WILLIAMS, GARDNER F. *The Diamond Mines of S. Africa.* New York, 1902. (Most valuable.)
REUNERT, TH. *Diamonds and Gold in S. Africa.* 1893.
PAYTON, CHAS. A. *The Diamond Diggings of S. Africa.* 1872.

(2) *Gold-fields of S. Africa.*

MATHERS, E. P. *Golden S. Africa.* 1887.
REUNERT, TH. See under Diamonds.
GOLDMAN, C. S. *Financial History of Gold and other Companies of Witwatersrand.* 1892.
South African Mines. 3 vols. 1895–96.
BAINES, THOMAS. *The Gold Regions of S.E. Africa.* P. Elizabeth, 1877.
South Africa. (Majority Special Number.) 1910.

(3) *The Scramble for (S.) Africa.*

HERTSLET, Sir E. *The Map of Africa by Treaty.* 3 vols, 1909.

FITZMAURICE, Lord E. *Life of 2nd Earl Granville.* 2 vols. 1905.
LOWE, C. *Prince Bismarck.* 2 vols. 1885.
BUSCH, Dr. MORITZ. *Bismarck, Some Pages from his History.* 3 vols. 1898.
ROBERTSON, C. GRANT. *Bismarck.* 1918.
ROSE, J. HOLLAND. *Development of European Nations,* 1870–90. 1905.
DEVILLE, M. VICTOR. *Partage de l'Afrique.* 1898.
KELTIE, J. SCOTT. *The Partition of Africa.* 1893.

Government Publications.

C. 4190. Angra Pequeña. 1884.
C. 4262. Angra Pequeña. 1884.
C. 4265. Angra Pequeña. 1884.
C. 5904. Africa No. 2. 1890.
C. 6495. Africa No. 7. 1891.

(4) *Bechuanaland and Transvaal.*

WILLIAMS, RALPH. *The British Lion in Bechuanaland.* 1885.
MACKENZIE, JOHN. *Ten Years North of the Orange River.* 1871.
Austral Africa. 2 vols. 1887.

Government Publications.

C. 2308. Bechuanaland. 1878–79.
C. 3419. Transvaal. 1882.
C. 3635. S. Africa. 1883.
C. 3686. Transvaal. 1883.
C. 3841, 3947, 4036, 4194, 4213, 4251. Transvaal. 1884.
C. 4275, 4310, 4432, 4588. Transvaal. 1885.
C. 4643, 4890. Transvaal. 1886.
C. 7932. British Bechuanaland. 1896.
C. 7962. South Africa. 1896.
C. 8474. Transvaal (Drifts question). 1897.

(5) *Rhodesia, Pioneers, Matabele Wars, etc.*

WILLS, W. A., and COLLINGRIDGE, L. T. *Downfall of Lo Bengula.* 1894.
BLENNERHASSET, R., and SLEEMAN, L. *Adventures in Mashonaland.* 1893.
LEONARD, A. G. *How We Made Rhodesia.* 1896.
THOMAS, T. M. *Eleven Years in Central S. Africa.* 1872.
HYATT, S. PORTAL. *Diary of a Soldier of Fortune.* (n.d.)
The Northward Trek. 1909.
COLQUHOUN, A. R. *Matabeleland.* 1893.
Dan to Beersheba. 1908.
WOOD, J. G. *Through Matabeleland.* 1893.
KNIGHT BRUCE, G. W. H. *Memories of Mashonaland.* 1895.
DU TOIT, S. J. *Rhodesia Past and Present.* 1897.
GROGAN, E. S., and SHARP, A. H. *From the Cape to Cairo.* 1900.

THE B.S.A. Co. *General Information, etc.* 1889.
Regulations for Pioneer Corps. Cape Town, 1890.
HONE, PERCY F. *Southern Rhodesia.* 1909.
SELOUS, F. C. *Travel and Adventure in S.E. Africa.* 1893.
Sunshine and Storm in Rhodesia. 1896.
JOHNSTON, Sir H. H. *British Central Africa.* 1897.
The Colonization of Africa. 1899.
Britain Across the Seas—Africa. (n.d.)
DUFF, H. L. *Nyasaland under the Foreign Office.* 1906.
LUGARD, F. D. *The Rise of our E. African Empire.* 2 vols. 1893.
PETERS, Dr. CARL. *The Eldorado of the Ancients.* 1902.
MAUCH, CARL. *Reisen in Inneren v. Süd-Afrika, 1865–72.* Gotha, 1874.
FOX-BOURNE, H. R. *Matabeleland and the Chartered Co.* 1897.
BLUNT, WILFRID S. *My Diaries, I.* 1888–1900. 1919.
GREY, ALBERT, Earl. *Hubert Hervey, Student and Imperialist.* 1899.
DARTER, ADRIAN. *The Pioneers of Mashonaland.* 1914.
JOHNSON, Lieut.-Col. F. "Reminiscences" in *R. Sussex Herald*, vol. iii. Lahore, 1918.
HENSMAN, H. *History of Rhodesia.* 1900.
THOMSON, H. C. *Rhodesia and its Government.* 1898.
COOPER-CHADWICK, J. *Three Years with Lo Bengula.* 1894.
MILLAIS, J. G. *Life of F. C. Selous, D.S.O.* 1918.
CHURCHILL, Lord RANDOLPH. *Men, Mines, and Animals in S. Africa.* 1892.

Government Publications.

C. 2220. Bechuanaland. 1878.
C. 4890. Transvaal. 1886.
C. 5237. Bechuanaland. 1887.
C. 5363. Bechuanaland. 1888.
C. 5588. S.A.R. 1888.
C. 5524. Bechuanaland. 1888.
C. 5918. Bechuanaland. 1890.
C. 7171, 7190. S. Africa. 1893–94.
C. 7196. Mashonaland. 1893.
C. 7284, 7290, 7383, 7555. B.S.A. Co. 1894.
C. 8547. B.S.A. Co. 1897.
C. 9138, 9323. B.S.A. Co. 1899.

The *Directors' Reports* and *Proceedings* at meetings of the British S. Africa Co. and the proceedings before the Privy Council on the *Special Reference in the Matter of S. Rhodesia* all throw light on the early history of Rhodesia.

I have especially to thank the Directors of the B.S.A. Co. for kindly allowing me to see these and other papers in their possession, some of them of a confidential nature.

(6) *The Raid.*

There is a large literature on this subject: the following books are specially useful:

GARRETT, F. E., and EDWARDS, E. J. *Story of an African Crisis: the Raid.* 1897.

[TERRAIL, G.] MERMEIX (pseud.). *Le Transvaal et la Chartered.* Paris, 1897.

FITZPATRICK, J. PERCY. *The Transvaal from Within.* 1899.

STEAD, W. T. *Joseph Chamberlain, Conspirator or Statesman?* 1900.

YOUNGHUSBAND, F. *South Africa of To-day.* 1898.

JEYES, S. H. *Mr. Chamberlain.* 1903.

Government Publications.

C. 7933. Transvaal. 1896.

C. 8380. 1897. (The Cape Inquiry.)

H.C. 311. 1898. (The House of Commons Committee's Inquiry.)

CHRONOLOGICAL TABLE

1852. Jan. 16. Sand River Convention (S.A.R. established).
1853. Feb. 9. L. S. Jameson b.
July 5. *Cecil John Rhodes b.*
Livingstone's first journey to Zambesi country.
1854. March 11. Convention of Bloemfontein (O.F.S. established).
1854–6. [Crimean War.]
1857–8. [Indian Mutiny.]
1859. Inyati Mission founded by Moffat.
1861. *Rhodes goes to Bishop Stortford Grammar School.*
1861–5. [American Civil War.]
1864. [Schleswig-Holstein War.]
1866. [Austro-Prussian War.]
1867. First diamond discovered in South Africa.
Mauch discovers gold at Tati.
July 1. [Dominion of Canada established.]
1869. Basutoland declared British.
Rhodes leaves school.
1870. Kimberley dry diggings discovered.
Sept. 1. *Rhodes lands at Durban.*
1870–1. [Franco-Prussian War.]
1871. Oct. 17. Keate award ; Griqualand West annexed.
Rhodes goes to the Diamond Fields.
1872. Cape Colony gets Responsible Government.
1873. [Ashantee War.]
April 30. Death of Livingstone.
Oct. 13. *Rhodes matriculates at Oxford.*
Nov. *Death of Rhodes's mother.*
1874. [Disraeli Prime Minister.]
March. *Rhodes returns to Kimberley.*
1876 (Ap.)–78 (June). *Rhodes keeps terms at Oxford.*
1876. July. [Brussels Conference on Africa.]
1877. Sir Bartle Frere Governor of Cape.
Transvaal annexed.
Sept. *Rhodes's first Will.*
1877–8. [Russo-Turkish War.]
1878. Feb. *Rhodes's father dies.*
African Lakes Co. founded.

[German African Society founded.]
March 12. Walfisch Bay annexed.
[Stanley returns from Africa. Congo Association founded.]

1879. [Afghan War.]
Zulu War.

1879. Jan. *Rhodes in fight with Korannas near Christiana.*
March. Hofmeyr enters Cape House.
Nov. Herbert Rhodes dies in Nyassaland.

1880. [Gladstone's Second Ministry.]
April 1. *Rhodes founds De Beers Mining Co.*
Frere recalled; Sir Hercules Robinson, Governor of Cape.
Oct. Griqualand West incorporated in Cape Colony.
Nov. *Rhodes elected for Barkly West.*
Dec. Transvaal War begins.

1881. Feb. 27. Majuba.
April 19. *Rhodes's maiden speech on Basutoland.*
Aug. 3. Convention of Pretoria restores independence to Transvaal.
Oct. *Rhodes's last term at Oxford: takes degree* (Dec.).
Nov. [Charter to British North Borneo Company.]

1882. Stellaland and Goshen founded in Bechuanaland.
Rhodes meets Gordon in Basutoland.
[Arabi's revolt; Tel-el-Kebir.]

1883. April. *Rhodes visits Stellaland.*
May. Germans occupy Angra Pequeña.
Aug. *Rhodes's first speech about Bechuanaland.*

1884. Feb. Basutoland transferred to Imperial Government.
Feb. 27. Convention of London with S.A.R.
March-May. *Rhodes Treasurer of the Cape.*
June. Granville admits German claim to Angra Pequeña.
Aug. *Rhodes's mission to Stellaland and Goshen.*
Dec. Warren's expedition to Bechuanaland.

1885. Jan. 24. *Rhodes meets Kruger.*
Jan. 26. [Fall of Khartoum; death of Gordon.]
Feb. 26. Berlin Act regularizes scramble for Africa.
June 30. *Rhodes attacks Warren's conduct in Bechuanaland.*
Aug. [Independent State of Congo announced.]
Sept. British Bechuanaland a Crown Colony; Protectorate over rest of Bechuanaland.

1886. Gold discovered on Witwatersrand.
[Gladstone's first Home Rule Bill defeated: Salisbury's Ministry formed.]
July 10. [Charter to Royal Niger Co.]
Nov. 1. [Anglo-German agreement *re* East Africa.]

1887. May. *Rhodes acquires all holdings in De Beers mine.*
Rhodes founds Gold-fields of S. Africa.
July 30. Grobler Treaty with Lo Bengula.
[First Colonial Conference.]

1888. Feb. 11. Moffat Treaty with Lo Bengula.
March. De Beers Consolidated Mines formed.
Sept. 3. [Charter to Imperial British E. Africa Co. (I.B.E.A.).]
Oct. 30. Rudd Concession granted by Lo Bengula.
1889. March. First S. African Customs Union (Cape and O.F.S.).
April 30. *Rhodes applies for Charter.*
Sept. 21. Brit. Protectorate over Nyasaland.
Oct. 29. Charter granted to British South Africa Co.
Robinson replaced by Sir H. Loch as Governor of Cape.
1890. March 6. *Rhodes and Loch meet Kruger at Fourteen Streams.*
June 27. Pioneer expedition starts.
July 1. Anglo-German agreement *re* Zanzibar, East and Central Africa, and Heligoland.
July 17. *Rhodes Prime Minister of Cape.*
Sept. 11. Pioneers reach Salisbury.
Oct.-Nov. *Rhodes's trip to Tuli and Pretoria.*
Nov. 15. Fight with Portuguese at Umtassa's Kraal.
1891. April. Adendorff Trek damped down by Kruger.
May 14. Brit. Protectorate over Nyasaland.
June 6. [Death of Sir John Macdonald (Canada).]
June 11. Anglo-Portuguese Treaty *re* African spheres.
July. Jameson Administrator of Mashonaland.
Rhodes's Bank Act passed.
Sept.-Nov. *Rhodes's first visit to Mashonaland.*
1892. [Gladstone's fourth Ministry.]
Rhodes's negotiations to acquire Delagoa Bay.
Rhodes's Franchise and Ballot Act passed.
Aug. Transvaal National Union founded (Uitlanders).
1893. [Gladstone's second Home Rule Bill.]
[Portal's Mission to Uganda.]
May. *Rhodes forms second Ministry.*
Kruger re-elected President.
June 26. Natal given Responsible Government.
July 18. Victoria affray starts Matabele War.
Nov. 4. Chartered troops occupy Buluwayo.
1894. Pondoland annexed to Cape.
June. Protectorate over Uganda.
Rhodes sends Hofmeyr and De Villiers to Ottawa Conference.
Rhodes passes Glen Grey Act and Scab Act.
Oct. Railway reaches Mafeking.
Nov. *Rhodes sees Kruger on railway and customs questions.*
Dec. Final agreement with Transvaal *re* Swaziland.
1895. Feb. 2. *Rhodes sworn of Privy Council.*
March. [I.B.E.A. surrender charter to Crown.]
April. Tongaland annexed.
Loch replaced by Sir Hercules Robinson.

May. *Chartered territories named Rhodesia by Proclamation.*
June. [Rosebery Ministry defeated; Salisbury forms Ministry—Chamberlain Colonial Secretary.]
Oct. Drifts incident.
Nov. 16. Brit. Bechuanaland annexed to Cape.
Dec. 29. Jameson's Raid.

1896. Jan. 2. Jameson surrenders at Doornkop.
Jan. 5. *Rhodes resigns.*
March 24. Matabele Rebellion begins.
June 26. *Rhodes resigns from B.S.A. Board.*
Sept.-Oct. *Rhodes's indabas in Matoppos.*

1897. Feb. *Rhodes before S. Africa Committee.*
Railway reaches Buluwayo and Umtali.
Lord Rosmead (Robinson) replaced by Sir Alfred Milner.
[Kitchener's advance on the Soudan.]

1898. April. *Rhodes restored to Board of B.S.A. Co.*
June. Cape elections; *Progressive party formed under Rhodes.*
Sept. 2. [Battle of Omdurman.—Fashoda.]
Oct. 20. New O. in C. for Southern Rhodesia.

1899. March. *Rhodes sees Kaiser; Telegraph agreement.*
May 2. *Rhodes's last speech to B.S.A. Co.*
June. *Rhodes D.C.L. at Oxford.*
Bloemfontein Conference (Milner and Kruger).
July 1. *Rhodes's last Will.*
Oct. 11. S. African War begins.
Rhodes at Kimberley.
Dec. 15. Colenso.

1901. Jan. 1. [Commonwealth of Australia established.]

1900. Feb. 15. Relief of Kimberley.
Feb. 27. Paardeberg.
Oct. *Rhodes's speech to S. African League.*

1902. Jan. 18. *Rhodes leaves England for last time.*
March 26. *Death of Rhodes*, aged 49.
May 31. Peace of Vereeniging.

1904. July 14. Death of Kruger, aged 79.

1909. Union of South Africa Act passed.

INDEX

Printed in Great Britain by R. & R. Clark, Limited, *Edinburgh.*